It Wasn't All Work

It Wasn't All Work

by

Stanley G. (Andy) Cooke

Regency Press (London & New York) Ltd.
125 High Holborn, London WC1V 6QA

ISBN 0 7212 0686 7

Printed and bound in Great Britain by
Buckland Press Ltd., Dover, Kent.

For
My Wife
MAME
(Frances Mabel)
To whom I owe so much
———

In this book she is referred
to as Mabel or Pidge

Over Alderley
1983

My thanks to my son Roger, for his encouragement to write this book, for his criticism and suggestions as it proceeded — and in particular 'My Earliest Memories'.

To Freda Adderley, for her help over many years and her suggestions for much of this book, in particular her part in making the Myers story.

To my close friends who have listened over the years to many anecdotes of my early memories, for their encouragement and friendship.

To all those who have helped in the preparation of the book over what seems a long time, particularly my secretary and, on the publishing side, John Thorpe who has been most helpful and co-operative.

Finally and very gratefully my thanks are due to all those who have helped in the making of this story; also to those who have worked for and with me over some fifty years, in a life that was exciting, hard at times, but never dull and invariably happy.

S.G.C.

Contents

ACKNOWLEDGEMENTS

The author and publishers wish to thank the following publishers and copyright holders for permission to use extracts from their books.

The Splendour That Was Egypt by Margaret Murray
Publishers Sidgwick and Jackson Ltd.

The Nylon Night by A. P. Herbert
A. P. Watt Literary Agents and Lady Herbert

A History of Ethiopia by A. H. M. Jones and Elizabeth Monroe
Published by Oxford University Press

The Shell Guide to England
Edited by John Hadfield
Published by Michael Joseph Ltd., in association with Rainbird Reference Books

Into India by John Keay
Published by John Murray (Publishers) Ltd.

Egypt (Architecture, Sculpture and Painting) in Three Thousand Years
by K. Lange and M. Hirmer
Published by Phaidon Press, London

The Wild Wheel by Garet Garrett
Published by The Cressett Press Ltd.

Wien by L. C. Friedländer
Published by Verlag Jugend und Volk, Austria

The T.I. Group Ltd. for permission to reproduce the old Hercules letterheading and also their permission (in so far as they are owners of the copyright) to reproduce the 1936 Hercules advertisement used on the jacket.

The Daily Mail for permission to reproduce (in so far as they are owners of the copyright) the Hercules advertisement used on the jacket.

My thanks to Mabel and Roger for the holiday photographs.

The Imperial War Museum for the illustration used on the jacket.

The Airborne Forces Museum for the illustration used on the jacket.

FOREWORD

This book came to be written at the suggestion or rather the persistence of my son who himself has children. He, Roger, was always fascinated by my recalling the memories of a very small boy of the First World War, of life and of the privations at that awful time.

I think he first absorbed them with the thought that the sufferings might have been exaggerated, but many history books on, and two visits to the battlefields of France and Belgium convinced him that I was understating the magnitude of the battles, the carnage and the sufferings.

Later he said he could almost feel the pangs of the great industrial depression through what were once my young eyes.

What perhaps fascinated him most was the sheer determination of men and women to lift themselves above the troubles — their ability to improve, to strive, even though the reward was small and security almost non-existent. In many cases the negation of ability itself and the limitations of finances could turn young minds so easily to communism.

The endeavours too that made it possible to enjoy one's limited leisure, even though the means were meagre, and through that to understand the meaning of the term 'the quality of life'.

He wanted me while I was still around to record the story for his children, of the way my generation had suffered, had not only survived but in some small way had proved the point that even though the odds may be stacked against you, the human spirit is a pretty handy tool to have around.

S. G. Cooke
September 1983

CHAPTER ONE

Early Memories

My earliest memories begin just before the First World War. We lived in a village about four miles from the centre of Birmingham, and about a mile further on the real countryside started, lovely and lonely country. I was just about four years old. At that time I had three brothers older than myself, one younger. That was only the beginning of our family, I eventually finished up with six brothers and two sisters — one had died in the awful whooping cough epidemic of 1916.

But first to that early summer of 1914. I was taken by my brother Norman on what was quite a long walk for me, some two miles each way — we could have travelled by tram-car, the old electric type, for half the journey to Alcester Lane End (the terminus) except that we had no money.

We left the cottages near the tramway terminus and in a very short time we were among the green fields covered with a profusion of wild flowers. I picked a bunch for my mum — there was a great variety, lady-smock, lady's lace, bluebells, fading a little, two or three different kinds of daisies and so many others; it looked like a magic carpet. What made the picture more memorable was a giant windmill towering over the lovely scene, now covered with bricks and mortar, on one of Birmingham's big estates.

It was magic to me, we lived in a terraced house with a garden of sorts and if you have ever tried making a postage stamp garden look elegant with lots of kids hell-bent on being 'road-repairers' or keepers of white mice, rabbits and rats, you'll know what I mean.

I can see even now the image of the front page of a tabloid newspaper when the Great War commenced. That first Christmas we had quite the biggest piece of beef I had ever seen. Our stockings were filled — one orange, two pennies and one tiny toy — quite the most lovely stocking I have ever had. No one would buy toys that had been made in Germany with the impressed marks, DRGM — our translation was Dirty Rotten German Make. My eldest brother had learned how to smoke and taught us all to make cigarettes with rolled brown paper and white paper as filling, or for the older boys a filling of dried tea-leaves. I was nearly a casualty with my first smoke and also failed to destroy my ersatz cigarettes and I gave the game away.

Soon after the war started there was the first war casualty from our neighbourhood — a young petty officer, Jesse Blood, had been killed. There was a full turn out, a naval band, gun carriage, lots of sailors and flags galore. To a child's mind it was impressive, to some young men it was perhaps a great thing to die. We had no more funerals like that one though — too many kids lost their fathers and I remember vividly one friend proudly showing me his father's wallet and general issue prayer book, stabbed through with a bayonet, his father's blood congealed around the vicious cut.

11

Not long after that the new village school was closed and surrounded with barbed wire and sentries. We had to go part-time to an older school, half a mile further to walk, where lessons for one shift started around eight o'clock and finished at lunchtime and the other shift then took over for the afternoon. We wondered why, but soon discovered the reason when the convoys of ambulances passed through our village. The red crosses to the child mind seemed to be a signal of victory instead of sorrow. If I had been much older it might well have provoked me to volunteer myself. Having since seen those unending rows of crosses in countless cemeteries on the Somme, one wonders perhaps cynically if that was the general idea.

My father was a civil servant, not in even reasonable health, with lots of children. When I was old enough to understand he told me that pressure from the press, the Derby recruitment schemes and finally the petulant women with their snide asides and white feathers, literally forced him to volunteer.

I was just six when he went to war. He was certainly full of cheer, in his office suit, and ready to be brave; he came back in about six weeks on embarkation leave, still in his suit — now caked with mud to the knees, with a stick, no gun, and an armlet marked BEF as a signal to let the white feather brigade know he was in the forces. We did not see him again for a long time but he sent us many of those lacey embroidered cards so beloved by the French and Belgians.

In the meantime things at home got serious. There was no real or fair rationing scheme. Potatoes were our staple diet and if we saw a potato lorry unloading at the greengrocers, one of us would run back to tell mother, while another would start queuing. The greengrocers only seemed to open when they had a delivery of potatoes and the other only things they seemed to sell were turnips and swedes.

One other event stuck in my young mind. My mother and a friend thought it would be a good idea if their children were dressed up to collect for the wounded. The little girls dressed as nurses with a couple of boys as walking wounded with substantial amounts of red paint as blood. The tiny procession was soon taken into the local police station after some 'well wishing folk' complained that children dressed up as wounded would provoke a feeling of anger in the population.

Civilians suffered too from terrible epidemics of influenza. I remember the long lines of funerals passing through the village. The men came back, many of them were wounded, some with waggling heads, shaking arms and staring eyes were suffering from shell shock. Others were laid flat in what were called long basket carriages, that did not last long and neither did the occupants. Just recently my son and I were in Arras strolling around the quiet town and in the fading Sunday evening light there was no hint of war or carnage. We were obviously on the edge of what was and perhaps still is the red light district, when he turned to me and said, 'I reckon the old man must have had a pleasant night or two here in the dark days.' No answer to that when life could be calculated in minutes.

The war eventually ended, after much privation and hardship, of rationing when there was anything to ration, of so much sorrow, of pain, not only of the body but of the spirit. Have a look at the great battlefields on the continent or at home at the country village war memorials, recording young lives wiped out in the slaughter.

Some of the memorials bear the legend 'They gave their lives'; they didn't *give* their lives they were blasted to bits by shells and bombs. That they were brave and had been sacrificed there could be no doubt.

My father came back, sicker than he went out, bitter, but being a civil servant his salary had improved through inflation. It seemed that quite a few salary increases were in the pipeline for him. They were usually celebrated by official dinners — from which he would sometimes come home worse for wear, top hat and all.

The feeling of elation at the end of the war was short lived; more soldiers returned from distant places, some fit but so many cruelly wounded. They brought with them some awful diseases from being cooped up in trenches with the dead at every turn, living in appalling conditions, crowded together, with insufficient food, breeding shocking germs by the million.

The flu epidemic of an earlier year was bad enough, but there was hope of survival with that. The new killer was referred to as sleepy or sleeping sickness, *Encephalitis lethargica*. I understand from my doctor friends that the brain just goes to sleep and the patient sinks into unconsciousness. There never seemed to be any hope and so they just went to sleep for ever. In our little village we lost many children that way, including my friends the three Barnwell brothers. I called to see them one day but their mother could only say, 'Go away, there's a good boy; they have to stay in their room.'

Great things were planned for peace time, more and better education, but that was a long way off; full employment, that was even further off. Many of the wartime promises about a world fit for heroes did not mature. But one thing did survive, the indomitable spirit of the human race.

As I grew older I knew that the flower of the young men had been killed or maimed. There were still plenty who had a go at making a new life, and many spent the last few pounds of their gratuity on a little plot of land, a shed and some chickens that might lead them to a golden age. It did not even lead to a golden egg; in my youth I saw many of the sheds in decay and the plots overgrown; the place was called 'Happy Valley'!

Near our village an airman used a field to land his 'string and glue' plane — he walked the wing as the notice said as 'an exhibition' and also offered trips at about five shillings a time.

The most impressive thing to me in 1922 was the great triumph of wireless broadcasting. My father had an experimental receiving licence to use the so called cat's whiskers and headphones and an outward sign of one upmanship was the aerial in the garden, supported by a tall pole constructed by two spreaders made from broom handles (they were a convenient width), holding conductor wires with insulators which looked big enough to resist 10,000 volts. These wires were then connected to a single wire conveying the signal to the set. The whole outside contraption could be adjusted by a series of pulleys attached to the pole. Once the attachment was made to the mysterious crystal set the whole remarkable contrivance came to life. It seemed to me that *Annie Laurie* was always coming across the air. It was not long though before the countryside was festooned with double spreader aerials. They arose like forests, only to die away to single wires and then no wires at all. The great boon of wireless was the arrival of news into the house itself.

The main means of receiving news had previously been by newspaper. There always seemed to be a newsboy screaming from street to street—SPEECIAL MA-EL—SPEECIAL EEDITIAN. This freely translated from the Birmingham brogue meant 'Special Mail—Special Edition'—the editions seemed to come around almost hourly.

Following the wireless set era there was a growth of gramophone shops—with records galore to choose from. Having heard a great singer on the radio, you could again enjoy the performance in the quiet of your home. The gramophones too improved, our first one was the image of the label on His Master's Voice, dog and all. In 1921 there was the first portable gramophone, that was a wonderful advance.

In 1925 William Morris introduced his £200 bullet nosed car. My elder brother bought one and took me to London to see my great aunt. On our arrival my cousin suggested we all three of us go to Brighton. There were only seats for two so I had a perilous journey perched with one hand on the luggage boot handle and the other on my cousin's shoulder.

In my early days the main means of transport to the city was by tramways. The tram was originally pulled by horses, later by steam and finally by electricity. The steel rails were laid in the centre of the highways and each tram held between fifty and sixty passengers—a most economic means of travelling; when omnibuses were introduced the cost of travelling just about doubled.

There was much poverty in the years following the Great War. In the City of Birmingham the Lord Mayor and Corporation hit upon a fund raising idea, an Illuminated Tramcar, covered with electric lights. All tramway traffic stopped for some time before its arrival and this travelling piece of light surrounded by volunteer collectors, made its brilliant progress night after night to the various corners of the city. It raised much money for the poor, it was an attraction that was badly wanted in a world that had little to cheer about, and in some way it inspired people, well, they at least smiled a bit.

Another thing that sticks in my memory was the abundance in the poorer districts of what were called off-licences, where booze was sold to be consumed off the premises. Nearer the city it was quite a usual sight to see the beer of the day being conveyed in big white jugs often by little boys for their beer loving parents.

Then there was the delivery of fish, fruit and bread, delivered by cart to the door—both in town and village. The yelling of the monger announced the star value of the day, with herrings at a penny a piece, or apples at a penny a pound.

* * *

Our big family didn't do too badly for the back pay and gratuity helped enormously and more important still, my father had a job to go back to. That was a fundamental, a little self pride sucked from the slurry of life.

Any chance of a member of a big family going to a public school (unless the parents were very, very well off), was out of the question. In the closing years of the war, children (outside public schools), provided they were up to it and in the seventh standard (the top), were released to leave school at the age of twelve, more fodder for the factories and if the war had lasted, for the guns. The war released good teachers, who returned to their jobs as soon as their wounds were healed. There was Bacon, badly wounded but brim full of enthusiasm; Chesham with only one eye — and what a searching eye it was; Walker (strange with a name like that) with a limp. More than half of the teachers had been severely wounded. Most of them had been at Oxford or Cambridge and, after getting their degrees, went straight into battle.

Thin as times must have been, they always looked smart in suits with trousers so finely creased that I vowed when I grew up, I would have, like them, creases, a rolled umbrella and bowler hat to match! They walked miles to school, no bikes, no cars, but had enthusiasm backed by discipline.

There were special schools for the less proficient. They were small and provided very special and kind attention, yet on the other hand they were used as a threat, perhaps wrongly, to children who did not really try; the mention of a visit to the special school was enough for them. It seemed to work, and so did they.

I vividly recall three head teachers: Miss Ward, head of the primary and infants; George Howard Mann, headmaster of my first big boys' school and Lewis Rand, a comparatively young man who had the daunting task of handling a brave experiment by Birmingham's Education Department, with a brand new co-educational school.

Miss Ward was tall, slim, wore gold rimmed spectacles; a stern disciplinarian, but kind to a fault. She could sort out the problems of the tiniest toddler. She seemed always to wear a taffeta skirt with a blouse to match. She had a very thin black cane and for a severe offence she administered a one hander with it. It was not the cane that hurt, it was the swish of the follow through against that taffeta skirt — I can hear it now. Once that noise was sounded the offence was never, no never, committed again.

George Howard Mann was organist and choirmaster at one of the fashionable churches of the day, a man of God, a believer that boys should treat girls with respect. For the transgressor he had sharp and immediate treatment. In stature he was all you might expect and wish in a headmaster — short, greying on the temples and rugged, respected and obeyed. His record for entrances to secondary, grammar and high schools was second to none, yet he was very human and an Empire man to the core. Each year on Empire Day several of the girls from the senior school would give a tableau on the British Empire — much to the delight of the senior boys. *Land of Hope and Glory* was really meant then, and George Howard Mann made a very deep impression on me.

Finally, I come to the younger man to whom I owe much in the way of life and determination. Lewis Rand, too, was a musician. He came to an entirely new school that was purpose-built as a co-ed with a practical room which could be converted in a matter of minutes to a carpenters' shop, a science laboratory or a girls' cookery room.

A mixed school of eleven to fourteen year olds was new then. He taught that the most important thing was respect, not only for parents but boys for girls, likewise mate for mate, respect for the school and what it stood for. I have not mentioned respect for masters or mistresses — in later years he explained to me that if you got the former respects right the respect for teachers was automatic.

In next to no time he had a parents' society, senior scholars' debating forum, a football team — he insisted we asked for no quarter. We played football against the local schools; no-one doubted the result of the first game, we lost 12-nil but the lesson he taught us was that the game mattered, not the score and if our devotion to the game continued the scores would improve — they did. He had trees planted by the head scholars (paid for by collections, although pennies were hard to come by) to commemorate the first year of the school. He too always wore a suit.

I was head boy. He believed in head boys and head girls and that those positions should be honoured, not for personal gain but for the benefit of the school as a whole.

He introduced Saturday night dances for scholars and parents. All had to pay, nothing was free and with the passing of the years I agree with that principle more and more.

He also believed that children should be provided with the education that they warranted and could cope with, even if that meant separating the brightest from the not so bright, even if it made extra work for the staff.

As a matter of interest at thirteen I was well advanced in logarithms, trigonometry and had an outline of Euclid.

Lewis Rand gave us his most precious gift free, yet more precious than any of us knew then, 'his time', for he died comparatively young.

Above all he had a very moving love of great music with which he imbued his scholars. He had no problem in filling the assembly hall for an hour at least after normal going home time. He held us in rapture with the lives and music of Mozart, Beethoven, Brahms, all the greats. The spin offs were obvious too; no graffiti, no broken desks, no vandalism.

Why did I not go to a grammar school or university? I was one of a very big family and, while my father had a reasonably good position, in those days further education grants were made on quite a different basis. I understood from my headmaster that a reasonably good job held by your father militated against you if you were one of many. Only the total earnings were considered, not the number of mouths those earnings had to feed. My brother Hector, who was much brighter than I, won a scholarship and an exhibition to one of the great city schools but even then his books had to be provided from the family kitty from which there were so many to be fed. He left school early! No books! I passed into three of the top schools, but there was no spare money; inflation was vicious and unemployment rife.

However, thanks to my headmaster, I was thirsty for knowledge and I pressed on with his help determined to learn; due to him, I virtually had individual tuition, not only in the matter of book learning, but in the graces as well — as I grew older I was taken with his family to dances and dinners, meeting interesting people and having happy times.

I have left one story of my boyhood till the last. It was a development that made a deep impression on me and fired me with the prospects of what could be done by the simple process of the division of labour and economy of movement.

The subject matter is a homely one: milk. Near our home there was an old farmhouse where people bought their milk, served from a huge bowl by the cleanest of clean gill or pint measures.

The next development I remember was milk being delivered by horse drawn milk float, which had a pair of huge wheels. It was deep sided and filled with milk churns, pails and measures. The driver of the float would carry his can and measure to the household doors, dip in the right measure and tip the creamy liquid into jugs or basins. Not very hygienic you might think, but it always tasted good.

Then one day after I started work at Hercules I walked past a brand new building with a frontage of glass. Behind that front was a revelation: thousands of empty milk bottles, crowding conveyors, travelling at speed, washed, filled and stoppered, all seemingly without human aid. From then on I stopped almost every morning to look and marvel at the amazing arrangement of conveyors — revealing a new system of milk preparation and the basis of door to door delivery of bottled milk which has lasted to this day.

Over so many years that layout and system have always been an inspiration to me.

In the nineteen twenties there was a type of evening class promoted not by the City Education Authorities, but by the Co-operative movement. We were introduced to stories quite unconnected with socialist theories — just interesting stories like Jason and the Golden Fleece — on reflection that possibly had some political implications!

Quietly we learned of the birth of the co-operative movement in Rochdale, the corner shop between the cotton mills; it struck me at the time that it was not a very good thing. Later sessions dealt with Lord Shaftesbury and his work among the underprivileged and the lack of education among children. From then on lessons covered problems of the poor, the unemployed, the wickedness of the rich mill and mine owners (who were sometimes generous even by the teachers' standards) and the filthy rich, who acquired their wealth by birth and were not so generous; comparisons followed to the bright new world that was on the horizon if the working class worked together. Prizes for essays were awarded by way of further education; my brother Hector was quite brilliant and won many. With us all, some of the messages stuck, with one of my brothers they stuck well and truly as he was very close to being at least one with communist tendencies. I suppose in those early days there was every reason to think of a bright new world. But in later years the stealthy insidious approach of these evening lessons seemed obnoxious and was a system of brainwashing the young.

The other evening classes I attended were for drama. These were great fun — the fee 1/6d (7½p) for a term, held in the local school. We paid for everything then including our own text books and scripts. The master insisted on a serious approach; speak properly, first learn your character, express the character in movement and so on. In a season we usually did two plays; *The Merchant of Venice* was a must with plenty of scope for males and females, for histrionics and the like. Then to balance we had a more modern play. The one that vividly comes to mind was *Abraham Lincoln* by John Drinkwater who lived only about a mile away from the school. I had the part of Grant, a good part, but I wished I could have been Abe Lincoln as the part of Mrs Lincoln was taken by Josephine, a girl who had quite the longest legs I had ever seen and who felt, as she climbed on to the top of a desk, there was no particular reason to hide them. I am quite sure Mrs Lincoln did not act quite like that, but having said that I did not recall any youth rushing off to ravish Josephine! I would have liked to have been Abe Lincoln though!

CHAPTER TWO

Warwickshire County Cricket Club

On leaving school my headmaster, Lewis Rand, gave me a piece of advice—
'Cooke,' he said, 'There are millions looking for jobs; turn nothing down, never be
without work, remember there is a first step on every ladder and if the first step is
low the second one will appear that much higher. I have the feeling,' he continued,
'That one day you will be taking many steps at a time.'

I got a job first time round and nearly lost it the next day. My wages, ten whole
bob a week (50p); my title, office boy at the Warwickshire County Cricket Club.
The staff consisted of (and I quote for the reason of the third name)

R.V. Ryder—Secretary

'Mr' Mason—the Clerk

R. E. S. Wyatt—Assistant Secretary (later captain of England)

Myself—I can't get the type small enough!

On my second day there was a near disaster, R.V. Ryder fixed me with an ice cool
eye demanding, 'Boy! Do you like cricket?' I must have thought that's a daft
question and answered with an almost enthusiastic yell, 'Yes!' A sound like thunder
emitted from Ryder. 'Stand up boy and answer properly!' 'Yes, sir,' I replied. For
good measure he continued, 'That's the trouble with you council school boys, you
don't know how to answer your betters.' That taught me a good lesson, I
determined that when I made it, I would command respect and not demand it. It
was my first and only brush with the old man, and in the days ahead he gave me
great encouragement and advice. I soon picked up all there was to know about club
subscriptions, gate receipts, lady members, professionals, insurance cards. When
the clerk was away I carried on. One day Mr. Ryder said to me, 'I am going to take
you with me to the bank with the takings.' He hired a horse and cab and the cheery
cabby seemed to appear the moment we phoned. On the way Ryder talked to me
like a father, 'Cooke,' he said, 'You are wasting your time. We could find you a job
during the winter, but that's no good. Start job hunting now. But first, you are
going to take the money to the bank on your own in the cab from tomorrow, that
shows my trust.' Whatever old Ryder had said to me on my second day was
forgotten.

It wasn't all work (there wasn't enough of it). I had a marvellous little office at
the top of the pavilion right behind the wicket, the envy of any commentator. I was
responsible during the morning for receipts and for the issue of pass-out and re-
entry tickets and more important on match days, the free tickets for ginger beer,
including one for me. I have savoured many scents throughout the world but that
smell of ginger beer and curling tobacco smoke speaks to me of lazy summer days. I
also had to phone the score at regular intervals to one of the city shops to attract
customers.

19

From that elevated position and lowly job I watched many of the great cricketers of this country, Jack Hobbs, Herbert Sutcliffe, Maurice Tate, A. E. R. Gilligan (captain of England), Harry Howell, Tiger Smith, W. G. Quaife, P. G. H. Fender and the colourful captain of Warwickshire the Hon F. S. G. Calthorpe who one day kindly gave me a bat. I saw Tate and Gilligan bowl out the South Africans for some thirty runs and the little upset that caused the great Lancashire bowler Cecil Parkin to lose a large part of his test career—frivolous to a degree compared with the amorous antics of the cricketers here and down under.

At that time professionals went out of one gate and amateurs through another. Even then it struck me how funny that Jack Hobbs, one of the world's great batsmen, was kept waiting at the amateur gate for some aspiring young amateur to accompany him to the wicket. Needless to say the amateur and professional dressing rooms were also well away from each other.

There were those two great Yorkshire all-rounders, Wilfred Rhodes and Roy Kilner, kind and courteous to everyone. E. J. (Tiger) Smith, a hero of mine, was the great Warwickshire wicket keeper, a good striker with the bat too. I remember with shock and horror, when I was stamping his insurance card, to learn that he lived in Station Road, Kings Heath; not a bad road, but in my hero worshipping stage I thought he would have lived in a minor mansion. The pro's wages (regular that is) were something like £4 a week with 1/7d deduction for an insurance stamp!

I still have vivid memories of one man and his job. R. E. S. Wyatt was the official assistant secretary and was later to become captain of England. I am sure that I shall be doing Bob Wyatt no harm by saying that at least in those days he loved cricket much better than he did office work and that lunchtime could never come too soon. The lunch, my lunch too was always bolted—why? Bob Wyatt always wanted to be in the nets when there was a moment to spare. Part of the time would be spent in trying to teach me to bat. More important, I had to bowl to him for the remainder of the time—this was real fun and competitive too—for he didn't use a bat, he used a wicket and on the middle stump he placed a sixpence which was mine if I could hit it. A sixpence then was worth bowling for, and I tried very hard.

I have a memory of Wyatt which probably he has long forgotten. An episode that took place in the holy of holies, the long room on the first floor of the pavilion. It contained a huge mahogany committee table with chairs to match. Around the walls were photographs of the great Warwickshire cricketers of the past; the biggest picture was of that great player Frank Foster, with many memorable games to his credit; whose most sensational effort was against Worcestershire when he made over 300 runs in one innings and took six Worcestershire wickets for a handful of runs.

One morning when Mason the clerk was away and Ryder had important business at the bank, Wyatt and I were waiting for the click of the door announcing that R.V. Ryder was on his way to the city. At a speed which would have done credit to even the fastest fielders the pictures were removed and carefully stacked, the august committee chairs were dealt with likewise—that is all but two—one for Wyatt at one end of the table, one for me at the other. The removal job completed, Wyatt whipped out of his pocket a hard rubber ball, quickly explained to me the grip for an off spin or a break and so on. Wyatt went through all the motions of the grips again, 'Put your first finger there and twist it as you release.' The ball would thump along the mahogany table, break inwards or outwards as the fingers contrived. This absorbing exercise was brought to a sudden and abrupt end for we hadn't heard the click of the door but we did hear the first footfall on the stairs, and with the speed of light we had the committee chairs back in position but alas not the pictures. Ryder looked around, 'Something wrong with the pictures?' he asked. We raised our busy heads from the papers so diligently being examined. 'Really, oh! yes,' we exclaimed. I was never sure, but I thought I detected a knowing smile on old Ryder's face.

CHAPTER THREE

Motor Cycles and Boiled Mutton

I took Mr Ryder's advice and before the end of the season I found myself another job. I joined the motor cycle division of Dunford & Elliot, founders of the Dunelt two stroke motor cycle. I was now a junior clerk, with an increase of 2/6d (12½p) in salary. At times I had reason to think that the title must have embraced accountant, filing clerk, deputy telephone operator, and, the most disgusting job of all, collector of two directors' lunches from the pub next door. Somehow or other the menu seemed always to consist of boiled mutton, potatoes and a goodly dose of concentrated onion sauce.

To get to the pub kitchen I had to pass through the sawdust bar, yes, a bar with sawdust on the floor complete with spittoons, reeking with the smell of last night's beer. Onion sauce, boiled mutton and sawdust stuck in my nostrils for a long time!

The offices were in Bath Street, Birmingham, a very seedy quarter and the works had seen better days. The directors were eager, full of enthusiasm and new ideas, but even to my young mind they seemed short of money. The motor cycles looked good, they entered all the trials, the TT as well for they had not only the ability to design the models, they had the courage to ride them.

They had bad luck (or was it lack of cash?) for whenever things looked like going well a serious defect would reveal itself. In one ACU six-day trial all of our bikes were out in a couple of days.

In the TT we would be going strongly and bang would go the engine! As I foraged around I could see that little, if any, of the work was inspected. In any large scale production, examination and inspection are vital; the price paid for this omission was high; in my opinion, terminal.

They suffered too from a competent, but unapproachable works manager. He never talked, he always shouted; he never barked, he always bit. Some seven years afterwards he worked for me as a shop superintendent at Hercules; to his great credit he was a changed man and thanked me for the way I handled him.

As for my job, at least it was varied. I progressed to the top office, the source of the ledgers, correspondence and accounts. I was told I would learn much; I did much, but learned little. At times I thought I was a latter-day Bob Cratchit, but perhaps Dickens would not have rated me that high! Conditions were not exactly the last word, the desks were high and sloping, which must have made me think of Dickens. If you got a ledger in position it usually slipped down and could at times be even dangerous to your person. Because the desks were tall, the back-less horse hair upholstered stools were very high. I suspect that the idea of these high stools was two-fold, firstly that to keep well balanced you had to keep your head down at the sloping desk, while if you relaxed and stretched, the odds were you would tip backwards with a mighty thump.

I complained to Mr Clements, the accountant, that I wasn't learning much. He suggested that I should read through all the correspondence before filing it. I did and it revealed what was going wrong.

So with more failures in competitions prospects did not look very bright. I said to Clements that if times were better I would be looking for another job. 'Don't do that,' he said. 'Let me speak to Mr Slater'—the managing director. I was duly sent for by the big man and asked to stay. There were great prospects, which I doubted. I was stubborn; could he speak to my father? 'Of course,' I answered, but I added that wouldn't necessarily mean I would stay. 'No,' he said, 'But perhaps you would give things a chance.'

He spoke to my father, who talked things over with me; his theme was that the threat of strikes was ever present and there was terrible unemployment. He pleaded that no real harm would be done if I gave it another chance, which I did.

I was given an insight into costings, that was interesting and helpful, but it made me more doubtful. I dealt with wages and came into contact with workers and piecework. I wasn't happy; I couldn't see the future that I yearned for here, or, what was more important, any way leading to it, so I left.

CHAPTER FOUR

Hercules, first rung on the ladder

It was 1926 and I was sixteen years old. I told myself that this was the time I had to go places. I had high hopes (quickly shattered) that I might join the Indian Civil Service and become a judge. I had studied the text books at the public library on how to enter the examination and I did the specimen examination papers quite easily. There was a long paragraph on sport; I wasn't too bad at cricket and football and reasonable at athletics — so far so good! I then turned to the rules and details of entry at the back of the book. The dreaded truth appeared, 'Applicants would have to have a private allowance of . . . hundreds of pounds per year and a clothing allowance of . . . pounds per year.' My father couldn't have raised even the odd pound, there were too many of us!

I continued to visit the same public library, to read all the newspapers, particularly the situations vacant which were pitifully few. These libraries were provided by the great steel magnate, Andrew Carnegie.

One day I spotted an advertisement for a junior cost clerk — it wasn't the job that later excited me so much as the company, Hercules Cycle Co Ltd. It had the reputation for demanding hard work and it was thriving. I got the job at the then princely wages of £1 for a forty-seven hour week. I still have and treasure that letter of appointment; somehow I felt I might be on the way, but nationally very black clouds were on the horizon.

The City of Birmingham in the early 1900s had the title of the 'Cycle City of the World' — Hercules in the late 1920s was the greatest cycle company in the world.

Formed by the brothers Edmund and Harry Crane, two Birmingham High School boys, their start in the early days was incredibly small. They commenced business in two adjoining cottages. Folk-lore had it that Harry cooked breakfast on a shovel over a fire, Edmund, or Ted as he was called, dealt with the sales and invoicing; they never dreamed of disaster, they always thought of success.

When I joined them they already had one very large factory in Aston. Nothing was wasted in these hard times; any finance that was available was always for new machines or new methods, and Ted Crane drove a very, very small car for many years; he also worked late into the night. There were no board dining rooms; meals for the top men were simple and served up on a tray.

Hercules were pioneers in automation, conveyorizing, automatic plating and enamelling, sandblasting and brazing. This was over fifty years ago and I know that for bewildering mental excitement perhaps it did not compare with microchips; the end result did though — for we made the cheapest cycle in the world, then claimed and proved it was the best.

On the assembly lines the naked frames started at one end and came off as finished cycles at the other. We did have a maintenance man on the lines who stepped in when an operator had to leave for the call of nature, we did have a chargehand too on each line who dealt with any assembly difficulty. *The lines did not stop.*

The cycles must have been very good, for over a very long period Hercules claimed, rightly, that they sold more than 60% of all cycles imported into India. True, we were flung out of that country one year by the Japanese, but next year we were back — the Japs were out for as long as I can remember.

As more money became available, the company turned its attention to advertising in the home market, they entirely dominated the trade. Another huge plant was rapidly acquired.

The export salesmen were widely travelled, and no country seemed to escape Hercules attention. The export sales ledgers were a veritable atlas of the world.

Edmund Crane, eventually Sir Edmund, was a bulldog of a man, tough and astute. Harry, on the other hand, was a kind sensitive man, always looking for a young man to encourage and always acting as a salve to the intensive and dynamic approach of his brother. Their greatest advance was made in the days of the deepest depression.

Harry Crane died young, in his 40s; Edmund eventually sold out to what is now Tube Investments and died a multi-millionaire.

I have just finished reading through a very old catalogue published nearly one hundred years ago, cycles were then being sold (by Myers, the company which I shall finally write about) at the very cheap price of £15.15s.0d. Just about forty years later almost the identical machine was being sold by Hercules at £3.19s.9d.

This surely was a miracle by any standard of pricing. It was made possible by mass production and fanatical application of the principle of the division of labour — heavy investment in the most advanced machine tools for the job and above all the conveyor system. There was something else too, not to be bought with money, the complete dedication of both management and men — the product and the company were all important. We never had a strike.

Over the years we have heard of numbered machine tools, robots, computerized tools and now microchips. I have yet to see, as a result, any substantial reduction in prices, or anything to compare with the dramatic illustration quoted above.

How nice it would be to read once again, 'Now at the reduced price of . . .'

I started at the standard time of 8.30 am. Saturday was a working day until 1 pm. My immediate chief was Mr Tom Collins, a kind man, a good teacher but like us all at that time afraid someone else might pinch his job. But lucky for me and for the company, he had no children and treated me as his, so I learned quickly.

I was deeply interested in the work and continually searched for information. There was an atmosphere of confidence and purpose, a feeling that if you wanted to 'go places', you certainly could, but you would have to work hard for it.

In 1926 black clouds gathered ominously and an industrial storm seemed about to break and the fear of losing your job sent a sickening shudder through even the youngest worker. The miners had threatened to strike and many were locked out. They tried to raise funds for their various marches and I remember the marchers singing their Welsh songs and hymns. I recall also their hollow cheeks, drawn faces and their pathetic collecting boxes. Looking back I felt then as I feel now, that they had a case, but this was bungled by the General Strike which followed. At best, sympathy turned to a denial of their cause, at worst it turned to downright opposition by the ordinary people — and they, in the end as always, determined the outcome.

I was still at Hercules as a junior cost clerk, hardly the position or the time to 'go places'. I repeat with good reason that I was still at Hercules, the importance of that remark was that the ability to hang on to a job was in itself an achievement at that time, let alone progress. Jobs were very scarce, for the General Strike affected everybody.

When the General Strike hit us in May, everyone at Hercules was sacked and told not to return until the emergency was over, when we would receive a telegram in confirmation. I registered on the Lord Mayor of Birmingham's Appeal for boys, girls, men and women who would volunteer to do anything. I volunteered as a tram conductor but happily for passengers I was not called upon to conduct.

It is difficult to convey the public spirit that was abroad; even in young people it welled up to meet the challenge.

It is no good pretending that things did not alter in the early days of the strike. Food was short and almost all work except by volunteers had stopped; but there was no shortage of helpers. Flat hand-carts were common at many street corners; they were a mobile way of selling fruit and vegetables in the city. The carts were immediately turned into carriages to convey girls to their office work, or to help in food distribution.

I remember too standing at the corner of New Street and Corporation Street in Birmingham to grab hold of a copy of the miniature newspaper, *The British Gazette* edited by Winston Churchill; somehow or other this pathetic news strip seemed to keep the people together, and stiffen their determination; the anxious desire to obtain a copy showed the tempo of the people, and their ultimate resolve.

Some might not agree but I felt that it was the united will of the people that prevailed in strength and the strike was brought to a sudden end. It had lasted only nine days, an episode our nation could well have done without.

This feeling of rising of a national spirit is perhaps best described in the words of a great Canadian, MacKenzie King, its one time prime minister, who, in a much later crisis said in a speech on 'Britain, its source and strength':

> The spirit of a nation is not readily defined. It is known only as it is revealed. It resembles the flow of waters hidden beneath the earth's surface. From time to time and from place to place the waters, having their origin in some secret source reveal themselves as springs or rivers. So also from time to time a nation's spirit wells up from its source and manifests itself in the collective acts of its people.

* * *

The strike was over but after twenty-four hours no telegram had arrived so my father insisted that I telephone Tom Collins, the chief cost clerk. 'Oh! you are too late,' he replied. 'You should have turned up when you had the telegram.' 'There was no telegram,' I said, 'And I've checked that too!' 'Then you had better come along and see what can be done. Turn up at my desk in forty minutes.' I did, and then came one of those quirks of fate — the cost clerk was taken seriously ill. I was left alone, at sixteen, to face real problems; my first chance and my first real test.

In the growing days of Hercules, Government contracts for bicycles were of major importance. This was the hey-day of the telegraph boy who delivered all telegrams on a bicycle (and they were delivered promptly). Consequently the Post Office contract for cycles was a big one, and in the off season it was essential for us to obtain it, for it provided work for many of our workers. However before we could even scent a contract, the tender (a huge document) had to be completed, which necessitated costing to a fine degree, obtaining promises from suppliers of guaranteed delivery dates for parts. Now, I was alone, I had to complete this very big tender with only a few days to go. I worked from early in the morning till late at night; I badgered the general works manager for labour details, the chief buyer for raw material prices, the accountant for on costs and after two days I was working to a steady conclusion.

The inter-departmental phone blinked its red light, signifying it was the managing director, Edmund Crane (Mr Ted) calling. He barked, 'Collins!' 'No sir! Cooke.' He continued, 'Where's Collins?' 'He's ill sir.' 'You say you're Cooke?' 'Yes sir!' 'Never heard of you!' 'Well I am Cooke, sir, Collins' assistant and I do know quite a lot about things sir!' 'Well, what do you know about the Post Office tender?' I answered, 'That's all right, I've nearly finished it.' 'You!' he growled, and the light went out. My lights nearly went out too, and minutes afterwards a breathless company secretary (Alfred Rowe) rushed in, gasping, 'Have you been talking to Mr Ted and promised him the Post Office tender?' 'Yes, sir, I have.' At that moment I must have appeared confident if not down right brash. 'Where is it?' he choked. 'Here, nearly finished.' He continued, 'My word, it's big and complicated — are you sure it's all right?' 'I am certain,' I answered and Alfred Rowe departed to his office.

Minutes passed, the red light blinked again, 'Cooke,' growled Edmund Crane. 'Come down to my office with whatever you have on that tender.' 'Yes, sir!' I replied somewhat meekly.

I picked up my papers and marched down three flights of stairs, knocked on the heavy oak door, listened intently for the voice, which seemed like a whisper. 'Come in.' I gingerly pushed the door open and stepped on to a carpet which must have had the deepest pile in the world. I swear even now that the rich deep pile tickled the back of my knees. There, seated behind his desk was the great man himself. He had a bullet head, nearly bald, a chin that jutted just a bit too far, with a face not normally given to smiles but which just at that moment carried I am sure a suggestion of a smile. 'So, you are Cooke. Good! Just draw up a chair opposite me,' he said.

I did so and faced him across what seemed to be a very, very large walnut desk.

'Those are your papers?' 'Yes,' I said. 'Put them away then,' he replied, 'I just want to talk to you.'

'You are very young Cooke, just over sixteen, and yet you are confident that you can produce a tender that not only will be good for the company, the men, but the Government as well.' 'Yes, sir' I replied. 'Well,' he said, 'I just want to say a few things to you before you finish it.'

He continued, 'Suppose you produce a wrong tender, say too costly, we shall lose the contract. That would be disastrous for the men, more unemployed, and disastrous for the company, for without work our overheads continue and we would make a loss. Suppose you are wrong and we lose money — disaster for us all. Suppose you are right and we win the contract, that will mean more work for the men and a bright future for the company. Do you still then say you can produce the right tender?' 'I do, sir,' I replied. 'Then go,' he said, 'And see me two days before the due date and we will have a final talk. If you want help quote me; if details are hard to come by tell me.'

After that I worked as never before. When the tender was ready, I checked the legal details with the company secretary and he cast an eye across the figures. 'Now,' he said, 'I will ring Ed. Crane and you can take the papers to him yourself. Down you go.'

Once more the long wait at the door, the difficult walk across the deep pile carpet. 'This is the tender sir,' and I gave it to him. 'And here are the papers.' He looked at me again saying, 'You remember what I said to you the other day and the consequences if we're wrong (it was "we" now) and the benefits if we are right? Then give the tender to me. I will surprise you, perhaps shock you. I am going to sign it right here and now.' And he did. Of course you have already guessed, we won a handsome contract and I was on the way up.

* * *

One day, and I knew it had to come, my chief recovered from his serious operation and I was the junior again, but for forty-eight hours only. I was told then I would not be expected to do a junior's job again and was to be promoted to supervise the shipping department, a very important operation covering the freight costs, bills of lading, harbour dues and documents, and the handling of the forwarding agents; it was a job previously done by a woman and to say that Lucy Copestake was efficient would be an understatement. She was also a second mother to me and in later years even tried her hand at match making.

Our export business was very big with shipments to almost the entire world — Brazil, Canada, New Zealand, Australia, Lithuania, Holland, Sweden, Norway, India, Belgium, Argentina, Peru, all parts of Africa, particularly the west coast and the Cape. It was interesting to see the various specifications for the west coast of Africa; this market demanded everything that ever appeared on a cycle — chain guard cases, three speed gears, horns, bells and above all mottled paint (this was a very simple process of delicately passing a candle over the fresh enamel causing a singeing which resulted in a mottled effect). Very often we were asked in pleading terms for tins of this 'mottled paint'.

I pitched into every item of cost, from timber imported from Russia for the crates to the small items of bills of lading at Southampton and Liverpool. At that time Southampton was fighting hard for business and its charge for documents was much cheaper than Liverpool. In Liverpool we had a fine firm of forwarding agents headed by a Mr Taylor; I politely told him that unless Liverpool charges could be brought into line with Southampton he would lose a big slice of our business. 'That's an ultimatum I suppose,' he cried. 'I would think so,' I added. 'Then will you hold off until I have seen you? I can dash down tomorrow.' 'Of course,' I agreed; tomorrow arrived. 'There's a Mr Taylor to see you,' said the receptionist. I went along. Mr Taylor was a very well dressed city man. I stuck out my hand; he looked at it rather peculiarly perhaps checking whether it was clean or not, coughed slightly and said, 'You do know I presume that I have come from Liverpool to see Mr Cooke?' 'Of course,' I replied. 'I am Cooke.' The colour rose to his face. 'You! You! You're Mr Cooke!' he stammered. 'Told me I would lose your business, yes you did!' 'True, true, but not as savage as that,' I replied. 'Come along then to my office.' He coughed once more then slapped his hand on my shoulder. 'Well done, though,' he stammered. 'Let's see how we can help.'

Help he did, by the time we had finished the company achieved much lower costs and he increased his business. I suppose some of my Socialist friends (I have quite a few) will say even at that age I was motivated by profit but that would only be true in part. I was interested in efficiency; profit was merely the visual end to efficiency. Taylor and I were friends from that moment onwards but for ever respecting the relative bargaining positions.

* * *

Work was still difficult to find and news that a company was taking on a few new employees spread like a bush fire. I remember once at Hercules we wanted four labourers, next morning there was a queue nearly a mile long; men who were hungry for work and for food stood four deep. Our personnel manager walked up and down the line, touched one here on the shoulder, felt another across his middle, touched another's arms, selecting as we select cattle for market today; it was a sorry sight that I never want to experience again; I felt scarred and I vowed that if I had any say it would not happen again.

I was nearly seventeen now and making my way. The one pound weekly increase was welcome.

Our plant at Aston Cross was in a unique position for on one side of us was Ansell's brewery from which a ripe old smell of booze pervaded the atmosphere, while on the other side was a vinegar company and the HP Sauce factory, both giving forth highly spiced smells. Towards the city was a great gas works filling the atmosphere with choking fumes. Below in our own basement was the lingering smell of naphtha from the old Dunlop days; here beneath the office block the reserve stocks of cycle frames were stored. I was taken through this holy of holies for the first time and was amazed to see row upon row of frames bearing names of famous cycle firms, BSA, Rudge, etc — an Aladdin's cave; it was an accepted secret that we were making for the great as well as for the masses.

In the factory, liquid refreshment was provided by the tea boys. On every landing and at various places in the big assembly shops giant tanks of boiling water bubbled away ready for break time. The tea-boys collected a motley array of tea pots, tea cans (about seven inches high with cups forming the lid), mugs or if supplies were a bit thin just cups; the precious tea was dropped by the owner in the appropriate pot and the tea boys collected them on to several big trays, filled them with boiling water, then distributed the brew. If you wanted, or rather if you could afford a smoke you went into the yard as smoking inside was forbidden.

If the weather was good I went with my previous boss, now a colleague, to Aston Hall, a particularly lovely Jacobean building (built 1619-35) where Charles I was entertained in 1642; about a mile away from the factory, it is a beautiful and historic site overlooking Holy Trinity Church and close to the Aston Villa Football Club.

We would sit and eat our lunch looking at this beautiful old building. I suppose it was then that I first got an appetite for ancient houses, an appetite that has developed with the years; I now live in a lovely old house built in the time of Henry VIII.

I was just seventeen in 1927, a spectacular year when Lindbergh flew solo across the Atlantic. There was a reminder of that Great War that ended just nine years earlier with the opening of the Menin Gate at Ypres. I did not see this great memorial till fifty years later but the deep feeling of sadness was still there. It was the year when the parliament buildings of India in Delhi were opened. I saw this spectacular complex on a tour of India many years later, and though by then they had passed from the keeping of the British, I still had a feeling of pride. In the Hercules days these events were just pictures in a newspaper, or a news item on the old wireless set that stirred the imagination.

The close association with world shipping had its spin-off for later in life when travelling to various parts of the world, I had a feeling that I had been before, nowhere more so than in India. It was to India that we exported vast quantities of cycles in a knocked down state in a case that could be carried by pack animal or coolie. From time to time claims for almost total damage were made and increased so much that the insurers sent an investigator into the hills of India. He discovered that a large number of the packing cases 'accidentally on purpose' rolled off the coolies' back down the side of the track to be recovered later of course and disposed of! That enquiry stopped the problem.

Shipping was thrilling then with the exciting names of ships and the knowledge that our ports were loading for this country and that, which up to my initiation to shipping were no more than names in an atlas. Even the terms were fascinating — time required for delivery alongside, FOB, CIF, and so on.

Hercules were pioneers in conveyors; if anything was carried by a labourer, then it could be carried by mechanical means. That was the slogan and conveyors sprouted up throughout the factory. Everyone was striving, we had no strikes, no downing of tools, very little clock watching. I know it can be said the economy of the times enforced the discipline. This would not have been entirely true though. There was a definite collective pride in the company and an overwhelming desire by staff to do their best in an economy that was friendly neither to company nor employees.

These were the days of original publicity when newspapers carried full page advertisements on the front page; we once had a spectacular advertisement using a picture of Hercules himself, with the hand thrust slightly forward. Unfortunately no one made any allowance for the folding of the paper which made Hercules look decidedly suggestive if not downright pornographic. The paper sold very well indeed and so did the cycles!

Through its advertising agents the company strove to take advantage of any position or event to increase its sales. For instance we had an annual works outing to the seaside or country to which every employee from directors downwards were allowed to go, or rather supposed to go. The one I have in mind now was to Tewkesbury. We used nearly a hundred motor coaches which joined the procession at various intervals, and a vast number of motor cars. There was to be a push ball match (the game where a gigantic ball about five feet high was pushed along the pitch to score). The big ball was carried on the first lorry bedecked with the firm's emblem and colours, the great cavalcade (naturally we had a police car leading the procession) got stuck at the first set of traffic lights. The amusement was terrific and the advertising impact enormous.

We had another advertising stunt which was entitled 'All for exports'. For many weeks we had been informing the press that our export orders were increasing tremendously and a great push was being made to clear the backlog (I am not suggesting that a few cases had not been saved up). Monday was deemed the right day for lorries to drive from all over the Midlands to load cases for export from very early that morning. Traffic movement was difficult, and by 10 o'clock every main road for miles around was jammed with lorries either loaded or waiting for loading. The police had been notified and did their best to unscramble the jams. The advertising value, particularly abroad via the press photographs and handouts was terrific. I remembered these tactics and put them into practice many years afterwards to good advantage.

* * *

The next move up in business followed soon after my eighteenth birthday. The company had an idea that good though the factory output was we were not getting value for money in every section because of 'fiddling'. I was told I could engage twenty booking clerks to record all completed work, excluding assembly which was covered by a card system, and was charged with organising a complete checking system throughout the whole factory. This gave me the chance I was looking for — to get to know more about production and what made things tick.

First of all I extracted from the wages records the total number of items booked and paid for, running in operational sequence from the first operation to the last, e.g. assembling lugs to tubes, to making frames on jigs and so on. It was quite obvious from this check that certain operations had been heavily overbooked. One item, 'patching', stood out. This operation was necessary because after the semi-automatic liquid brazing of the frame, small spots of metal remained exposed from the brass, and these required a hand process of patching. Judging by the number of patches booked against the number of frames produced, each frame should have looked like a spotted dick, but a test check revealed that each frame on average carried only one and a half patches. We at once installed a booking clerk who recorded man by man the number of patches completed, the total number of patches booked dropped dramatically. Half of the men involved were out of work but they were found other productive jobs — a great saving, which provided half the cost of the total clerks engaged in the entire factory. This immediate small success was mine, but the major credit was due elsewhere, to the person who thought up the idea and inspired one young man to concentrate on the basic and elementary principles.

And so the year rolled on, the booking systems were refined, statistics and controls were built up and this brought me into very close touch with Harry Crane who was the works director. He got to know what I was doing and asked for a number of items to be translated into charts. As I dealt with these, I had access to his office and his criticisms and suggestions which was another very helpful leg up.

I was then promoted to have a 'free thinking' couple of years. I had authority to walk, stand, look or enquire into any operation, room, building or method, and question whom I liked. I was in fact an efficiency man. Anything that looked inefficient I was to report on, first to the man in immediate command, secondly to the works manager, thirdly to the directors. There was great wisdom in this, for it did away entirely with the possibility of factory or office politics. The fellow on the job knew first and very often he could offer suggestions too, so could the works manager. Thus in the end we got the best ideas on each level with no politics.

I had long thought of a particular operation which seemed to involve a disproportionate amount of walking. This job was the lining of mudguards. I should explain that after the mudguards were enamelled a thin gold or red line was lacquered on them for decoration. This was done by means of a colouring box, an invention of an engineer from Redditch. A simple enough affair, a metal box not quite as big as a match box was filled almost full with coloured lacquer; at the bottom of the box was a tiny valve which allowed a small amount of lacquer to pass through and a gauge which the operator pressed hard against the mudguard thus ensuring that the lacquered line was in exactly the right position; the operation was very fast.

The important thing was to keep the operators fed, and to remove the mudguards once the lacquer was dry. A number of girls simply took about a dozen mudguards over their outstretched hands and carried them down the steps to the mudguard stores. I sketched out a carrying stretcher which would convey ten times as many mudguards at one move. The cost of my method against the existing system represented a tremendous potential saving. All this I committed to paper and the foreman, supervisors and even the girls were enthusiastic. I waited for a whole fortnight, nothing happened and I couldn't wait any longer. Next time I saw a relaxed Harry Crane, I said, 'What do you think of the idea of conveying mudguards?' Normally not a swearing man he answered, 'Bloody daft.' Well I don't know if there is any water colder than iced water, if there is, I was drenched in it at that very moment. He was a kindly chap though, and must have noticed the effect for he at once countered, 'Bloody daft, yes. It's made us all look bloody daft too—we can put a small conveyor in there and save the lot!' He added, 'Now remember Cooke, anything that can be moved by hand can be moved by machine.' The ice-cold water still trickled a little though.

I stuck harder then ever to my theme of eliminating carrying and was busy looking everywhere for ideas and studied many books on the division of labour. My next big breakthrough was in the press room, another holy of holies. There was a good technical superintendent in charge and I would ply him with a continuous barrage of questions. I had the idea that where components needed more than one pressing operation, we could avoid any carrying by resiting the power presses so that each operation was in the correct sequence. This was of course difficult because a gang of presses occupied on say a four successive operation schedule would need to be reasonably fully employed.

I was told it was a bit daft anyway because presses were already overworked and we were about to spend approximately £100,000 on additional plant, a lot of money in those days. We were only just thinking of installing what today would be called time and motion study, so I had nothing to go on except my own observations. I acquired a stop watch and started timing the various operations which would form the basis of my scheme. At this point the superintendent said he had had enough and he would kick me out of the press plant. I was ruffled and countered, 'One day you might have to worry you said that.' So I continued and the kick never came.

Timing presses was exciting for at once I had the feeling that here was a chance to make an immediate and considerable saving, both in time and the amount of plant required, but I had to bear in mind it was quite impossible to 'catch' or use more than a fraction of the strokes of the press unless it was fully automatic. So from time to time my enthusiasm waned, but notwithstanding, I gradually built up enough information showing that with proper handling and re-alignment of presses, we not only had enough presses but too many of some sorts. The re-siting of the presses was put in hand and the major part of the new investment apart from that required for new models was cancelled.

You might ask why this was an easy field? In a way it was simple because the business was growing at an enormous rate and the staff and management usually had to turn somersaults each and every day to keep pace, but they were well led. Here I must pay tribute to John Furniss, the general works manager, long gone from this world, who was dynamic yet tolerant, firm but fair, willing to listen to any new ideas which would assist in the vast increases required in production. He was very kind to me, carefully explaining why this idea would not work, but just how it could be made to work, and from time to time he would say, 'There's another fruitful field you could investigate.' No politics, that was his constant aim.

He and the directors had a very simple way of dealing with kitchen politics. Suppose someone said *sotto voce,* 'I don't like the way Jack is going about this, perhaps he's got something in mind but I doubt it.' He would at once say, 'Let's have Jack in to find out.' If it were anything but totally true, the informer would stumble with, 'Perhaps not now, some other time.' 'No, now!' Furniss would exclaim. If the falterer interrupted again he would say, 'You know our way of dealing with internal politics; if we find the guilty one he goes at once. If there's any doubt the two go.' It worked, it saved time, it gave peace of mind, and men and management could concentrate on their jobs.

* * *

It was felt that I should try my hand at looking around the office and its installations with the same enquiring eyes as I had done in the factory. This was a very useful exercise because I had not quite made my mind up about what I wanted to do when my industrial education was finished — did I eventually want to be a production expert creating something, or an administrator?

To widen my horizon I learned all I could about production and office routine during the day and studied commercial practice in the evenings. I would leave the factory at six o'clock, get home about seven, have a bath, put on a dressing gown and swot into the early hours of the morning for the intermediate and then the final examinations of the Incorporated Secretaries' Association, to become an Associate (AISA) just after my twenty-first birthday. Later this body became the Chartered Institute of Secretaries.

These were the days before computers, but even then the company had a neat little way of controlling its biggest non-productive expenses. A weekly record covered the wages paid to everyone who was not a piece-worker. It had to be prepared by the time wages were paid on Friday and every non-productive operation, was costed down to two decimal points. The grand total of the expenses then had to be compared and equated with the cash discount obtained on our purchases. If there was a variation of even a hundredth part of a penny per cycle produced there was an inquest. We thus knew all labour costs were covered. The marvellous tool that enabled us to do this rapid check was one single comptometer; indeed so keen was everyone on costs that consideration as to whether we purchased that comptometer or another calculator took up a great deal of executive time.

It was at this time that we also branched out on an automatic scrubbing machine to clean the wood blocked flooring, that was subject to costing too. These little matters in retrospect seemed perhaps petty when I came to spend millions in later years, but the basic lesson that was laid down was never forgotten by anyone who experienced it. In those far off days capital expenses on tools or equipment of any kind had to be recovered within three years from installation, in other words, to compete efficiently in a difficult world each pound spent had to play its part in reducing costs or that pound was never spent.

It is interesting to recall that our cost of producing a standard bicycle including all raw materials and fitments, ready for delivery, but not including advertising and delivery charges was slightly under £2 (selling in the shops at £3.19s.9d). To meet the Japanese competition we sold these machines delivered into India, at 39/9d – a risk in those days but it achieved a major break-through.

Every worker's aim be he or she a production worker, office clerk or administrator was to keep things moving and to look for cheaper and more efficient ways to do a job. At the time the going seemed hard but after many years in big business, they were for me golden days.

My tour of the offices was exciting. They occupied four very large floors though when we got to grips they were reduced to three. There was quite a big staff, particularly invoice clerks. We were sending out some 15/20,000 cycles a week now, so I fastened on to the largest operation, invoicing. Mr Hirons who was in charge of the operation expressed similar comments to my friend in the tool room that my posterior was in danger. Relationships were not improved in that year when I beat him for the first time in winning the sprint championship.

At that time we had a contract for a big direct mail order business, J. G. Graves Ltd, of Sheffield (very many years afterwards I was engaged in an attempted bid for the company) and we despatched many hundreds of cycles weekly direct to their customers. As the routeing tags came in from the factory an invoice was made out for each cycle, many typists were involved. To economise we simply took one typewriter and obtained big rolls of paper of invoice width and fed them through the machine. We allowed the routeing tags to accumulate for several hours, then one of the typists moved across to the reserved machine and typed a line for each cycle tag. The roll was kept in the machine for one week, on Friday night it was totalled up and despatched to Graves. There was a four way saving – far fewer pieces of paper, less postage, less work on ledger cards and one cheque in payment from Graves with the same economies for them.

Alongside this office survey we studied all wage sheets, looking for wages which were above the norm (sometimes due to fiddling) or for other reasons. Finally they were studied where the total cost of any item pointed to unproductive methods.

If any idea came to mind the procedure for action was very simple. A management circular was issued, the top copy went to the time study department (one chap) who first re-checked the timing. He in turn gave his views and very often the removal of a seat or the re-siting of a bin could affect results. Many of the ideas came to nothing, others produced ordinary results and savings, but occasionally a thought sparked off another thought and produced a brand new approach to an operation. I should say here in case of any misinterpretation that exactly the same approach was adopted in the case of low earnings. Was the timing right? Had the procedure been altered making it impossible for the operator to earn worthwhile pay? This was very important. Was there something wrong with an approach? Was there another way of doing the job? Was there extra keenness by an inspector? Finally, was the particular operator up to doing that job? On the other hand a sudden increase in earnings could signal a deterioration in quality.

I remember one vital job that revolutionized our sales ledger department. Yes, we had sales ledgers with loose leaves. To speed up posting we had junior clerks to stuff the ledgers, placing the appropriate invoice next to the customer's ledger sheet, the ledger clerk had only to flick her eye to the name on the invoice and check with the ledger sheet and post, withdrawing the invoice replacing it with a plastic marker. The invoices were clipped together and the ledgers passed over to the comptometer operator who: (a) Totted up the value of the invoices; (b) Totted up the value posted, put a red dot against the item in the ledger; (c) Agreed both totals; (d) Then finally entered her sales total on the list provided.

By very early the following morning we had our sales figures, fully analysed, and knew that the charging up process was correct and up to date too.

That system was easy to read, easy to interpret, and it gave one a feel of the quality of work and the tempo of sales by our salesmen in any area.

The managing director had a hatred of bad debts and twice a month he would stay in his office until late into the night to study the sales ledgers which had been trucked down to his office. He would go through them minutely for bad debts or slow payers, he could obviously read at a glance the history of an account and it was woe betide the sales ledger manager if a bad debt or slow payer had not been actioned. The result was very few bad debts.

In the present day higher computerized business, this kind of control would be laughed at, that would be wrong. A managing director would be as right today as he was then, for at one glance he knew the 'state of the poll' and at the end of two days he knew the state of his business. Also his executives were always on their toes knowing that a close check was being kept on day to day work. This is a lesson I have never forgotten and some forty years afterwards in the position of chairman of a very much bigger company, I kept my fingers on the pulse by looking (at random maybe) at precisely the same kind of records as my boss did some generations before. I am for ever mindful of that regimental motto *Knowledge dispels fear*—I believe it does in war, or for that matter in peace and in any walk of life at any time.

* * *

During these years I was always in close touch with my headmaster. He thought I should try and be of some help to less fortunate 'brothers and sisters' in the poorer parts of Birmingham. The City of Birmingham's Education Committee had what they called an 'After Care Committee' which meant in short a follow up after kids left school. The Committee recruited a number of volunteers (this work undoubtedly forms a substantial part of our education bill today) to go to the homes of boys and girls who had recently left school and they (the volunteers) would have three questions in mind: 1. To see if the boy or girl had found a job. 2. If they had found a job, their wages rate and how they were getting on, and if the conditions were fair. 3. If the boy or girl had not found a job or work of any description, the investigators would want to know what kind of work they were looking for and after further questioning by the visitor, could he or she or the Committee help?

I said I would try, and duly turned up at the offices of the Committee. In those days it was an evening job and I sat awaiting an interview. I must have looked very young, for one Committee member came along and said 'Yes son, are you looking for a job?' I was on my dignity immediately. 'No,' I retorted, 'I have an excellent job, I thought it was the Committee needed help with your "after care".' I handed the now shaken member a letter of introduction from my former headmaster. That changed things. But I always thought they had the last laugh. Yes, they certainly did want help, he gulped, but unfortunately it was in one of the worst quarters of the city with stinking courts and back alleyways, filthy hovels lit by gas with open burners, no proper sanitation, bare bottomed children roamed around like little animals, dirty and messy. The air was foetid. For my area of work stretched from the lower end of Hurst Street (a very dubious place) to about a mile further south. Hurst Street was one of the arteries leading from the city centre of Birmingham. It contained two theatres, one at the bottom end was so-called the Hippodrome. It was also a parade ground for the ladies of easy virtue. From the theatre onwards, the shop property gave way to slums. The addresses themselves, once you understood the jargon, gave a fair idea of what you were in for. For example, No 12 back of No 4 Court, back 14 Blank Street. Or No 8 Court 2 back of No 6 — they meant just that. One walked down a dismal entry (corridor) at the side of No 14 into a wide alley, cobbled paths, one dreary gas lamp fastened to the side of a hovel, Dickensian like, casting a fitful glow on the seemingly endless line of slums. Eventually I came to hovel No 12. It was bad enough in the winter, but the overwhelming heat and stink in the summer was awful, the atmosphere was choking.

All this work was 'for free', in fact you would probably not have done the job if you were paid, for it touched at the very heart of human suffering. At that time there was a sweet on the market called 'Chiclets' — a peppermint covered chewing gum. On my visits I would nip into the street corner shop for a packet, chew a 'Chiclet' avidly, to clear my mouth, and throat, of the smells that were about, and spit out the residue and hurry quickly to my call. I will just pick out a few calls from my memory.

The first call I ever made was to a very dingy hovel back of No 14. It seemed a lot further than that. After much knocking on the door it was opened by an emaciated woman. My mind boggled — was it Harry's mother or grandmother? 'Are you Mrs . . .?' I tried. 'I am, what you want?' she panted. 'I have called about your son Harry, has he got a job?' 'Come in,' she gasped. I went in. The red tiles on the floor were coated with filth and were only visible in parts. The wallpaper was peeling off, the gas light was an open burner. The furniture consisted of two chair frames with wooden boards about 9″ wide for seats—whilst the table was three planks across two old packing cases. The little fireplace was full of dead ashes. An enamel washing-up bowl was in the corner (water came from a communal pump in the court). There was a text on the wall 'Jesus loves me'. I had my doubts about that—if he did he must have shed bitter tears.

I coughed 'And now, about Harry.' 'Well sir, 'e aint very strong, 'e suffers with his chest.' I had not yet learned the right approaches. 'What does his Dad do?' I asked. 'He aint got no dad 'e's dead with the consumption.' (I thought yes, and you will be soon, from the same trouble.) 'Have you got any more children?' 'Yes,' she said, 'One daughter still alive—but not for long—she has a chest. Would you like to see her?' 'No.' I couldn't face that, so back to Harry. 'So you don't think Harry will be strong enough for factory work?' 'No,' she said. 'Or shop work?' I asked. 'No, only strong enough for office work.' Eventually little Harry came in. I questioned him—he certainly wasn't very strong, you couldn't expect otherwise, and his education was not of the best. But yes, I said, we would somehow try and fix Harry with an interview and hopefully with a job which joyfully we did. But I had the feeling first time that the family would not be around for long. That was the saddest call.

My next call, still in the same district was not so touching. I sucked another 'Chiclet' and made for another court. I knocked on the door, it did not open. I knocked again and again, it still did not open. Eventually a window, a sash window opened and a comparatively young woman, who, but for the ravages of time and her trade might well have been a bit of a beauty, poked her head out. I was subjected to a battery of unprintable four letter words, but I shouted 'I've only called about your son.' 'I tell you now,' she screamed from that upstairs window, 'Get off this bleeding plot.' I shook my head, swallowed another 'Chiclet' and suddenly realised the reason for her anger—I was obviously upsetting the rhythm of her occupation.

The hot summer nights drew on. I still did my visiting twice a week. Some calls were very heart tugging but here and there there was the funny side. I went to a back of beyond court; my knock was greeted by a man who was not unlike Doolittle in *My Fair Lady*. 'Yes, what do you want?' he asked. I told him. 'You had better come in,' he said, and the way he said it you knew he was quite proud. This little terraced cottage was so different; no peeling wallpaper but everywhere and everything was spotless, floors, windows, hearth. The cheap brass ornaments glittered in the evening light, the home-made pegged type rugs were clean and bright and there were even a few flowers in a vase. 'Yes,' I repeated, 'I've called about Jack. Has he got a job yet?' I enquired. 'It's good of you to ask,' said Dad, 'But yes, I have got him a job with me, a scavenger lad he is, works alongside.' 'So you're a dustman,' I observed.

Then in a slightly louder voice which Mom could certainly hear (she was busy making tea) he said, 'He brings ten bob home to his Mom every week doesn't he Mom?' he boomed. 'If he behaves himself he will be like me one day, a dustman, and that is a job for keeps.' Those two words 'for keeps' were vitally important.

'Now you'll have a cup of tea,' he chirped. 'Could give you something a bit stronger but I think tea's better for you.' Again in a very loud tone he said, 'Yes, he's got a good job, brings home like I told you 10/- every week to his Mom, so he can come off your list now.' I had my tea, I said thanks. 'Now,' he said, 'I'll show you along the terrace to the road.' On the way he whispered, 'Told you a lie, a bit of a lie in front of his Mom. He doesn't get ten bob a week, he gets 12/6d, but I open his packet and give him 2/6d for himself. Better that way—his Mom's a bit tight. I don't like telling lies really,' he declared.

* * *

I was about to finish my last big assignment on the administrative side before real promotion came. Hercules had made great in-roads in the cycle business and it was a big enterprise. The foresight and courage of Edmund Crane to win the Indian market had been rewarded where we were by far the biggest supplier. The Japanese had been knocked out and what appeared to be the suicidal price policy turned out to be a money maker, for the extra demand increased our buying power and our purchasing prices were reduced. Our ability to increase mechanisation resulted in a tremendous surge in production which in turn trimmed our overheads and increased profits. We engaged many more hundreds of operatives and had two large factories.

The payment of wages to the ever increasing number of employees posed a real problem. It was a rule never to be broken that wages had to be ready on the factory floor at 12.55 pm on Friday—payment was to be completed by 1 pm.

The payment was never a problem but the preparation was. A new system had to be devised. I was given the assignment as part of my efficiency job and it gave me control of all payment systems. I was about twenty-three and little did I know this was my last job in office administration. I got down to it by the simple procedure of doing each job myself and then making an assessment, lining up the works clerks to give and present the information in the simplest form to the wages department which at that time was catering for several thousand people. Came the great week when the new innovation went into action and all calculations and wages packets should have been ready by 5.30 on Thursday evening for the pay out on Friday. I was so confident that things would go well that I arranged to meet Mabel, my wife-to-be, in town at 6.30 pm. But things did not go right; in fact everything seemed to go wrong, nothing would balance and it looked as if we would be lucky to be ready the next night. In our hearts though, we knew we had to pay out at 12.55 next day—the hours rolled on inexorably. I thought of the appointment, I couldn't leave, I couldn't contact Mabel. I was sure she would understand, just as she had done before. The wages clerks were marvellous. We determined to break the back by 10 pm that Thursday night, come hell or high water; some of us at least would return next morning at 6 am. The light gleamed through. I sent out for chocolates, tea and cakes to keep the staff happy; they were great. At 10 o'clock we packed up with a fair degree of confidence that at 6 am the following day we would see things right. Meanwhile Mabel phoned and all was well. The clerks had a fixed salary and there were no promises of anything extra, but, to a woman, they all stayed on late, and they all turned up early at 6 am next morning. The job came first. They did get extra, but they did not expect it.

Just three days before Christmas I had a visit to my office from the company secretary who was also a director. He said, 'Cooke, you've always been in first with your request for a salary raise, well we've beaten you to it this year, your salary goes up by quite a slice!' I gulped. I suppose I really had got a reputation. I had been outwitted in a kindly way. He continued, 'In addition I've got a letter for you from Ted Crane, just to wish you well.' That letter is still one of my treasured possessions.

I quote it not because of its references to me but to show that labour and staff relations on a high and personal level are not new. As far as I am concerned, nearly fifty years ago they were well established. The letter dated 22.12.1933 reads:

> It gives me great pleasure to express to you, my brother's and my own appreciation of your energy, whole-hearted support and loyalty to the firm during the years you have been with us.
>
> It is of considerable help to both of us to know that we have men such as yourself on whom we can absolutely depend. 1933 has been a record year for the Hercules Company, although the financial results have not yet been ascertained they will be satisfactory and as a bonus on these results enclosed is a cheque, etc.

* * *

As the company expanded it acquired a new works manager, who sold the idea of measured daywork to the company chairman.

Many of the senior staff (I was one) protested that this system, whilst saving booking, and in theory, inspection, did nothing of the kind; in practice it protected the slow or bad worker and indeed it penalised the fast worker by depressing his earnings to the level of the slow or poor operative. We pleaded that we already had the best of both worlds and our assembly lines, like the Windmill Theatre, *never closed* for the final adjustments were made by the leader, the highest paid man. The many assembly lines were graded—the fastest line carried the fastest workers and it was the reverse as far as the slowest line was concerned. Therefore good and fast workers earned and were paid more than others. In addition each individual operation was priced so that if a line was clogged up on an operation a fast operator from another line would help out and his line was credited with the wages. The proponents perhaps assured us that measured daywork ensured that:—(a) Costs would be reduced (less booking, less inspection); (b) Less inspection—therefore less inspectors (this assumed the next point); (c) Quality would be improved—again because operators would not be impelled to sacrifice quality for speed; (d) There would be no unrest between workers because one group would not earn more than another. We never had any unrest anyway. It seemed curious that all manual workers were supposed to be equally skilled.

Production fell, so did wages, so did quality. Because quality fell, we needed more inspectors, because quality was challenged operators became restive. Indeed after a couple of weeks, output fell by half.

The men did not strike for two very good reasons — they could not get another job easily and they had faith in the management that the system would be reviewed. They appealed, they showed their wages packets, they pointed to the stacks of cycles which still needed adjustment.

The orders were rolling in fast. We were losing ground and some of us realised that would be a setback for the company. Daily we appealed for a return to the previous system. It was not too easy to convince the managing director after so short a period, but after a few more days, when his precious company could have been in jeopardy, he acted and we returned to the original system.

First all lines were cleared of repairs and adjustments. Once this was done, production was re-started and within days it was even higher than before. Improved quality followed, and we were set for new horizons. It was a narrow escape.

I read just recently of the problems caused by maintenance men on the motor car assembly lines. Even the tools and men had to be selected before a plant repair could be carried out. In the meantime the plant I gather stood still. I reflect technical advance has been terrific. If we had had the kind of tools available then, as BL has today — where might we have been. What we did have in good measure though was management, real management, from the floor upwards and above all great co-operation from the workforce — perhaps what we are lacking is a bit from both management and men.

We had maintenance points on the conveyors, maintenance men jumped on a breakdown; no arguments, the lines were kept running.

No factory is ever without problems but we did have a way of dealing with them quickly. Some were even amusing. I remember a case when the polishing and mopping supervisor had to deal with a young woman operative who was moved to a new mezzanine floor we had built for extra accommodation. She did not like it at all — she said the spindle was too high. The supervisor said to her, 'Come with me love; together we'll measure the height of your old spindle.' I think it was 3′ 6″. 'Now,' said he, 'Let's go to your new spindle and measure that too. There we are lass,' he exclaimed triumphantly, 'That's 3′ 6″ too.' 'Now-ow, it's wrung somewhere, if spindle isn't 'igher the flo-ower must be lower!'

Many years ago the two great railway systems which were then in existence, the GWR and LM & SR both carried their initials on the sides of their coaches and trucks, they appeared in gold leaf and paint. The story goes that some thoughtful employee or passenger had the bright idea that it was pretty obvious to anybody with eyes to see that as the coaches and trucks ran on rails, the said coaches and trucks were in fact railways, so the question was posed 'Why have "R" after the initials GW and LM & S?' Why indeed? The point went home, the 'R' was dropped, and from this simple act great savings were effected.

* * *

Early in 1935 I was invited to visit the secretary/director. He pushed a chair out for me and poured a cup of tea. He enquired how all the new systems were going — did I think I could find a replacement on at least one part of my job and search round for another chap for the other half.

'Well, Cooke,' he said. 'I had better come to the point. You've been with us now for eight years. You've had a good insight into every part of the business. I am told that I must now release you to the works side. I can tell you in advance, but not in detail, you are going to be offered the assistant works manager's job at Manor Mills.' It produced all the components for the assembly plant; in fact if production failed on any component manufactured at that plant, output and delivery was affected at the assembly plant.

Alfred Rowe continued, 'During the morning Harry Crane will send for you and spell out the details of the job. Answer yes, if you feel you're right for it, or no, if you feel otherwise. Don't at this stage argue too much financially, that will follow; you'll obviously get a good increase in salary anyway. Above all remember the responsibility. You are very young, just eight years ago you joined us as a junior clerk at a pound per week and you probably now know more about production and administrative systems than any of us. I'm sure you can and will do the job.' I felt very humble, and thought that the latter statement was more than flattering. I left his office and kicked my heels for the next hour or so, thinking of my good fortune.

Eventually the phone rang, would I go along to Harry Crane's office? He was a calm yet determined man, quietly spoken, fair but firm. He outlined the job and said that in arriving at his decision to give me this post at twenty-four years of age, they realised that some people might think they were taking a risk. He was confident they were not. With all the new developments particularly in nickel and chrome plating taking place they were looking for someone who would be young enough to stand the strain and fair enough to deal with the staff if problems arose.

He congratulated me and thanked me for accepting the post, I would have a fortnight to clean up, but no notice announcing the appointment would be made until I was ready. This was due to the fact that I would have working under me many supervisors and managers who were old enough to be my father. At least two had threatened they would kick my arse to 'kingdom come' if I ventured on their preserves again. I was also to work alongside or rather be the assistant to the gentleman who had advised on the measured daywork system; it would be difficult for he now allowed smoking on the shop floor, the theory being, that if the men smoked on the shop floor, they wouldn't dodge off to lavatories and waste precious time. On the other hand to some of us there was the appalling risk of fire which we experienced all too soon.

I took up my position of assistant works manager. It was a real break — my meals were served in my office and I had a full time secretary.

I knew what I was in for that first morning. I had to meet all the managers particularly those two who years before had threatened to damage my posterior. I did not have to wait long. I arrived at 7.45 am, the works opened at 8 am. At 7.50 there was a knock on my door. 'Come in,' I called. There stood this big man, the superintendent of the press shop, twiddling his cap in his hand, he was more nervous than I. 'I was determined to be the first to see you on your big morning,' he said. 'Do you remember years ago when you were asking so many questions that I said I would kick your arse out of the place?' 'Yes,' I said, 'I do.' 'Well,' he said with just a touch of emotion, 'I want you to know that if there is anything I can do, anything at any time for you I'm here to do it. Good luck, sir!' 'I couldn't have a better start,' I replied. 'You did spur me on with your threatened booting of my bottom, but thank you again.'

Some months before this appointment I was engaged to be married. The drawings for our house were completed, costs were obtained and the land was bought in a beautiful piece of country south of the city, my new job was in the north of the city and I had to be close at hand for any emergency in the new operations. I talked it over with my wife-to-be and we decided that the land had to be given up and the plans scrapped. We searched for another house and found one about four miles from the factory, so with the prospect of a married life, a new home and an exciting business life, it was good to be alive.

There were problems of course and these were the days before company cars were perks. If you wanted a car you had to buy one and frankly with a new home, etc I could not afford it or rather we were not prepared to pledge anything or indulge in a mortgage.

If there was a breakdown at night (and many sections of the plant worked around the clock) it was the assistant works manager who was called on first. Only if he could not deal with the problem (but he better had) was he privileged to ring up his senior colleague. This meant that the chemists (vital in plating), engineers and electrical management staff had to be on good terms and have the same outlook on life as mine and turn out in any emergency at any time. Happily in the main we did share the one essential aim — *the firm came first*. I cannot stress that point too much.

We were married, set up house and shouldered responsibilities at the age of twenty-five. Even though I was called to serious problems in the middle of the night and hired a taxi to bustle down to Aston only to show up again for a shave in the morning, my wife never grumbled. She, having been in the medical business, agreed, as you would expect, that service came before self.

* * *

The story of producing even a simple item like a bicycle is too long to tell in detail, but one of the most interesting yet simple processes was wheel truing for which we used German machines. The spokes were laced in the wheels by girls and then trued by men. The wheel was lifted on to a bench, the spindle screwed into a holder and a little mirror or reflector rested on the top of the rim; above this mirror was a light shining down on the mirror which reflected on to what looked like a skeleton dart board; as the operator tightened up the spokes and the wheel became more balanced the light moved to the centre of the board until finally when the wheel was completely true, the light was bang on the bull's-eye; it was most effective. I was so deeply impressed and I still vividly remember it. Then there were those thrilling assembly lines, automatic sandblasting, conveyorized enamelling and plating plants, the big press shop and so much more.

We always had a very big exhibition stand at the Motor Cycle and Cycle Show usually at Olympia. In the trade it was the event of the year. A bright idea was hatched up, it was decided that our cycles had not only to look the best — the machines on show had to be mechanically the best too. Deep thought was given as to how this could be assured.

It was decided that all the component parts were to be made in our tool room — for the very good reason that the tool makers were our best engineers. The parts had to meet up within the original tolerances shown on the drawings or blue prints. The components were duly produced and looked marvellous.

Came the day for assembly, and a mild panic set in. On assembly very, very few cycles worked correctly. Time was now precious. We compared these specially made and very costly models with others taken from stock and without question the stock machines worked best. There was only one way out — we had to use standard cycles with extra spit and polish. There was a rush to ensure a shine on component parts and frames from stock sufficient to make thirty to forty machines. When assembled they all worked perfectly.

But we did not leave it there. We wanted to know why the mass produced article worked better and the answer was really quite simple: once the tools for mass production were produced, with no tolerances, and set dead on, the production of almost perfect components was assured. In short the sum total of all the tolerances on the tool room job was not nearly so accurate as the dead accurate tool producing a dead accurate job. But out of that problem emerged the answer that mass produced cycles, engineered from perfect tools and tightly inspected, were indeed better than hand crafted articles. But the original tools had to be dead right. Needless to say our advertising people used this revelation to good effect. *Not only were our bikes the best — they were cheaper too.*

I mentioned earlier that one of the exciting developments was the installation of what we claimed to be the first automatic conveyorized nickel plating and chromium plating plants in Europe, possibly in the world. I only came on the scene as they were becoming operational so this enables me to go into some little detail purely as an observer.

For that age, the plants were quite revolutionary and even by today's standard would be regarded as big. Both plants covered a huge floor and stood several feet high. Each were immediately over their feeding operation, *ie* nickel over polishing, chrome over mopping (brightening). Each consisted of numerous vats and a large drying oven. There were seven or eight vats in the nickel plant containing different liquids, sulphuric acid, cooled by water filled cathodes, the huge plating vat with about 20,000 gallons of nickel solution and a fortune in nickel anodes, etc.

Previously there would have been several operators working on each vat with a time lag at each for loading. The new process was continuous for twenty-four hours a day and the components were loaded at one end by a couple of operators with another couple unloading at the drying end.

All this was made possible by the use of one continuous horizontal conveyor and seven or eight vertical conveyors which lifted up the racks and placed them on the horizontal conveyor for their passage through each separate process. As the vertical conveyor dropped the transport bar in position on the horizontal chain it was conveyed through the particular vat of solution to be lifted up again on completion and likewise until every process was finished. The chrome plant operated likewise, but chrome plating used a much more dangerous solution. Prior to this innovation we employed much more space and perhaps seven times as much labour with a more difficult job of controlling the ultimate quality of output. Obviously there must by now be even more refinements to the job, but the cut in costs achieved by just that breakthrough, I feel, will never be repeated.

There were the critics. It was regarded as a joke that the plants were located on the top floor above everything else. This was deliberate for it allowed the 'swill' to drain off, but above all the very location ensured the quickest passage from the preceding to the concluding operations. Time was precious; time wasted cost money.

A contribution was made by all — capital from the company, planning by the management and understanding and assistance by the operators. Although we met difficulties, there were no walk-outs or strikes.

Harry Crane was right when he told me there were difficulties ahead. If the conveyors on the plating plant were not in perfect rhythm disaster could follow. If one rack jammed with another (the amount of swing varied with the loading) the vertical conveyor would shudder and that could throw strain on the main conveyor causing a pile up. Yet the balancing process could not be completed until the plant had dealt with many varied loads. Trouble came too soon and my phone rang at 2 am with the urgent message, 'main conveyor jammed on the chrome plant'. I was at the works very quickly together with the design director of the plant suppliers. The plant had jammed and a cog wheel (about 3½ feet in diameter) had cracked in three parts, so the plant just could not run — that was serious, for little or no stock of work was kept between operations as we were at peak season. The designer took a look at the fractured wheel and pronounced, 'The plant will be down for eight or nine hours. We have to dismantle the chains forming the conveyor, the fractured wheel has to be removed from its spindle and rushed away to the factory for welding, strapping and truing.' We had no spares as the plant was very new.

Getting the wheel off proved a difficult job. We tried freezing with ether, and many other ideas too, for operating space was restricted. It was off at last and rushed for repairs. In the meantime the night staff waited for the drying oven to cool and then removed the plated components both from there and from the various swills; that gave us at least a breather. The day staff were switched quickly to the static plants to give some cover. Nine hours later the wheel, duly trussed up and strapped was refitted, the delicate job of taking the plant through a trial run was commenced with a man standing at each of the many change-overs. Thankfully, very thankfully, no further assistance was required and I made good use that morning of my emergency shaving set. The breakdown illustrated vividly the tremendous time and labour saving virtues of the new idea—that was not unimportant.

* * *

The orders for Hercules cycles continued to pour in, far above anticipation and production was strained to the limit. The component plant had been planned to produce a maximum of 20,000 sets of parts a week but we needed many more.

It was at that time I received a real lesson in the responsibility of management. The phone rang, 'Ed Crane here,' came the clipped staccato voice. 'Cooke here, sir,' I replied. 'Oh, yes,' he said a little more relaxed; 'How are things?' 'Quite well, sir.' 'How many sets are you producing?' he asked. 'Approximately 25,000 a week.' 'Oh! really,' he countered. 'You know of course how the order book reads?' 'Yes about 38,000.' 'Then what about it?' 'We are already producing about 25% above the plant norm.' I thought this a good point to get in. 'Really, is that of importance?' I hesitated, 'What?' he said, 'Would you say if you ordered a cycle and it arrived without hubs, gears, handlebars, free-wheels?' 'I have the point,' I replied. 'Now, who is responsible for the provision of these parts?' He had given me enough lead not to fail on this one. 'Me, sir!' 'Good, good!' he continued; 'Now what's the problem?' 'The machinery is running flat out, we shall have to spend capital on extra machines in some sections.' 'Have I ever said you can't?' 'No.' 'Then you know the drill. Send two copies of your request and good luck, you'll soon beat the targets!'

I should explain the reference to two copies of the note requesting capital expenditure. If you required capital you simply sent Ted Crane a note itemising the plant required with an estimate as to what the plant cost would be and the period over which the cost would be recovered, normally three years. Ted Crane would then send one copy back signed in red EFC—he was the only one allowed a red pencil. He would keep the other copy and three years hence you would be asked, how this or that particular piece of plant was paying off.

However, the demand for cycles was very seasonal. It reached its peak in May, eased down in June and slid very rapidly in the last weeks of July. In one way that was useful, for the tradition was for factories to take the first or second week in August for the annual holiday; adding on the bank holiday closure it gave eight days. There were no package holidays then. The whole factory was closed down and management too took their break. Just a caretaker crew was left.

As the last week in July approached I was conscious that the annual ritual of lay-offs was to begin. Now I had the responsibility of deciding how many men had to go on the eve of a holiday. I felt ghastly. I think our share of the lay-off was just over one thousand. It did not seem to upset the employees a great deal. I swallowed. I had to get down to the slaughter and in terms of human suffering it was just that. The job was done, the instructions were given and my soul was seared. I knew that these lay-offs were common practice but I vowed that we would find a way out. The spectre of men going home to their wives and children with the trip to Blackpool cut down to a local day out at Sutton Park or Aston Hall never left me throughout the journey to Ireland.

Normally you would expect it to be a very happy time. We were off on the Friday to Ireland and the Glens of Antrim and the Mountains of Mourne—they really do come down to the sea. However it was a sad time to think about the victims of lay-offs.

On the return from holiday I contacted my works management colleagues. I also went to see the company secretary. I asked him what the chances were of avoiding lay-offs if we devised a scheme that gave a more even production during the year with a schedule that could provide some work for all throughout the year, even on the basis of shorter hours.

We reckoned that by reducing our stocks of components, frames and all fitments down to almost zero in the summer we could slowly build up to a high stock figure by the following January, running from then on at a more even rate although increased a little during the summer. All we should have to spend extra was a tiny bit of additional labour in storekeeping, a few thousand pounds on racks and the cost of the bank interest. Against this we could offset the cost of overtime, delivery would be very prompt and a more stable labour force would result in higher quality.

By offering more stable jobs we would attract the cream of labour, if, as looked possible, we would later have to increase our labour strength.

On paper this experiment looked very simple, but much heart searching went on, before it was agreed that we put the proposition to the directors. It was a hard-headed project with a very sympathetic appeal. We won a trial run provided the operation cost nothing except the interest on the extra money being temporarily employed. It paid off handsomely and the horrors of holiday lay-offs were avoided.

I feel that this was one of my better jobs, and one of which I have always been proud.

* * *

It may be asked why many of the queries were directed to me and not the works manager. I suppose doubts were beginning to enter the minds of the older heads that too many problems had been arising of late. Perhaps I had even been put there with this in mind—I wonder. I too was shocked at the number of 'friendly staff' being engaged using the then new idea of head hunting. By head hunting I mean pinching or luring a man from another company or a supplier who could not answer back, and offering him a salary which he could never achieve in his old position. Some said it was an attempt to buy loyalty; old heads knew you couldn't do that. Much head hunting went on and much doubt spread. Measured daywork systems and the fire incident gave way to unease.

The men who were brought in were decent fellows but they were a band of brothers and step brothers who had no inbuilt loyalty to the company. So eventually political cells were created. If there is anything that destroys the determination and strength of a company it is *politics*. In addition to this problem there was, after the sudden death of Harry Crane, no binding authority for the two plants. There was a second political build up between the two plants that should have been ended at once but was only to be satisfied by the appointment of a general works manager, my old friend John Furniss. The cells faded away. However it seems nationwide head hunting today is a professional job.

* * *

So political elements during the last twelve months of my stay with Hercules had built up, factory was against factory. It just had to be stopped and in the Hercules manner it was dealt with overnight. The pressure on my immediate chief was great, but his ideas were never accepted. He resigned. Eventually a number of heads he had hunted rolled or followed his way and resigned. I wondered who would get the job. I knew immediately after it was filled that I should have applied but I was too busy keeping the plant calm and steady. Be that as it may, the man appointed came from Rocky Lane, our assembly plant. I knew him well and liked him. He was much older than I, had a longer experience and deserved the job. But I was young, ambitious and therefore had to consider my own position, which I will refer to later.

Most of my colleagues of those far off days have gone! Alfred Rowe retired early and died early. Eventually Edmund Crane sold out. It would be only right for me to say that no-one could have had a better chance or better teaching than I had. Throughout my whole business life I have been eternally grateful for those early days. It could be said of the Cranes:

They built their best in the worst of times and thought them in the most calamitous. (Staunton Harold Church, Derbyshire)

I realized that recent events meant that I might be waiting for dead men's shoes and my youth was no longer on my side. If I wanted to go to the top at Hercules I would have to wait a long time for preferment so I decided to spread my wings and use whatever other talents I had.

I thought it only right to warn Hercules that I wanted to widen my scope both industrially and financially. There was sympathy and sadness. Some time afterwards I learned from John Furniss that he had read my stars right. His view was that money might be a temporary sop but sooner or later he was sure I would spread my wings elsewhere. He said that even if the company had a bigger job to offer it would not prove challenging enough.

I did not have long to wait for an opportunity for a few days after I had made up my mind, an attractive advertisement appeared in the national press.

'Young men of director stature for training, etc, etc. Littlewoods Mail Order Stores Ltd, Liverpool.'

I forget the exact wording, but the message was clear 'Director stature'. It was as if some fairy godmother had listened to my innermost thoughts.

The advert was attractive. The title (to be) was attractive likewise. Littlewoods were proving to be a great British company of considerable potential. I posted off my letter.

I had not long to wait for a reply. Arthur Moores, brother of John Moores, offered me an interview in Liverpool.

It seemed that while the slump in the country as a whole was making its mark, in Liverpool it was devastating. Buildings were empty, windows were unwashed, papers were blowing along the gutters, Lime Street Station was grubby. The wind always contrived somehow to blow from the Mersey. Estate Agents' windows were plastered with details of houses to sell or let and to crown it all there did not seem many people about. No bustle except at Littlewoods where even the commissionaire seemed to be on the ball. Yes, I was expected.

In minutes I was ushered into a small but well appointed office — beautiful carpet and curtains with a lovely fireplace. Behind a large desk was quite a small man who rose from his seat and said very cheerfully, 'I'm John Moores, have a chair.' I sat down. He walked round and stood quite close. He was very interested in my letter. 'Now what more can you tell me about yourself?' he went on. We obviously had something in common and seemed to get on well. He probed me for about half an hour and then told me that he had an estate fellow waiting to do a deal with him for over £300,000, but that could wait.

He talked with justifiable pride about his venture into the mail order business. He was frank with his figures. He told me too of his break into the chain store system of trading, and how difficult that was. There was great scope there. He explained that he and his brother Cecil were the only Directors. That was a good bait. He explained how vital it was in these new businesses to have men with fresh minds, free from thought of other competitors, GUS, M&S, BHS, Woolworths and the like. In short he wanted to carve out a Littlewoods philosophy. 'Now!' he said, 'You will join me, won't you!' 'No!' I said. 'I can't say that yet, there are many things I would like to know more about.'

He walked around his desk, picked up a packet of cigarettes, chucked them at me and said, all smiles, 'You are a cheeky young bugger. Have a smoke. That estate chap will still have to wait. Carry on with your questions.' I said, 'I will run through them as quickly as possible.' 'No!' he said, 'Not as quickly, as carefully as possible.' I started, 'I already have a position of considerable authority and prestige, consequently I control a great number of employees. I have a title.' To me somehow that seemed very important. 'Last and by no means least, what are the possibilities of rising to the position of director or in any event to the top?' He said, 'I will deal with your points backwards. On your last point, someone or some two will some day be appointed to the top jobs. There are other people of course beside you.' He made that quite clear. In fact they engaged fifty would-be directors for training. Of that fifty, only two remained after two years. 'The going will be hard,' he said, 'But I'm impressed with you. Now the question of a title and control of staff. I understand that point. You can have a title,' and he reeled three off. 'They could be starters. On the other hand I know what I am after and I don't advise you to start that way.

If you want to move the right way, and I would want you to; for after all I wouldn't be spending all this time with you unless I wanted you to go the right way.' I thought at least he was making no promises.

'As regards prestige that will automatically be settled if you make the last point. Move in now. In short I am offering you not a title, not a position, but a challenge and a chance. Will you now say yes?' I said, 'I really couldn't. I want to think things over, particularly your answers to me. I want to talk things over with my wife.' 'Fair enough,' he concluded. While the horizon seemed wide the risks were considerable. 'But,' I said, 'I will write to you tomorrow and tell you my answer and my reaction to your suggestion that I should seek no title and no particular position.' 'I know your answer will be yes,' he smiled. 'We shall get on well.' We shook hands and I departed.

I walked back to Lime Street Station, Liverpool, to board the train to Birmingham. I had many thoughts on the way home. Here was I, rising twenty-seven years, already in a sound and commanding position with one of the most exciting manufacturing companies in the country, contemplating packing things up, moving house to another city among new people, to an unknown job and possibly unknown future. No long term contract — they didn't exist. The only things that were really being offered were a chance and a challenge.

I pondered. Could I be sure of anything? No, I could not, except that I had struck up an accord with John Moores. Was that enough? There was one other director, Cecil who commanded the Pools and had the reputation, rightfully, of being a very nice chap. There were several other relations, brothers, brother-in-law, cousins and they could cause problems.

My wife and I talked the position over — the decision had to be made quickly. It seemed to boil down to this: — on the one hand the certainty at Hercules of a good position but now with no great challenge; on the other hand *very great uncertainty* but with a great challenge and possibly an advance to entirely new horizons. We talked long into the night and came to the conclusion that I would never really be happy in business again if I let the challenge pass.

What if it worked out wrong? We concluded we would just have another go, somewhere else. That was pretty forbidding, but once we made the decision we would carry it through. Forbidding, it certainly was, in view of the terrible unemployment and trade in general, to say nothing of Hitler and his threats. It was of course a much more challenging position than one would ever be offered today. You risked the lot. Today there are company houses, company cars, moving expenses and the like. In those days nothing, no nothing. These perks were only to grow as the years passed by and today I suppose few executives would ever consider taking on an appointment that did not carry a car, a long term agreement, a house and moving expenses. I merely make these points to illustrate the risk and the motivation, the power of challenge and the will to win. I make them not as apologies or from any mean streak of mind, because I suppose I as much as anybody else was responsible for bringing in new amenities, but whether they all do good is doubtful. Certainly they do nothing for the motivation of challenge and on reflection I think that is a bad thing. What they did do was to assist the head hunters and that I am certain must have had disastrous results; I have witnessed them.

I accepted John Moores' suggestion and wrote accordingly. The die was cast.

CHAPTER FIVE

Littlewoods

There was a time when Littlewoods meant just the pools firm. Today the Littlewoods organisation is one of the biggest private companies with a wide variety of interests.

Littlewoods entered the mail order field in what was then known as the club business. Trading by mail was not new, and I tell about it in the story of Myers. A club organiser got together twenty members or more each paying a shilling a week. The members drew lots for who should have first turn. A member with the first turn could choose goods to the value of a pound with delivery at once; the member with the twentieth turn paid for twenty weeks before she got her goods. It was a self supporting credit system with no risk of bad debts to the company.

It was mainly of interest to the lower income groups. Two important things were required for this venture: money and names. Money was needed to provide the costly catalogue, advertising, a warehouse stock and all the normal requirements of business; this was no problem. It enabled them to lose money in a substantial way to generate business. Littlewoods had ready access through their pools mailing lists to the names of people who did business by post, and in the right strata too. This was a gift from the gods!

Certain sections of the press cited the Lottery and Gaming Acts to prevent the use of the pools names. This was niggling, but it was useful in a way because the name Littlewoods was brought to the forefront. John Moores used to say that any kind of publicity was valuable and he certainly was right about this.

Next came the entry into chain stores. When I joined the company there were four or five mediocre stores. Trading through chain stores was a hard slog in the early days—though helped by the Littlewoods name.

Then the war came, bringing with it a series of serious problems but opportunities too.

Early in the war Littlewoods had many factories producing a wide variety of war equipment from balloons to dinghies, fuses to flying suits, components for Wellington bombers to pontoons. Above all, parachutes were produced by the million; in fact, one group I ran, produced every known type of parachute, including the escape type for pilots, the X type for airborne armies and the mighty clusters of parachutes to drop jeeps, guns and boats.

After the war buildings were available, labour could be retrained and reorganised, so the attack on the retail trade was launched. Many of the factories were used as ready made supply lines and an important link in the speedy supply of goods to both mail order and chain stores.

The old mail order club system virtually disappeared and an agency system with credit facilities developed rapidly. Growth was the order of the day. For a credit business money was vital and Littlewoods had money. Progress continued and on the other side the chain stores grew too.

Just like Hercules, Littlewoods invested heavily in capital goods and advertising (sites were the tools of chain stores). Only the best would do.

Of course, every business has more than one facet. In its early days at least it suffered sadly from internal politics which was to me by far the least attractive part. I suppose it might have appeared even worse to me after the thorough way Hercules dealt with the problem. I hope I played some part in quietening the problem, but eradication was not easy.

The company indulged, like most big companies, in head hunting. It was a modern approach in recruiting top people but I hated it then and I hate it now!

I was with them for twenty years, for nearly eleven years as one of the two first non family executive directors. They were always exciting and often very happy days. If any of my writings appear critical, they are not personal. I have tried to show the tensions, personalities, personal preferences, ideas, philosophies and above all the determination involved in operating a great business.

* * *

Having left Hercules on Friday I made my way north on the Sunday for my debut at Littlewoods on Monday. That perhaps is a day best forgotten. John Moores was abroad, Arthur Moores was away. The personnel department handed me over like many other 'would be directors' to the planning department. All day my mind was in a turmoil; if this was the way men of director status were treated what hope for the lesser fry? However, I was told that the acknowledged system for getting to know the business was to know its faults and that meant a stint in the inspection department. Dependent on your outlook, you either got to know the good points of the system or the bad things — come to think of it knowing the faults is not a bad introduction.

I wrote to my wife:

12th October 1937

> I am beginning to find my way around now — one or two things are a bit irksome but they of course have to be swallowed for the next few months. It's certainly a wonderful organisation.

At my small table I had a pile of copy correspondence together with an inspection report on its quality, how many typist errors, etc. I also had dumped at my side a bottle of milk, which I did not drink, although I should say that the provision of milk was forward thinking as it ensured that employees took a break and food in an age when food and drink was at a premium. My refusal to drink the milk was duly noted — my second brush in a short time. This one was irritating, even funny on reflection. But my first brush was more serious and fundamental. It was the demand that everyone should clock on. I refused on the grounds that it was quite wrong that management, who had to undertake all the responsibility, had to line up with the hourly paid employees whom the managers sought to manage. John Moores was keen on this and often clocked on himself but I never agreed with this either.

Back to the milk: I was reported to matron. Yes, they were well advanced in that sphere too with matron and nurses. I had a visit from her and she tried very hard to impress on me that the milk would do me good. If I did not like milk, what about orange juice? I must have one or the other or my refusal would be reported to Mr John. I rebelled at this. I said, 'Just you do that! But if I were you I would leave a bottle of orange juice each day on my desk and if I feel like it I will drink it.' She was delighted with this way out. It was this system of reporting and being reported, and certainly the threat of it, that I was sure was in need of dilution not the orange juice. I thought it should be eliminated and, though it was never entirely cut out in my time, it was diluted very substantially.

However the inspection system as a check on quality was a vital link in the mail order production chain. That is just what it started as. The whole office and warehouse system was scientifically planned, by AIC (Bedaux) and operations had been appropriately staffed.

It was important that a check on quality be kept, so that high wages were not handed out for poor quality work.

That was the basic idea for inspection but unfortunately the system went far beyond a production check and became a commentary on ideas and ideals and eventually on individuals. The amount of paper used was mountainous. I well remember an inspection report on petty cash, obviously a very small portion of the duties of the company accountant. Some withdrawal chits had not been fully dated, or full names had not been recorded. Little things, but the report was blown up to such a degree that it appeared that the crown jewels had been stolen. Even that method of reporting could have been tolerated if the report had been made to the head of department, but in my early days it was made to the chairman himself, with copies to everybody in authority, Uncle Tom Cobley and all, with the poor old chap in charge of the department well at the bottom of the list.

An excellent innovation of the time was the introduction of experts from the National Institute of Industrial Psychology, headed by a Mrs Raphael. The operation worked very simply. When a new system was introduced and after it had run for a week or two, the girls were at liberty to seek an interview with the NIIP, but the arrangement went even further and the NIIP investigated stresses, strains and frustrations, that were involved in so many operations. Trouble was looked for well before it developed; apart from being fair it meant good industrial relations.

* * *

To my wife:

13th October 1937

I have now found a very quick way of getting to Liverpool from New Brighton (just thirty minutes) by the underground railway — quite cheap too, only 10d return. It is also possible to get cheap ferry tickets too — 1/5d per week as many times as you like.

As I said I joined Littlewoods before the age of perks like motor cars, homes, long contracts, etc. So in the very early days in Liverpool when my wife was still in Birmingham, I stayed in a hotel in New Brighton which was quite a seaside resort. The cost of a hotel room and meals made a big hole in our savings. I wondered from time to time how long I could stand the job, and if by any chance I might be called back by Hercules.

I returned to the hotel one night to find awaiting me a large yellow envelope, the hallmark of Hercules. I thought, 'This is it — the recall.' It was not; but it was a marvellous letter from one of the directors who was away when I left, wishing me good luck and saying he knew I would do very well. That was it — I rang my wife and said, 'We move.' So we started house hunting.

House hunting in a huge area that was so depressed and seemingly full of house agents was a different experience to what it is today in a prosperous county like Cheshire. There were so many houses to choose from for sale or to rent at low prices.

A call to estate agents brought offers to meet the train, on Saturday and Sunday too, a car always standing by. 'What are you doing for lunch? We'll send you lists for each district.' The agents vied with each other in offering extras. The lists arrived, and in the meantime I did some hunting around eliminating areas that would not suit.

We saw four agents at intervals from nine o'clock on a Saturday morning. We looked at various districts and numerous houses. No, this wouldn't suit — that wouldn't do. What if the price were reduced? No, it just was not the thing. We narrowed down the first list to one district, the Wirral, that piece of land opposite Liverpool across the Mersey, still almost unspoiled in 1937. History has it that the whole of the area was the last part of the British Isles to be overrun by wild animals. True it is that the Romans had their convalescent camp at Meols, that Handel stayed at the inn in Parkgate before he sailed to Dublin for the first performance of *Messiah;* that King William III stationed his fleet in the Hoyle (Hoylake). Wallasey once had a racecourse patronised by royalty and at Birkenhead one of the first paying ferries in the world was established by the monks. Above all that the Wirral contained some very pretty villages, to say nothing of the mansions of the cotton kings of the past, the biscuit and drug manufacturing kings. It was the habitat too of many other prosperous tycoons of the time. Their houses flanked the Royal Liverpool Golf Course at Hoylake, whilst the old windmill on top of Bidston Hill gave a quiet country flavour to the whole area and the heather at Thornton Hough (home of Lord Leverhulme) was delightful. New Brighton, Wallasey and Noctorum were not built up as they are today but beautiful Caldy was becoming enriched with lovely houses; then the oases were more obvious than the buildings — it is the opposite today.

We searched around, tempting offers were made but in view of my experience in business to date we decided only to rent. That was no obstacle for the estate agents were joyful to get the properties off their hands anyway. Still another blank weekend but we decided to stick it out until something more suitable came along and anyway despite the drain on our reserves it was better to feel just a little more settled, so I travelled back to Birmingham each weekend.

One evening I noticed in a Liverpool evening paper an advertisement which seemed to fit the bill — a house in a little unspoilt village close to the sea with beautiful woods, a very old church, and an attractive tennis and badminton club too.

Upton, just a few miles from Birkenhead was then still a typical country village with the old cake shop up ancient stone steps, a general shop for everything from paraffin to linen and hen food, a real butcher's shop (not a retailing unit of an abattoir), and a grocer that was a general provider. I phoned the advertiser who was an agent for a great building society. I saw him that evening. 'Here are the keys,' he said shoving them into my hand. 'The rental is extremely reasonable. The property is in first class condition, and I feel certain you'll like it.' I visited the house that evening; it was in very good condition and the only fault there was not enough ground but there was a piece of land available the agent said his clients would buy if we decided we wanted it.

I called my wife and she came up to Liverpool the next day. Everything was first class except she did not like the colour of a couple of rooms. 'Well,' said the estate agent, 'It's all been redecorated but if your wife doesn't like the colour of her bedroom let her have the colour she likes and send the bill to me, and if there is another room she wants in a different colour have that redecorated as well.' Could it happen now?

* * *

Around the various sections of Littlewoods, the reception to all newcomers was generally hostile. Any suggestions were received with the retort that they had all been tried before and that the people who made those suggestions had long since departed. I realised why John Moores wanted bigger men and I determined at that moment to help forge a Littlewood philosophy. To do that the internal political set-up had to be weakened or destroyed, otherwise the peaceful dream of a Littlewood trading philosophy would never be fulfilled. I feel I helped.

In the next few weeks with vigour I covered personnel, planning, costing, stock control, buying, warehouse, mailing, sales, promotion and canvassing. The latter was most absorbing. Littlewoods wanted to grow quickly and to recruit agents they employed press advertising, circulars, magazines and of course canvassing which was always the most costly and unacceptable. It was part of the sales promotion department and had a manager with assistants each covering a section of Great Britain. Sections were divided into territories, each with an assistant manager. The territory was sub-divided into areas, each with a supervisor. That area was sub-divided into towns or villages, with a leader in each. Under a leader a number of women would carry catalogues around and canvas on the doorstep to persuade a housewife or workmate to become an agent. The agent in turn would persuade her friends or relatives to become her customers and she would get 10% commission on all the orders obtained. That part of the job worked well, providing the application forms submitted were genuine. We had our fair share, or rather unfair share, of non-existent householders and had to be certain that those who existed were honest and trustworthy. At that stage the supervisor was supposed to check the applications submitted via the canvasser, and re-visit the householder to express an opinion as to the applicants' suitability.

If acceptable, orders would be collected, attached to the application form, and forwarded to head office for checking by the area manager. They were finally vetted, accepted or rejected and bonus payments sanctioned. Unfortunately, many of the applications were faked—a hazard of the trade. Some were in respect of canvassers themselves. Sometimes, on counting heads, we found the area managers took the canvassers to the cinema or for a day out in the country! There was much to clean up. We quickly set out to increase the cross and spot checks, both on the ground and against schedules. Quotas were fixed, teams became tied to plans and, as both these systems began to bite, resignations from that part of the business were very brisk.

* * *

I set off on a new assignment a few days after I had written the following to my wife, addressed to The Poplars, Hilary Drive, Upton:

27th October 1937

My own Dear Pidge—Here is a short letter to welcome you to your new home—I know you will be happy there in fact I know I could be happy anywhere with you.

I had survived a few weeks and in doing that created something of a minor record. My wife was to move to Upton the next day when I was faced with a sudden change which would for a while take me up and down the country. John Moores put the case to me—would I manage a chain store to get to know more about the operation? I replied that I could not until I knew what it entailed, but no doubt I could learn and quickly. (We only operated eight stores then.) Would I go to Brixton Store then, with a couple of assistants, and learn merchandising from the stockroom upwards. Merchandising was an important door to open and the key to that door was in the stockroom.

I should explain the term 'from the stockroom upwards'. It has long been a tradition in store trading that the only sound way of learning the business was by first handling the merchandise. That idea cannot be faulted.

The stockroom was in the basement. Therefore progress could only be upwards for the simple reason that you could not go any lower, the sales staff never failed to make that point. But there is an old northern and midland expression 'if yer wants to learn properly lad, thee starts at the bottom.'

It undoubtedly is in the physical handling of the stock that the basic learning begins, whether in issuing to the sales floor, or recording and counting inward deliveries. The very feel of all types of merchandise makes its impression on the memory—you knew what things looked like, those items you handled most frequently you knew were best sellers, those items that stared at you from the racks without moving were non-sellers, or in the jargon 'lemons'. I cannot emphasise that matter of feel too much; I was to learn the classical, if not the glossy way. Merchandising is the blood in the veins of any retail enterprise and no sales records, no computers, no reams of paper can substitute that physical contact. Today, forty years on, I can remember many of the best sellers and certainly most of the lemons. My own task was to get and absorb information and establish a Littlewood System of merchandising.

Moving to London made me very sad. My wife moved north and just three days after she arrived I moved south to Brixton. So there was my wife, alone in a new area in a new house with friends only as she made them.

I stayed for a while in a hotel in London, returning to Upton each Saturday evening on the Liverpool sleeper, met by my wife on Sunday morning and back again on the sleeper on Sunday night to London. To pass the time from store closing on Saturday evening to sleeper time, I used to walk from Brixton to Euston. At least I could see some of the sights of London though the suitcase got heavier as Euston approached. The extra expense of this sleeper travelling was borne by me. My bank balance suffered what with moving house, hotel expenses, rail fares, phone calls and the like. It was tough but I liked to think I was tough too and that spirit saw me through.

To my wife:

16th November 1937

Moved into Cora Hotel rather Slaters Tea Bar now. This hotel is right opposite the Ambassadors—one of the real swanky shows, and I am writing this letter in a room dead level with the neon illuminated foyer . . .

Work is going down pretty well but what a mess it is in. I certainly don't want the job until it is cleared up a bit. Why it has been allowed to get like it goodness only knows. I'm getting quite used to the cockney slang—but Blimey yer dorn alf af to lissen.

17th November 1937

Well I have only done half a day's work today (Wed) the store closes at one so I went and had a lovely two hours in the Brixton Astoria—a swell cinema too—Jean Harlow in Saratoga was the picture—her last one, you know she died whilst it was being made—so you can imagine it would appeal to my morbid sentiments.

58

18th November 1937

You say I am not mentioning much about work—well it's really donkey work at present, real donkey work at that, but I would dread taking over quite in its present state. It is however proving extremely difficult to keep down to the '£250 a year man's' stuff idea [a reference to the fact that SGC was supposed to be just that—prepared for a short term to do the most menial store room job to get information on which to build].

I did not and do not complain. I was offered the job to manage and it was my idea to get to know things from the bottom, but the feelings I relate were real. I knew little about chain stores, but I did understand the fundamentals—expensive High Street sites with the resultant high rentals and rates and big capital expenditure could only be justified by high sales per counter foot. This in turn meant the introduction and maintenance of a detailed merchandise system which meant best sellers would have to justify the space allocated to them; poor sellers would be out. There was to be no room for two or three variations of one line unless it was an extremely fast seller. In short the whole range had to be made up of very fast moving lines.

At Brixton and throughout the whole chain of stores there was a tremendous amount of duplication. For example there were ladies' pure silk fully fashioned stockings at 1/11½d per pair, taking about £150 per week which justified just one line yet there were something like six almost identical lines so the cost of counter space and handling was excessive. In the corsetry department there were sizes to fit anyone from Mae West to Skinny Lizzy.

There was also the ever present problem of *shrinkage,* the erosion of the profit margin caused by a variety of human failings, breakages, damage and the never absent problem of theft.

There were many ways for the counter hand to pinch from the cash register, ringing up a lower price for a relative, stealing the odd coin and depositing it in the heel of a shoe. The choice of Brixton for investigation was a good and obvious one with its low sales, high stock loss and the shrinkage.

With the three assistants from Liverpool I set about the stockroom. There were so many lines it was like a poor man's Aladdin's cave of items never to see the light of the selling floor. There were two classical pottery examples, 'the boy with the thorn in his foot' and 'the girls with bunches of grapes'. There were hundreds of them in the racks and on the floor, and we did not sell one a week. There was the stationery department, a pretty deadly department in a chain store at the best of times; at Brixton there were twelve different writing pads and eleven never did sell.

Because so many articles were on offer no line, however good, ever got an adequate display which was vital. The only means of selling fast, the basis of success in any chain store, is to give adequate space to those items which are attractive with potentially high demand.

Again in food there were too many lines. Some sold very fast, some never sold at all. Many were sold at a loss to gain interest and volume.

There was one that sold only on Saturday and it was this that gave us a lead to one of the most common methods of stealing. This superb culinary item was prunes in loganberry juice which only moved on Saturday and in the evening at that. A dozen tins would sell in one go. One of my assistants was installed in the cafe bar opposite the food counter from early Saturday morning. There was a long, long wait and then at 5.45 pm there was a quick sales movement, one dozen tins of prunes, and many other items too. The sale was completed but only sixpence was shown on the cash register. Both the sales girl and the customer were questioned; both denied any collusion, but under prolonged questioning they admitted they were mother and daughter. The fiddling finished, as did the sale of prunes in loganberry juice — and the assistant.

The lack of proper merchandise listing meant overcrowded counters — resulting in insufficient display, with slow moving stocks cluttering up counter and store rooms alike and sales suffered. The cause of this serious position was simple to identify: we had too many men at the top, with too many different views and on the counters the result was too many items, the emphasis depending on the standing or strength of a particular group of the moment. Sometimes ex-Marks and Spencer staff were in the ascendant, at another ex-Woolworths, further down the line ex-British Home Stores. So if each group had their ideas in force for only a short while, the counters were littered with merchandise representing their different preferences, and finally our own mail order section's experience was thrown in for good measure. It was evident that the need for a Littlewoods philosophy as John Moores identified to me was very, very necessary.

I rented a flat at Montrose Court, Clapham Common. It was very pleasant though the Clapham to Brixton journey was hardly to my liking. The best thing about Clapham was the common which was pretty pleasant. Having a flat meant my wife could come to London, I would avoid expensive sleepers, I was nearer the store, I could shorten my stay and I could have my assistants round in the evening to prepare in advance for the next day, so things began to move along very quickly.

Meantime, the operations chief came to see me. He was a brilliant man, an ex-Woolworth district manager, a high position for one so young. He had no time, as he said, for some of the 'wallahs' in Liverpool. He said, 'Look Cooke, old boy, you can't fool me. You are going much further than merely supervising this store.' 'Yes,' I said, 'I guess that's natural.' 'Well,' he said, 'I know you don't like London, so you will want to get your ideas over quickly. I'll stay away from here for six months, then if you are ready to move on, I'll stand you a bloody good drink. Shake!' and he stuck out his hand. 'Good. I'm off.' That really freed me.

We had been carrying things through to logical conclusions with counter displays devoted to best sellers. The sad hosiery department of the past was attacked with enthusiasm — silk stockings were an appealing line to all women, young and old. We cleared the counters of dead stock, producing extra space for a full display of potential winners. We extended a range only for an obvious fashion colour, or size that had been omitted. Whole collections of poor sellers were tipped out. The effect was terrific, sales rose astonishingly and stock was reduced. Other departments were treated likewise.

We were now able to produce an intelligent 'check list' consisting of fast selling lines and their prices—in short, items which should always be on sale—it was then an indispensable guide to management. A superintendent's job on entering a store was to call for this list and check both the display and the price. The latter was very important to avoid what is commonly known as *price crowding,* a means of temporarily putting a higher price on a display to cover a potential loss or shrinkage.

* * *

Stealing was an ever present problem and it was continuously watched from every angle. In those days counters had an assistant in the middle with a good all round vision. The height of the counter was studied so slipping goods into a shopping bag was not easy. A nine inch glass kerbing went around the outside of the counter top; to take anything the hand had to be lifted *up and over* which was quite a deterrent. Open displays were few and far between.

Today, selling is virtually all self service. Fewer assistants are required, but the extra cost of ticketing, store detectives and shrinkage amounting to millions of pounds cannot be all magic as far as profit is concerned.

At Brixton, everything began to fit into place, weekly stock and sales figures were spot on, ordering was on time, deliveries were better because of regular ordering, sales figures enabled redundant stock to be moved promptly.

The Christmas season came on all too quickly and with it the very big crowds. One of my instructions was not to miss a week with the figures. However I resolved it would be absolute disaster to keep the system going during Christmas week, because increasing shopping crowds and movement would make accuracy of recording impossible. I therefore opted for a three week period covering Christmas and the New Year sales. There was no other way and that quick decision was necessary.

I decided we couldn't come to any harm, because if we ran out of merchandise there was no time to replenish stocks.

To my wife:

29th December 1937

I have this morning had a letter from H asking my opinion on two ideas—so it does seem, although I of course still take everything with a *pinch of salt,* that I am being appreciated—it helps so much.

30th December 1937

The job is still going along OK—lot of prejudice but at the right moment I shall sit on that with a capital S.

After my decision it seemed I was fighting my battle of Waterloo, except it was nearly my Waterloo. My proposal not to send weekly stock and sales figures over Christmas and New Year was thrown around by those seeking to protect their own ideas (I did not blame them—jobs were hard to come by) but they sought to give the impression that the planned system would not survive any normal pressure (but

61

Christmas isn't normal). That would not have been good for John Moores (who was anxious for a Littlewoods way of doing things), the company or myself. I fully understood that and had written to John Moores explaining the position but two days after Christmas John Moores, with a deadpan look, walked into the store very briskly. He came straight to me, 'You've bloody-well let me down; we shall be the laughing stock of the whole chain store crowd,' he growled. 'We have failed.' 'Sorry,' I said, 'We would have failed and been laughing stocks if we had done otherwise. Have you read my letter to you?' 'No,' he said, 'But I've finished with you.' 'I am sorry,' I replied, 'But with respect that could go for both of us.'

'That's it then,' he said. 'Would you,' I countered, 'Just read my letter, because on this very day we have everything as it should be, figures are correct and no damage has been done! Will you please read my letter? Then if you think this matter is seriously wrong, just tell me and I shall know what to do.' He said brusquely, 'Good afternoon,' and as an afterthought, 'I'll read your letter but it won't alter my feelings.'

To my wife:

31st December 1937

There has been a serious disagreement with J. M.

But it did alter his feelings. Within two days I received a charming note from him saying, 'Yes, of course you were right, absolutely right, it's I who would have been wrong.' An act of a big thinking man and it endeared me to him during the next twenty years that I worked with and for him. It also gave heart to me and my associates to polish off this part of the job and get back to the north to bind the whole rapidly growing chain of stores to a Littlewoods merchandising system.

* * *

So came the day to return north. There was no better view of London than that of Euston Station fading away as the train moved out! Mickey Riley was my chief assistant and I shall always be grateful to him. He had courage, wit and resource, and was with me for many years. He was worthy of a top job, which he never got, for reasons outside his making.

Although we had won an initial victory and were developing quickly, the whole of the merchandise and buying depended not only on the stores system but on a complete re-organisation of the buying section in Liverpool, using the figures provided by the chain. For many reasons this re-organisation was vital—checking overall stocks, making transfers, reviewing sales, adjusting orders (pending introductions of new items), providing bulk estimates on which buyers could negotiate larger contracts at lower prices, and above all chasing 'delinquent' shippers to expedite deliveries. There was now a collective approach.

I was moving fast through the field and was now a senior executive with quite an amount of power, and enemies, but not a directorship in sight. That would be a few years and a great war off. As the business progressed we were frequently opening new stores and the Moores' philosophy was very much like Cranes' at Hercules — publicity, crowds, queues, the use of big personalities from famous pilots to comedians, whoever was in the public eye at the moment of opening, and we certainly did get the crowds. We often had to fight our own way through the crowds to get into the stores. As openers or loss leaders merchandise was virtually given away — real bargains like pineapple cubes just 2¾d a tin, sugar 2lb for 3½d (just 1½p at today's currency), men's trousers 2/11½d per pair, women's dresses at 2/11d and so on. When we opened the Belfast store we sold out of trousers in minutes. Belfast was the home of cheap clothing and taxis were used to collect stocks from manufacturers, for we had to satisfy the great crowds of shoppers that were waiting then and in the days that followed.

This idea of opening a store with a near 100% check list became a talisman. A great drive was made by the merchandisers to get the goods delivered in the shortest time from the drying out of the bricks and mortar to when the first customers entered. It was split second timing. I introduced a scheme of sending out shoals of telegrams to all wayward manufacturers. Then managers of stores already open plagued us with telegrams for help. If the merchandisers could not shift the suppliers, the buyers had a go; if the buyers could not move them, then the head buyer and finally it was my turn.

The aim was to open new stores with every fast selling line on offer. Our new systems provided vital knowledge and a hope that if we opened correctly, we would continue that way.

* * *

By the spring of 1939 I was well established and making good progress despite politics; the company was showing its heels in the mail order and chain stores business.

Things looked bright and my wife was pregnant with our son and heir to be born in November 1939, but there was one cloud as the threats of war became louder. Everybody hoped for the best and tried to keep business going normally, which for me meant more and more visits to our stores, getting the feel of things and trying to put over the company philosophy.

On one visit I spent the night in Rochdale and my operations friend said he would fix me up at the best hotel. I realised when I arrived there were only two hotels, so it was not a very difficult choice. The one he secured was off Yorkshire Street — we had a store there. I wanted to see how this store operated, particularly at closing time. With that exercise over I went looking for the hotel. I made my way up Yorkshire Street but could see no hotel. I quickly came down again, still no hotel. I asked a policeman, 'Where's the hotel in this street?' 'Eh!' he said, 'I don't rightly know of one.' (I thought I had been taken for a ride.) 'Now wait a minute,' he continued, 'Ooh! Aye, go up left hand side until you come to a kind of opening, go through there and then in a far corner you will find a pub — sorry, hotel.' So I followed the directions—yes, a building was there. I tentatively pushed the door open; the sawdust bar was one side and 'Dad', obviously Dad, was at the back of the beer engine. 'Good evening,' I coughed, for I had a terrible cold. 'Evening,' came the reply. 'I think you have a room for me.' 'Aye, thee name is Cooke.' 'Yes, that's me,' I answered. 'Aye, well does yer mind waiting a bit, mother looks after them things, and she's taken daughter to the first house of the flicks, be home soon. Aye! You're ready for a meal too—she's got a very nice mix grill for yer. Thee's got a cold,' he carried on, 'Wants looking after—what about a drink?' 'Good idea,' I agreed. 'Thee'll want a big jug of lemon juice when thee goes to bed.' Yes! Mother eventually came home, I was to ''ave her son's room, the "neet" but ah must eat first.' A magnificent meal was served. Dad eventually directed me to son's room; it obviously was son's room for his boots were still under the bed!

In the country as a whole the war clouds gathered; at times it still seemed impossible that the worst would happen, though some signs left little doubt. On the ferry one evening from Liverpool to Birkenhead I leaned on the deck rail as the blood red sunset coloured the cheeks of the young soldiers, searing the sky and staining the Mersey. Turning to the young chaps I said—'Ah well! If it comes I suppose it will soon be over.' There came a clamour of replies 'Not this time mate, it won't. It'll be years. We're up against something bad!' That scene was etched on my mind. These young men who were going to fight had a feel for the position and what it meant. In the industrial mess that we are in at this present time men twice their age cannot comprehend that we are in trouble at home, losing our markets abroad, and pricing ourselves out of jobs.

In the event of war Littlewoods had already offered one of its big properties to the government, indeed it had been fully equipped with additional telephones. All too soon 3rd September arrived, and the Prime Minister announced Britain was once again at war with Germany. First, there was the impact of the blackout—it was forbidden for any spot of light to be visible at night—air raid wardens and police saw to that. Gas masks and evacuations were the order of the day; school children by the trainload were evacuated to the countryside, each tiny tot carried the inevitable gas mask and a little bag of belongings. Companies as a whole reacted immediately, and volunteers with help were ever ready. What we seemed to lack was leadership but shortly the country was to have a world leader in Winston Churchill.

On a company level our 'offer' of help came to fruition very quickly (except it was not really an offer). A brigadier descended on us with his supporting officers with a very important piece of paper. 'In the name of King and Country' he required possession of our stocks of sheets, blankets, pillows, pillow slips, quilts, gum boots and the like. Yes, we would be paid for them but he had to have them there and then. These homely items were the backbone of the mail order catalogue business and we paid very dearly for this in the mail order company. Then nothing much seemed to happen for a few months except the odd air raid warning, or the appearance on the streets of more and more army vehicles. Shortages of this and that were felt and many more men were being enlisted. The French believed their

Maginot Line was impregnable, and, while Neville Chamberlain has been blamed by so many for being taken in by Hitler, we had gained precious time for on the declaration of war we certainly were not ready.

However, a most important event happened in our personal life, on November 30th (incidentally Winston Churchill's birthday) our son, Roger, was born. For that important moment, war was forgotten. Humans have a spirit that rises above even the perils of war and ours did. All went well with Mabel and Roger and in the quiet of the Poplars in Upton on the Wirral the war could have been a million miles away. Of course the war didn't go away; it came with a vengeance. But it did not stop our little celebration, curtailed yes, abandoned no!

* * *

The company began to suffer, and, to its credit, it plunged into the war effort; within weeks parachutes were being made in Hanover Street, Liverpool (later to be bombed out of existence). Many of Littlewoods' buildings were switched to war work with unbelievable speed; resulting eventually in a whole spectrum of war work from parachutes, flying suits, balloons and dinghies, to fuses and shells and airplane frames and so on, and thousands of workers were transferred and trained to new skills. It seemed a great deal of this enormous amount of work was soon forgotten by the powers-that-be after the war for we had to fight very hard to maintain jobs for our staff. That was never easy.

In the days of the phoney war we had bought a very aged and decrepit business in Manchester; it had already been run down to the last spool of thread and the last piece of workable machinery. My task was to form a Manchester group of war factories.

The building was littered with the remains and bits of work of other generations. Somehow the conditions did not seem to matter; no one argued, the big floors were cleaned up, useless items were thrown out, black-out blinds were fixed, lavatories and canteens completed. Now we had our first factory in Manchester but no war work to go with it.

We tramped from one government department to another in search of contracts but with little effect. It seemed that in some ivory towers there was no war on! After titanic efforts, the Ministry of Supply asked us to quote for a large contract of WAAFS pyjamas. The WAAFS had a reputation of being attractive but the pyjamas certainly were not — indeed they earned the title of 'passion killers'. For me it was a far cry from producing cycles by the tens of thousands. In the old Hercules fashion we determined to win a substantial part, if not the whole, of this anything but imaginative contract. We would then at least have a foot in the door. We got the contract — I have the feeling that nobody else wanted it. We were in production and, being new contractors, we were subject to the most rigid government inspection, but that really did us no harm, it prepared us for the exciting and difficult work that lay ahead.

We were not happy though for we wanted more challenging work. In short we wanted big parachute orders, so the search for this type of work was on, and management time was spent mainly on canvassing for work. Together with my assistant we tramped around the various ministries, Aircraft, Supply, Naval and all, in both London and Leeds. From the replies we got, it still seemed that even then there was no war on, but time would tell—and for the country it only just 'told in time'—it all seemed so strange. Finally we decided to check with the Contracts Directorate to see if they would at least confirm whether they were fully committed. If they were it would be surprising; if they were not it would be downright crazy to turn us away.

The Director of Contracts was engaged but we had an interview with his deputy, Dan Levey (father of Sir Michael Levey, Director of the National Gallery), a most honourable and pleasant man, who never drank and who never seemed to eat. He worked very much to the book, but with a humanity that was Christian to the core, and the type of man who, pre-war, was the cream of the Civil Service. He said, 'Tell me what facilities you've got? What are your finances like and above all what's your labour position?' This was a fine approach and he got the answers frankly and truthfully. They had to be correct, he couldn't be hoodwinked.

He flicked over his papers. 'Suppose,' he said, 'We offered you a trial contract, for parachutes, would you be prepared to stand or fall by its results, and would you be prepared to do it on a fully competitive basis?' 'What kind of 'chutes have you in mind?' we questioned. 'Oh! simple ones to begin with; flare and star shell parachutes, they all take a certain amount of wire splicing—can you handle that?' We eagerly agreed it all; stage one had been reached.

The conversation continued, 'Now suppose the demand escalated and contracts became very much bigger, and the 'chutes got more and more complicated until eventually you became involved in the big supply dropping 'chutes and even man droppers; can you honestly say you could handle them?' I said, 'With great respect I have handled enormous production problems, sheet steel entering the factory on Monday, with the finished cycles leaving that same factory in tens of thousands within days.'

'Where was that?' he enquired. I told him and he was satisfied. 'Let me tell you finally,' he concluded, 'That if you are successful there's stacks of work, but you will have to be right on at least three major points: quality, production and price.' The three points were vital, I agreed. We shook hands. 'I've got quite a bit of work to do on it; be in touch with you sometime tomorrow.' We shook hands and were on our way.

The hard pavement outside Thames House had never felt so springy; we almost ran to Euston—there were few taxis about anyway in those anxious days. It has been said by an outstanding statesman that seven days in politics is a long time—twenty-four hours awaiting the yes or no on a contract is a hell of a long time. But at three o'clock the next afternoon Dan Levey phoned. Yes, there was great pressure for flare parachutes (used in bombing raids) and he was prepared, subject to us signing the documents, to give us a trial.

He emphasized there was a big demand for star shell parachutes for the navy and it might be better to lay out for this job first as it was simpler. He had notified the technical branch to send drawings and advised the AID (Aeronautical Inspection Department) to instal their factory inspection unit. We were ready to go and we did.

About this time the evacuation of Dunkirk fired the imagination — the little ships, the great acts of bravery, devotion and heroism have been recorded, filmed and talked about down the years and are now part of our history. I recall the railway stations seemingly full of train loads of troops, with grimed faces, stained with perspiration, with tattered uniforms, and those men tired beyond belief, grabbing the cups of steaming tea from the shaking hands of the tired ladies, working as required around the clock.

Vividly, I recall two brothers, rescued from Dunkirk, who made their first call to our office to make sure that their jobs would be alright when it was all over. Never will I forget that tired couple, their blood-shot eyes staring from blackened faces, no hats, their hair soaked by the sea and dried by the smoke of battle, their battle dress virtually without sleeves, and tattered trouser legs reaching only to the knees.

So now, the defence of Britain itself was more important than battles abroad. Sign posts on the roads were removed, as was any other indicator which would guide an enemy and, although we were reminded by Churchill that the retreat from Dunkirk was no victory, no one could deny it was a deliverance. The tale has been told many times of how really desperate the country was for arms (it seemed very strange that we had to search for war work) for we were to be prepared to fight on the beaches, in the fields and villages.

I remember a broadcast appeal made to the nation for everyone without delay to take any kind of weapon they had to the nearest police station. My wife had her great great uncle's gun, beautifully chased, complete with ram rod loader; she urged me to take it along. To say I was fearful of the reception was an under-statement, but I went. The policeman looked at it with admiration, but with no particular desire to acquire it as a weapon. 'Beautifully made!' he opined. 'Lovely chasing too! Bit of an antique, sir,' he said. 'Yes,' I agreed, 'But the appeal was for weapons.' 'Yes I know,' he concluded, 'But do you think a German would stand still while you pushed home the ram rod?' That was enough! We still have it at home.

* * *

The hours were long and the journeys to and from Manchester made night and day as one; so I had to move my family once more though it was not so easy to find an isolated place and be within easy reach of the factories.

After much searching I phoned a country estate agent, told him I wanted a house to rent for up to three years, either very modern or very old and it had to be south of Manchester. I nearly fell off my perch when he said I could have either. I was off like a shot. The new house was out, we had seen it before. 'Where's the key to the old house?' 'It's out,' he replied, 'Somebody else wants it too.' He described the old house and its location. I went to see it without a key. After some miles along the main road, I turned left as directed, drove nearly a mile up a cobbled lane (itself full of history) with a deer wood on my right. Further ahead, huddled among the trees was an old Georgian farmhouse set deep in the heart of lovely country. True, despite its leaded light and shuttered windows, stone roof and hand-made bricks, it was pretty run down. The garden was dominated by a huge bed of blackcurrants; the fruit was very useful in the hard winter when the snow which came under the door seemed deeper than it was outside the house. But above all there was peace, with the old walnut tree that had seen two or three serious wars in its time of guarding the gate, and there was the soft smell of the rich earth.

I fell in love with it. On the phone Mabel urged me to take it, but added 'You make it sound like a manor house.' It was hardly that, but it looked safe and in beautiful country too.

I went back to the agent, now in deep argument with the other would-be client. 'What about you?' coughed John Shapley. 'Me! I'll take it now.' 'Done! It needs decorating, water, sewage and electricity.' 'We'll see to that (in truth it needed much more than that). It'll be alright.'

No, it did not start alright, for on removal day the decorators had just started work. We arrived near mid-day on Saturday; we pleaded with the men, the boss and his wife, to work overtime, and all was well. They borrowed the keys and turned up again at 4 am on the Sunday morning. There was no electricity, above all no water; plumbing had been completed but did not work, so the 'two seater' away up the garden had to suffice some of our needs.

As for water — there was just a well, but the pump had not arrived. Life with a baby was hard — for a long time we fetched our water in milk churns from old Sam and Mary Slater, the farmer up the lane; we had our baths up there too. As for cooking we had to make do on a little Georgian hob grate.

To celebrate the arrival of the removal vans the heavens opened. That would not have been so bad except the removers had packed the kitchen and garden stuff in the van and our lovely antiques on top.

At last the pump arrived; it looked terribly small but I was assured, 'Our firm's done jobs around here for a hundred years, so it will be alright.' We would know when the electricity was connected.

The great day arrived for laying the water on; the electricity was connected, and a sickly trickle came forth to be witnessed by them 'what had put pumps in for nigh on a hundred years'. 'Sir,' came the suggestion, 'We can drop pump to bottom of well.' I reckoned the end result would be the same sickly trickle. It was. Finally there was a triumphant cry: 'We want a bigger pump, guvnor!'

In the meantime our demand for water got greater. Our old help from Birmingham arrived and she fetched water daily from up the lane, until one day as she was trudging back from the farm with a bucket of water in each hand a herd of cows approached. Helen just did not like cows. She promptly put down her buckets and nipped behind the hedge. She liked them even less as from her vantage point she watched them take long cool drinks, until her buckets were completely empty. Poor Helen.

The bigger pump arrived just two weeks from ordering; it was war time too — but by today's standards a minor miracle. Water at last, our main troubles would be over. No! No! The countryside in Cheshire took a long time to adopt us. We were not quite there yet. My wife and her mother were violently ill, awful sickness, headaches, the lot. The doctor came quickly — his questions were like rifle fire. Had I been sick? No! The baby! No. Drink any water? No! Drink any milk? Yes. He pronounced it either water or milk, and supplies must be changed at once. They were and so back to Sam and Mary for the water.

Doctor Allison said he would get the milk analysed. I was to take the water to town for analysis. I sent the specimen round and phoned the analyst. 'How soon can you get it through?' with some anxiety in my plea. 'Two to three days.' 'What!' I exclaimed incredulously. 'My family is ill.' He agreed to speed things up.

In next to no time he phoned. 'Where's that water come from?' 'A well,' I answered. 'Anybody using it now?' 'No, the doctor forbade it, but I'll confirm. Why?' I asked, 'Is it serious?' 'Serious, It's . . . lethal. It's about seventy-five per cent sewage.' I phoned home. They all recovered but it was a near thing.

Back again to the agent! The ground was opened up and pipes exposed. One was very near the well, but he said, 'I know it's alright we've poured water down.' He tried flushing the lavatories and empying a bath; the water cascaded like a minor Niagara Falls from under a big stone trough straight into the well! It transpired that the plumber in his anxiety to leave things looking right moved an ancient stone trough bang on top of a waste pipe. Systems were cleared and cleaned; we had water that we could drink, lights we could switch on and a house to sit down in.

We had our troubles but, through many extensions to the house and the creation of some lovely gardens surrounded by the beautiful countryside, we lived there for nearly forty years and, now, live only a few hundred yards away in another ancient house.

I thought as I came home late at night to a quiet and dark countryside that it was not really a bore to stop the car and shift the deer and their young from the lane so that I could get my car into the drive — but I do not think it was with any particular love for me that these beautiful animals lay waiting. I was sure of that when I looked at our garden in the mornings after; they rather liked our crops of vegetables which they devoured a-plenty.

* * *

We passed the test of the trial contract for flares and star shell 'chutes with flying colours; they were delivered before time, and up to quality. I say we because I have always endeavoured to make every job a team effort and to share out the success to all who contributed to its success.

The parachute production continued and in a short time we were employing many, many hundreds of operatives. Our relationship with the technical branch of the Royal Aircraft Establishment at Farnborough and later with the Parachute

Training School was first class. Our staff, particularly the management, was excellent; no job was too big, no assignment too difficult, and no day too long.

1940 drew to a close, we were settled in the old farmhouse; our evening enjoyment extended to a walk up the quiet lane.

In the early days of the new year, production was growing very rapidly, covering an ever widening range of newly developed parachutes. At that time the production of parachutes for laying mines in the sea lanes was urgent, almost desperate. The canopy was unusual being made of hessian, with rigging lines of very strong harness webbing. The whole outfit was assembled to a steel plate with its green multi-petalled canvas cover which held the release pin and static cord. As the mine and assembly was dropped it pulled out the pin ejecting a parachute drogue, which in turn deployed the main canopy. Made of hessian the 'chutes would sink with the mines leaving no trace. A tremendous amount of enemy shipping was damaged or sunk this way.

In that time of pressure in the late spring of 1941 John Moores phoned enquiring 'How's things going?' 'Quite well. We've got our troubles though here,' I replied. 'You might have your troubles but nothing like the one I've got here,' he continued. 'Can you come over quickly?' I did.

In Liverpool the atmosphere in the Mail Order Division was anything but cheerful and some of the permanent black outs did not help either. John was in the office where I first met him years before. He thanked me for coming over and plunged into the problems of mail order. He pulled no punches for the problems were very severe and he rightly said that without immediate strong and imaginative action, the mail order business might well be in jeopardy. He certainly did not under-estimate the problem; after listening, neither did I.

He asked me to return to Liverpool and deal with it — with the compliment that I was probably the only one who could put things right.

Having absorbed his review of the situation, I agreed immediate action, and tough at that, was necessary. This would mean I would be away from Manchester parachute production for some weeks but fortunately the management there was good.

I said that to succeed I would want a free hand on staff, merchandise, finance and, in fact, the lot. Without that free hand, success could not be obtained and the outlook would be grim.

The operation had to be original, quick and confident. Looking rather like Ted Crane did so many years before, he said, 'But I've never given a free hand to anybody in my life before and I doubt if I ever shall again.' Until his ageing years I don't think he ever did. He stood up and said, 'My secretary is in her room; dictate the authority you want and I will sign it.' And he did.

The company had taken a battering. Executive labour had been pulled out for war work; with bombing up and down the country the post and rail systems had become more than disorganised; Liverpool itself had suffered gravely; and finally we had had a lot of merchandise commandeered by the forces.

I was offered a tough go-getting assistant, Ray Evans, who proved of tremendous help and encouragement. Originally he was a chain store man, and very opposed to me in the early days; it was different now he was the man for the job.

The company had moved a large part of our clerical staff outside the city; some for reasons of safety, and others to make buildings available for war work. On the Wirral we occupied two mansions, Merle Dene at Bidston adjoining Upton, and Mere Hall, on the plain. Those two buildings held the mail order problems. John Moores told me that in Merle Dene over forty thousand letters remained unanswered, and we were losing ground every day. Unanswered correspondence, in the sophisticated mail order business is extremely important; it is the clotting of blood in the veins. With a good and up-to-date system of correspondence business is retained and often increased. When correspondence is ignored customers lose their faith and the company loses their business.

So having left the Wirral for Manchester I had made my way back again. It was difficult to find a local hotel as many had closed through shortage of labour. After a rapid run around I settled into the West Kirby Hydro, an imposing looking pile but desperately short on rations and service. For lack of labour it had to close its doors early and open them late; freely translated that meant there was little or no chance of getting breakfast and no chance of getting a meal at night except within restricted hours. That was difficult for I was anxious to get to grips with the problem, working from early in the morning until late at night. If there was an egg about in the morning the night man boiled it, otherwise it was bread and marge. If there was a cold dish at night it was very thoughtfully left on the table between plates, otherwise it was again bread and marge—that seemed to be my staple diet. Let me not convey that people were thoughtless or unkind. Not so; labour and food was just not available, and anyway at that time food and drink were the least of my troubles.

I looked over both mansions and talked with the managers and supervisors and some of the key staff. It was clear that Merle Dene was in a terrible mess: filing cabinets were bursting with unanswered letters, staff seemed to be walking this way and that and arriving nowhere. This elegant building had a baronial staircase, which went upwards from the reception hall to the very top of the building. The staircase was always crowded, with queues of girls going up, and queues coming down. I only needed one guess what the queue going up was for, but I journeyed upwards nevertheless and I enquired of the girls every so often, 'What are you waiting for?' Always the same answer, 'the lav' (loo had not reached us then). The downstairs queue was for another important human need: they were 'waiting to get a cuppa and a sandwich'. I watched those queues for a long time, then, as I often do now when anything troubles me, I walked around the garden; and that garden held something very important, for the very large glasshouses were full of tomatoes and the cold frames held lettuce by the hundred. These would help the sandwich problem. Continuing my walk I found an old coach house adjoining the 'baronial pile', and another thought clicked. I 'phoned the head of the chain stores cafeterias section seeking his help to feed a few hundred girls and quickly. 'What, today?' he cried. 'Yes, and we can start on tomato and lettuce sandwiches; bring some big tea urns with you too,' I concluded. He was first class and arrived very promptly with helpers, bread, marge, tea urns and all, they got to work with a will.

I checked the lavatories position with the head supervisor. We were indeed short on seats and required a substantial increase in facilities. I called the maintenance manager, always an old friend in need, pleading 'Look I just must have a new lavatory block for the women; we're losing half our working day whilst they queue up for their turn.' 'How soon?' he said. I laughed, and continued, 'Yesterday would be best but I'll take tomorrow.' 'Impossible but I'll try,' he said with a confidence that did me a lot of good. I thought with those two problems about to be solved I was on my way. I make these points merely to show how common everyday problems can snag up a good organisation.

Next I had to overcome a defeatist attitude that was abroad, the 'we will never get it right brigade'. This could have been difficult for I would have to be very firm but I would never give in.

However, I was able to trace the root of the 'we are beaten' battalion. I was sorry for him, he really was in a dicey position. He repeated 'the position is impossible' and just wanted to go; we let him. He was treated kindly and fairly for after all it probably did look a bit hopeless.

The effect of this one change was electric, for deep down the will to win was there and that corporate will to win is something no marvellous microchip or mighty computer can ever supply. Recovery started from that moment, for three essentials had been attended to, stomachs had been satisfied, so had the natural sanitary requirements. Above all their spirits had been lifted.

I now had to find a solution quickly to the main problem. I decided to cease answering any correspondence and re-sort the thousands of unanswered letters; I realised that this was at least very dangerous, yet it had a compelling attraction, for I thought many of the letters might be reminders from people who were writing a second time having failed to get a reply to their original letter. I guessed that if I was right this one act might halve the main problem; it was a gamble well worth taking.

It was essential to do the re-sorting operation outside normal working hours. The local management said this was impossible, because they had tried to obtain overtime and had failed. I suggested that perhaps hope might help and I could promise just that. I addressed the staff and explained my theory of reminder letters and pleaded for overtime, the response was full and enthusiastic.

The re-sorting idea worked like magic, and the guess had proved correct, for more than half the letters were in fact repeats. We analysed the complaint letters very quickly, immediate action was given and the healing started, heavy mail that continued to arrive for some time received similar treatment.

Thank goodness news travelled to Liverpool slowly in those war days and by the time the reports of the gamble had arrived there, we were 'on the way to winning the battle'. However across the Mersey various whispers were going around of impending catastrophe. I thought then of Whistler, the artist, and the story of the critic who on seeing one of his pictures, cried 'I have never seen a sunset like that.'

To which Whistler snapped back 'I don't suppose you have!' I felt a bit like that too.

John Moores phoned me and asked me if I had made this so called catastrophic decision. 'Yes, I made the decision alright, and it wasn't catastrophic,' I replied, 'And what's more it's worked. Just as we hoped more than half the backlog is repeat correspondence, therefore the problem now is only half the size.'

Shortly afterwards I thought it a good idea to go over to Liverpool for lunch and 'test the water with my toes'. My instinct was right for as I pushed open the executive dining room door the babble of conversation stopped, just as if the conductor of the orchestra had dropped his baton. I said, 'Do carry on, the subject obviously affects me.' John Moores ventured, 'Yes, do tell him what you think.' Many of the executives around the table were those who had blundered and should have prevented the problem that threatened the heart of the business which was hardly fair to their chairman.

The air was suddenly full of spluttering remarks. 'No, no! It is not that serious! I am sure it will work out alright!' And so the gasping continued. The chairman chipped in with, 'No, just tell him what you were saying!' There were so many nervous coughs I though pneumonia was rife. At last one worthy volunteered, 'I was just saying that *somebody* had said that not all the correspondence has been replied to correctly,' and more joined in. 'You are quite right,' I answered. 'I should think something like a quarter are not as correct as I should like them to be.' 'Just as we were saying, very serious. Exactly, it is serious,' the brave ones burst forth like a Messiah chorus. Eventually the talk died down, I said, 'Of course one letter answered improperly is wrong, but let us look at things sensibly. A fortnight ago virtually no correspondence was being answered, and I was called in because the backlog was so great. Now we are answering thousands of letters a day and possibly a quarter are not correct. I do suggest though that even one letter answered is better than none, and thousands of agents being re-satisfied must surely be even better.'

I explained I was there especially to seek their help to cure any letters being answered incorrectly. I reminded the gathering that before the war we had a big team of correspondence readers; they no longer existed, and that in itself was one of the reasons for the very serious mess I was dealing with. I warmed to the subject, 'I have been thinking hard, and you can all assist. For example, if every executive, supervisor, young or old, male or female, gave just a couple of hours each day, at morning, noon or night, to help read each and every letter sent out and correct any which were wrong, we would be more than half way up the hill.'

The chairman was enthusiastic, even amused. 'You can count me in, my secretary and my assistant,' he exclaimed. Others chimed in with excuses of meetings on this or that, or somebody waiting to see them—shades of Rome burning! Excuses poured forth like water from a fire hose, but no-one was excused. Finally the last hopeful had a triumphant query, 'Will there be desks available tomorrow?' 'They are ready now,' I snapped. The idea worked!

The theme rubbed off and buyers worked like busy bees finding substitutes to give satisfaction, even to buying goods at prices much higher than the catalogue price. My feeling was that if these methods retained our agents, the price we were paying was cheap, for it was both costly and difficult to recruit agents in war time. Finally, if all efforts failed to find the right or similar lines, a very personal letter signed by myself was despatched explaining how stocks were seized by the military authorities, and how many of our staff were serving in the forces and how Liverpool was under the constant threat of bombing. In the main the great bulk of our customers accepted with good grace the simple truths. But even with the utmost generosity of thought I cannot deny that someone had blundered and let the company down.

A serious point arising from the correspondence was the alleged non-payment of commission. From the company's viewpoint this was awful for it was a key point of policy that come hell or high water commission had to be paid at once. Rapid action was required for it was a rock on which the temple of integrity had been built. The manager was emphatic that payments had been made and his records proved it! I said this was rubbish; they proved nothing except that the commissions had been authorised. The responsible planning executive explained the step by step procedure for obtaining postal and money orders. The commission sheets were cleared to the post office twice daily, using the tradesman's bicycle with the deep basket (petrol rationing did not allow otherwise) and returned with any postal orders that were ready. 'Do you bring back as many as you take out?' I asked, and his face clouded. 'Hardly.' 'How big is this post office then?' 'It's a sub-post office.' 'How many assistants?' 'None,' he muttered. 'There is just an old lady, a bit slow too.' It was my turn to gasp. He shot out to bring back the uncompleted items and then we all waited. Eventually the faithful bike groaning under the weight crunched up the gravel path. 'You've got them all there?' I asked. 'Oh, no! Only an odd item here and there has been dealt with on these sheets. It's serious,' he coughed. 'You're telling me,' I echoed, 'And the agents have been telling us for weeks. Get them all back quickly.' A squad went down to collect them. No more were sent to the little old lady. We now had mountains of unpaid commissions which made me both angry and sad: angry because the problem gave rise to the most unfair and virulent letters and sad because it cut right across company policy of paying on time of which it was justifiably and rightly proud. The odd summons arrived the next morning merely I suppose to rub salt in the wound. Someone had blundered and ours was only to do — we certainly wouldn't die! With enthusiasm the summaries were filed in datal order. This was the last problem; true the system would have to be altered, but that is another story. The senior staff worked late into the night and by noon next morning all was ready for the next stage — we allocated a wad of sheets for analysis to dozens of staff (it was before the days of computers), and shortly the complete statement of postal orders and money orders required to clear the job was ready in double quick time.

I phoned the head postmaster of Liverpool requesting thousands and thousands of postal orders. 'Now when do you want them?' I replied, 'At once.' 'Send tomorrow lunchtime for them.' he said. I could have jumped for joy. I knew for certain this operation was the last hurdle. The postal orders and money orders were collected — grabbed with relish would be a more appropriate term! All who could worked with a will and within a couple of days that vital job was over. Now the great clearing up took place and new guide-lines were laid down. The pass had been saved.

* * *

I have always felt that this episode in the company's history was appreciated and it was an important lesson. As for my own contribution, I would say I was propelled by the CDE of business, something you cannot put into a system, a computer or business guide — Courage, Determination and Enthusiasm. In a way I too was grateful for the opportunity it provided.

When the crisis was virtually over, and it had nearly crucified part of the business, I invited John Moores to visit two of the buildings with me but he hesitated in case the staff were still upset. I replied that they were only upset because they had reason to be; it was leadership and planning that was lacking. It was true as I have said before that executives had been drawn off for both the forces and the war effort, but there should have been a lead by those remaining, the remnants of the *force politique*. John Moores did come over to the Wirral, the then outpost of mail order, and made a couple of speeches, which were well received. He and I finished up having our lunch with the employees on the grass banks of Mere Hall; a modest lunch, he got the tea, I fetched the tomato sandwiches. All was at peace at least on that bit of turf, if not elsewhere in the world. It was fortunate that the chairman had identified two problems and fortunate for me that I accepted the challenge.

Thinking of that alfresco meal, I am reminded that pre-war we had excellent canteens for the work force; apart from the Wirral they were good even in the war.

For myself I usually had a luncheon tray and kept working. If I had someone of importance for a talk over lunch, my office or rather desk was converted to a luncheon table by means of a large linen cloth which served the purpose and looked well. I remember one luncheon party quite well. 'Our Gladys', who did for us and my feeding in particular, tried so hard, though not well versed in first class English. Gladys wanted to lay the 'white cloth' and I was on a long phone call so she could not get round. She tilted her head slightly and said, 'Please sir, could I excuse myself in front of you!' Good old Gladys!

* * *

In Manchester both in range and quantity parachute production was increasing rapidly. At one of our busiest times, I had an urgent call from Ringway Parachute Training School where senior officers of the forces were preparing a big exercise. They were in trouble with supply dropping parachutes, which were breaking up on opening. 'What ours?' I asked. 'No, everybody's. Can you come at once?'

75

An officer met me at the guard gate and led me to the rest of the squad, the chutes were certainly in tatters, but in a heap their pretty colours of blue, orange, green, yellow, black and white were a welcome change from the huge area of grassland (now Manchester Airport). The matter was serious and why the failures? I knew the limit of speed for dropping a given load and it seemed to me that the reason for the failures was either that the containers were overloaded or the planes were flying too fast. We were talking then of speeds of 150-200 mph.

At this time we were using two different fabrics to make supply droppers. While both had been tested I thought it advisable to dispose of the fabric point quickly. We all agreed and planes were loaded with an equal number of chutes made from the two different fabrics but carrying identical loads and flying at the same speed as on previous tests. All the chutes descended in tatters so it was not the fabric. These tests had dangers and for protection tractors were dotted all over the airfield. If a chute and container came too close you ducked behind a tractor and a hit was followed by an almighty thump.

I asked if speed was more important than load, I was told it was but the loads had already been fixed and containers were manufactured accordingly — but there was a margin. I suggested with some trepidation that we should test a selection of parachutes from each manufacturer, at the original maximum load dropped at the specified plane speed (this I think was 150 mph). They worked, that proved the manufacture was right.

The speed was then stepped up by stages of some 10 mph, until the chutes shattered. So eventually we reached a safe margin above the specified speed but still using the original maximum load. Experiments were then made the other way round, by flying at the specified speed, with the originally specified load, then working up the load factor until the chutes were shattered. By doing this the services would have two options, speed or weight, with both above the original specification. We then decided (and I think this was vital for confidence sake) that every maker's parachutes should be tested once again to prove the new options. They were and they worked; confidence was quickly re-established and extra precious cargo could now be dropped or speed increased. I was later told that the big exercise was indeed the first invasion of North Africa. I earned myself a good double gin and a lot of very good friends.

After the battle in North Africa, I was invited to the Parachute School to meet the commander of the 6th Airborne Division. Delivering a lecture to the parachute boys, standing on the stage with just a cane in his hand, the force of his personality came through — and I would wager that every man present felt he had been in the battle among the sands of Africa with Lt Gen Sir Richard Nelson Gale, DSO, OBE, MC. Before dawn on D Day he was the first allied general to enter France since its fall; the story goes that on D-Day, he rode a white horse across the Caen canal bridge at Ranville; in his own book he wrote that 'he took the horse along with him.'

During one of his visits to our factories he took out his wallet to give me a forwarding address, I could not but observe a four leaf clover all very carefully pressed, 'You, General,' I exclaimed, 'Carrying a four leaf clover around for luck!'

He leaned back and laughed, then in a confidential voice he said, 'You know Cooke, wars are dangerous things and I reckon if there is a likelihood of luck with a four leaf clover you should take it.'

* * *

The X type or static type parachutes were used for dropping men into battle and were required in ever increasing quantities, consequently both silk and nylon fabric for the canopy was in short supply. The ingenuity of the research men at Farnborough solved the problem by using two types of cotton fabric, one dark in colour and very strong for top panels to resist the initial opening shock while the main part of the canopy was made from the very fine cotton fabric of lighter shade.

This led to an odd problem, for as the parachute opened and the paratrooper looked upwards, he saw a very dark star. On a visit to the Parachute Training School at Ringway, I was questioned about this by the sergeant in charge of packing. I explained the process and asked the reason for the question. 'Well sir', he said, 'I 'ad a young chap come in here yesterday, all quivering like and he said, "Sarge, as I was dropping this morning I looked up to the sky and saw a dark star at the top."' Quick as lightning the sergeant had replied, 'What, a star at the top. You! You! You've 'ad a 'hossifers' parachute, they's reserved for the hossifers; 'ow did you get 'old of it?' The chap, agitated but now pleased, pleaded to keep it. Sarge was happy.

We made parachutes for dropping lifeboats and I quote the *Daily Despatch* (now only of happy memory).

> Our aircraft makes a straight run over the dinghy. A button is pressed, the lifeboat falls from about 700 feet six big parachutes opening in a flash to steady it as it floats gracefully down to make a perfect landing about 60 yards ahead of the dinghy. A host of mechanical contrivances come into action as a lifeboat is released . . .

The parachutes for this job were big and quite intricate but from a production angle not nearly as exciting as the parachute clusters for dropping jeeps and guns. These began as a twelve cluster job, but there had been continual trouble over some failures so I was asked to go along with the boffins to a testing site outside Pontefract to see what could be done. As there were no road signs we got lost near the town in trying to find the park. We stopped a road sweeper. 'Can you tell us where we are, we are looking for . . . park?' 'Oh! yes,' he said (we were on a highly secret mission). 'You'll be coming to see them there parachutes dropping jeeps and guns. Funny thing,' he said, 'There's twelve parachutes and only eleven of 'em open.' He was right, but his twelve were out of date very soon, followed by clusters of four 60 ft and even 96 ft diameter parachutes — 1,000 square yards of fabric in the sky, and at that time the largest textile item ever to be mass produced.

To produce these we took over another large building. These chutes were difficult to handle and even the slightest breeze or draught would cause the canopy to bellow. As we were required to pack them for immediate service use, great care had to be taken with not only the canopy but the very lengthy nylon rigging lines.

I remember a special event when an officer of the Special Air Services addressed the workers, I asked him if he was frightened when he dropped behind the enemy lines. Instantly he replied, 'Oh, yes!' But continued, 'As soon as your feet touch the ground it all changes—your training takes over. Bury your chute—one hand automatically feels for the knife, the other for the gun.' He told me that in one of the messages he received he was told that a jeep and gun would be dropped. He did not believe it but bang on time the RAF came over and there, he said, were these unbelievable additions to his armoury. It was a big job getting rid of the chutes but they managed. I asked, 'What did you do with the wires?' 'Oh!' he said, 'They were the best weapons we had. We stretched them across the road, windscreen height from tree to tree and just waited for the Jerries to come belting down the road. The havoc,' he repeated, 'Was terrific.' 'The havoc?' I repeated quietly. 'Yes, they lost their heads.' That young man was leaving for duty behind the lines in just a day or two and we never heard from him again.

It was as if some influence decided we had enough of the offensive type so finally came the blue riband of our range, the delayed free drop escape chute. Up until this time in the war, the manufacture of this chute was confined to two of the original parachute makers (Irvin himself designed and dropped with the delayed chute) while the late Raymond Quilter was the inventor of the paratrooper or X type.

For the test we were provided with 90 yards of silk fabric (the chute used 87) so the allowance for faults was very small. We were promised that, if this chute could be made and tested satisfactorily at RAF Henlow, we would obtain a contract. We did produce that parachute from that one length of fabric, it seemed a first class job to us and we (our team of three) proceeded with the 'men from the ministry' to Henlow. Squadron Leader Bunn opened it up to have 'a little look see'. He queried the lacing of the parachute cords but fortunately he was wrong. 'Right,' he said, 'We'll have it loaded on a dummy and soon you'll know.' The plane rumbled along the runway and it seemed hours before it was back over the dropping zone. 'There she goes,' cried Bunn as the dummy dropped out and the chute pulled out of its pack and hung, all tightly packed, for what seemed to me to be hours. In fact it was only a split second or so, then before our very eyes the lovely cream canopy blossomed out against a blue sky drifting quickly and softly down. We had made it; we had a drink on that. Despite the glory of the jeeps and guns and chutes, to save a life rather than take one had its attraction.

* * *

I must mention some of the principal members who took such an active part in building the business and, through them, pay tribute to all those who unselfishly contributed to its success. There was Jean Wilson, devoted and always faithful to employer and employees alike, and general boss of all women operators. Herbert Foxall, a real Lancashire lad who did not know what tiredness meant. Tom Greenhalgh, the boss of the night shift, and, until he went in the forces, Geoffrey

Seddon-Brown, who was my deputy and was later followed by David Galbraith. Finally Freda Adderley, first my secretary, then executive secretary, who was responsible for all meetings, statistics, follow-ups and of great assistance in the preparation of policy here and elsewhere — later to join me in the formation and organisation of the new John Myers of mail order history, eventually deputy managing director and deputy chairman.

There were so many, many hundreds of others that supported us in the whole operation from beginning to end — be it late at night or early morning. And to them and others it is an honour to repeat what I have said many times, 'Thank you.'

We realised early on that boredom for a lot of the women workers was a real problem, for they were doing the same job all day through, working on the same fabric and the same operation from morning till night. We tried to deal with this in a variety of ways: we had a ladies' Production Day when women from the office and women from the factories took over the entire factory production and the men merely acted as messengers, labourers or clerks; everybody had great fun — and above all production increased.

We had a good press, ever ready to stimulate. I give just a few quotes —

> *Daily Herald.* 1st December, 1944.
> 'Parachuted guns saved the day.'
> *Evening Chronicle.* 20th February, 1945.
> 'Production Drive to our 14th Army.'
> *Sunday Express* 16th May, 1943.
> 'Chute Girls mark Tunis with Output Drive 25% up.'
> *Daily Mirror.* 1st December, 1944.
> '4 chutes = 1 winged jeep.'
> *Evening Standard.*
> 'RAF mines sank 550 Nazi ships.'
> *Liverpool Daily Post.* 1st December, 1944.
> 'Guns flown from factory to front in two hours.'
> 'How Lancashire Girls answered an SOS.'
> *Daily Mail.* 1st December, 1944.
> 'Guns flown to Front direct from works.'
> *Evening Chronicle.* 1st December, 1944.
> 'Typists make the giant Chutes they supplied the men of Arnhem.'
> *Daily Worker.*
> 'Parachutes dropping with the new airborne lifeboat.'

We had special production efforts — for the 8th Army, the 14th Army and of course for the heart-throbs of the girls, the 1st and 6th Airborne Division, the boys in the red berets. Many were the letters received both from the troops and their commanders. Perhaps all of these things and thoughts are summarised in a speech by General Sir Richard Nelson Gale at our main factory — deep in sincerity — in historical interest and its humanity. He commenced: —

> I have something to tell you. To start off with I am a soldier and I know my job and that does not frighten me, but this public speaking is not up my street.
>
> The Airborne Division consists, according to the operation which it is going to undertake, of something like 12,000-16,000 men. The responsibility that rests upon the

shoulders of the commander of that number of men is a very great one and it is one of which I can assure you, one is deeply conscious all the time. You have in your hands the lives of a large number of men and everyone of those men who is fighting with you and who is being launched into battle is a responsibility. For everyone of those men there is someone at home here. That thought is constantly in my mind. It must, by the very nature of things, be in the minds of every commander. The task of the general is to see to it that his men are put into battle fit so that they stand every reasonable chance of succeeding in whatever enterprise they undertake.

Now I can tell you for a certainty because I was there and I have seen it, that the generalship of the British Army today is of a very high order from Monty, as we all call him, downwards.

The men, your men, have been brilliantly led and the Hun has been consistently out-manoeuvred, out-witted and out-generalled. Now that is one end of the stick. At the other end of the stick are the men themselves.

No words of mine can possibly pay the tribute that is really due to these men. The young men, young as far as an old buffer like myself is concerned, the chaps in the ranks are absolutely magnificent. Again, again and again I have been with them in the conditions under which they have to live and fight, and to me it is an absolute miracle. The moment they do sag, they fall straight to sleep from utter exhaustion, and when the call comes they get up and are on the job again. I think, at least I don't think, I know it, that they are fortified in their attitude towards life and in the way they do their job of winning this terrible war, by their women-folk at home. There is no shadow of doubt about it.

A commander has to look around, you know, and he has to think of what principles he is to be guided by, and one of the first principles I have had before me always, is that it is the men that count because ultimately the battle is in the hands of the private soldier with the gun or the rifle. To me it has always been abundantly obvious that the private soldier is one of two people, whether it be his mother, whether it be his sweetheart or whether it be his wife, there is somebody else and those two, although they may be separated by many miles of water and for long periods of time, those two are a team. In fact you are part of those chaps who are doing their stuff on the other side.

We landed in France, my Division, the 6th Airborne Division, before anyone else on the night before D Day. We had a certain amount of good fortune because we completely surprised the Boche and we always held the initiative. We had to take a piece of ground that was of vital importance and we had to hold it. You know, like most things in life, it is very easy to take something but very much harder to hold it. Hold it we did, at some cost.

It sounds a terrible thing to say but the cost was reasonable. The men who gave their lives, and those who were wounded and maimed, were reasonable in their numbers, when one considers the enormous advantage that was given to the army as a whole as a result of that operation. And then we, all of us, were able to have a crack at the Boche and kick him in the pants, and we kicked him in the pants from the River Orne outside Caen to the River Seine and we pushed him in the Seine and the Division that we fought ceased to exist. I was in SHAEF HQ until two days ago and I asked, 'Where are my old friends, the 716th German Division?' and they said, 'They don't exist.'

We liberated about 400 square miles of French territory. It cost us dear but in that ten days we advanced over that country, we lost 25% of the men, more than we had lost in three months of fighting. We took more prisoners than our total of wounded and we killed and wounded a great number of Germans—a great number.

Now these men of mine go into battle through the air—they go down to earth by parachute and some of them by glider and you are making the parachutes which carry them to earth. The confidence that these men have in your work is very great and it is very justified. I had to raise and train the 1st Parachute Brigade before there was ever thought of the 6th Airborne Division. I know it from the beginning and Group Captain Newham here has been training these chaps almost from the beginning and the number of fatal accidents that do occur are very, very rare and almost never have they been attributed to faulty workmanship.

In addition to the men coming down by parachute there is the equipment supplied by air. I want you to think in terms of that gallant, that terrifically gallant, band of men of the 1st Airborne Division which fought so magnificently at Arnhem. The only way those chaps could be supplied was from the air and your handiwork must have been a godsend to them. In France, at one of the very sticky periods, when we were being heavily attacked by the 21st Panzer Division (a Tank Division) I had a great number of my anti-tank guns knocked out and at that time the only way I could get some anti-tank guns quickly (with their jeeps) was to have them dropped by parachute. It might interest you to know that these big 60 ft clusters have brought down to us 6 pounder equipment with their jeeps which were in action against the Boche within two hours of having left this country.

It is a stupendous thought now, that this is what your work makes possible. I have been around this factory and I consider it a great privilege that the management have been kind enough to let me come and see you and a far greater privilege that I have been allowed to talk to you. I cannot say with what admiration I have viewed your work. I mean it from the bottom of my heart — to see you slogging away day after day, many of you with home ties as well, it is a most inspiring thing. When I get back to my Division tomorrow or the day after I shall make a point of telling my men that are in the ranks, and their officers, how great is your contribution to their efforts. Thank you very much.

At the conclusion of the great battle of Arnhem, we manufacturers received a note — from the Public Relations Directorate of the Ministry of Aircraft Production. I quote it in full — it is a simple message printed economically on general issue flimsy paper. It is the most moving document I think ever to emerge from a government anywhere.

THE MEN OF ARNHEM

Formed early in 1941, from the nucleus of a Commando unit, the First Airborne Division includes men from almost every regiment in the British Army. All are volunteers.

On November 11th, 1942, at Bone in Algeria, paratroops of the First Airborne Division first went into action. After further successes during this campaign they gained fresh laurels both in Sicily and Italy. At Taranto, in 1943, they fought with distinction as infantry.

Then on 16th September, 1944 — warned just before their take-off that they 'were taking part in one of the greatest airborne operations in military history' — the Division descended in force behind the German lines in Holland, near Arnhem.

No pen can describe what they endured in the days that followed. Against appalling odds and in appalling conditions, they fought as few men have ever fought in all the long years of recorded history. They fought in the spirit and with the ineffable courage of men who had gladly volunteered for the toughest, deadliest and most dramatic of all the War's most terrible tests.

A famous Dutch author spoke of them in a moving message 'For ten cruel nights and days the thoughts of the whole of Holland have been with your men West of Arnhem . . . Here . . . the word heroes takes tangible shape, before the eyes of our people who stand and bare their heads . . .'

British designers and workers gave them the tools, the best weapons and equipment that craftsmanship and ingenuity could devise. And they did the job. This was their final message: 'All will be ordered to break out rather than surrender. We have attempted our best and will continue to do our best as long as possible.'

Field-Marshal Montgomery said to them: 'There is no shadow of doubt that, had you

failed, operations elsewhere would have been gravely compromised. You did not fail . . .
in the annals of the British Army there are many glorious deeds . . . but there can be few
episodes more glorious than the epic of Arnhem, and those that follow after will find it
hard to live up to the standards you have set . . . In time to come it will be a great thing for
a man to be able to say "I fought at Arnhem".'

* * *

On 4th November, 1944, Sir Stafford Cripps, Minister of Aircraft Production,
visited our main factory in Manchester. In his speech, he said:

> You will remember, of course, very vividly the initial stages of the invasion of North-
> Western Europe when paratroops were dropped behind the beaches. Kept entirely
> supplied from the air, a great deal of very heavy equipment was dropped with them in
> order to give them the weapons with which they could attack the Germans and defend
> themselves. Not only in North-Western Europe, perhaps even more so in the jungles of
> Burma, the parachute has performed a tremendous task. Those troops who penetrated
> hundreds of miles into the jungle behind the Japanese lines, eventually linking up with
> some of General Stilwell's forces, were entirely supplied for months on end by parachutes.
> We have developed this technique of dropping from aircraft on every front where we have
> been fighting, and also you will, many of you, have read accounts of the way in which the
> fighting forces in the interior of France and other occupied countries, were kept supplied
> with offensive weapons of various kinds and with food, in the time before the invasion of
> Europe. We were able to build up stocks of materials inside the actual enemy-occupied
> territories and in that way when we attacked in the north-west there was developed
> throughout occupied Europe an internal attack upon the Germans which had a most
> disintegrating effect upon their transport and their supplies which contributed very
> greatly to the effectiveness and the swiftness with which we were able to advance through
> France and Belgium into Holland, it also assisted us by diminishing greatly the number of
> casualties that we should otherwise have had.
>
> In all these various ways, you have been making a great contribution to the offensive
> efforts of the forces, both on land and sea and in the air, and for that, those people who
> have used your parachutes and have had supplies dropped to them on your parachutes,
> are all of them, I am sure, very grateful to you for the work you have done, and as the war
> is developing today there is a great likelihood that more and more parachutes will be
> required for dropping supplies, in the Far Eastern War. . . We are not able to recover
> parachutes which are dropped over enemy territory and perhaps it is a comfort to us to
> think that many of the ladies of France and Belgium and Holland may now be using some
> of the parachutes that you have made, in order to clothe themselves. . .
>
> I dare say that some of you are turning your minds towards what your position will be in
> the future. You know that government policy is to provide full employment for all the
> people in this country and for the first time in our history, the government itself is taking
> the responsibility of saying that such a policy will be put through, and I am sure that, as it
> has been approved by Parliament, it will be approved by all the people in the country.

Sir Stafford Cripps was one of Britain's most brilliant lawyers. He was to me very
warm hearted, deeply interested not only in the past, but intensely concerned with
the future. Sometimes this feeling did not come through very clearly in official
speeches, but in the quiet personal chit-chat as one walked along with him it came
through crystal clear. I did not find him the ice cold minister sometimes suggested,

or the ascetic Tibetan type of man often portayed by his critics.

In our struggle to convert our labour force eventually we had much help and understanding from the Board of Trade of which Sir Stafford was President.

* * *

I have often wondered if I should have turned to politics (Sir Stafford indicated I could be of help elsewhere) which I suppose would have meant changing almost the whole of my philosophy, but not all, for on many things the major parties agree. I was young and eager to help put the world aright but I had quite a few ideas that would be a hindrance.

In my forty years in industry, I never had a strike, my door has always been open for any approach, be it by management or staff. This point must tempt my friends to say, 'Have you never had a union problem?' That wasn't quite true, for we did have workers' committees, etc; sometimes we have benefited from them, at other times they have been great yawns,

I believe if employees get good pay and work well, with reasonable hours, they should in return deliver a good day's work, work not blighted with long and costly stoppages. They should always have reasonable access to management. The working conditions should be good. But, over and above all that, they should have good leadership. We did however have one 'union', the important one that is between management and staff.

Taking a long and dispassionate look at the mass of employees, I repeat the mass, the things people do want most in their lives are good housing to make a comfortable home for themselves, good schooling for the kids, something to be proud of, and security, particularly as they get older. They do like to see enthusiasm, even dedication, on the part of the management, in short somebody to look up to. It has been said, 'If we hadn't got a God we would create one.' That may be out of date now, but I have the feeling it is there, just the same, for if we did not create a God we would possibly create a monster.

I do not believe any great number of workers want to see copies of the balance sheet and profit and loss accounts. No, this is a gimmick; it sounds very well from a platform of a few politicised members but they do not, I repeat, they do not in my opinion represent or measure up to the great body of workers who like their telly, their kids and the car and the home — somebody surely has got the story wrong!

Finally, I do believe in the reward or medal mentality, for the 'Star Operators' Medals' were first introduced in our Manchester factories — they were awarded to operators who had over a period made super efforts. The medal was simple, no big cash awards, just recognition by a little decoration. In making the presentation (I quote the *Sunday Express* 5th November, 1944): Sir Stafford Cripps, Minister of Aircraft Production, told the girls yesterday: 'You are the Stakhanovites of the Industry.'

NOTE: Stakhanovites — the Russian production experts named after Stakhanov, hewer of 102 tons of coal in a single shift.

I think it sad that we have lost the medal mentality; even in sport itself it is money, money and bigger money. In those days of not so long ago, it was the effort and achievement and the medal at the end that mattered.

Even in education the medal mentality has gone; the state scholarships were an excellent idea, for if parents had too much income for their child to have the full value there was always the small award direct to the child. That was vision, critics may say the carrot, perhaps so. One wonders how many Stakhanovites we have in the NCB or British Steel — no it is money and more money and usually less work.

We have heard in these last two years the cry that we are back to the 1930s. That is a load of rubbish. What is more the cry is often made by people whose mother was at that time no more than a twinkle in their granny's eye. No, perhaps after all I would be no good at all in the political arena!

* * *

Very early one Sunday morning I had a phone call advising me of a very urgent parachute requirement and that all other work would be delayed, if necessary, to meet a vital timetable. For obvious reasons he could not give details, except that the objects requiring attention would be delivered next morning and would cause considerable road congestion for many long low loaders (commonly called Queen Marys) were being used. The Ministry of Transport and the police had that in hand, I was to say nothing to anyone but to be at the factory by 7 am. We were to be given just three days and nights to clear the operation whatever it was.

I arrived in Manchester about 6 am, the roads to our factory for some distance around were clogged with the huge lorries, carrying tremendous packing cases. The man from the ministry in the comparative quiet of my office unfolded the story. The cases contained American parachutes, already packed for action. The American packs had to be removed, the parachutes had to be repacked in British covers with new drogues and release gear for use with British containers. The work on the new components went ahead in minutes; repacking followed immediately. The job was of great urgency for I was told in confidence that a battleship had to be loaded and would leave early on the Thursday morning unescorted for India. The parachutes were required to supply our troops who might be in trouble in the Battle of Kohima Gap in India/Burma.

The police agreed we could have lights on for the loading of lorries, and in the event of a threatened raid we would be blacked out immediately. The Ministry of Transport man would be on site throughout the operation and give the routing chits and instructions to the drivers.

We used the drivers in strict rotation. Those normally living in or near Manchester wanted to know when they were likely to be required — some had not been home for weeks. The man from the ministry had to be fair and impartial. One very restive driver lived just outside Manchester and had not seen his wife for some time so he asked the ministry man when he was likely to be wanted. He was told to see the boss. I was understanding but in the early stages it was difficult to say anything about timing. Every few hours my friend the lorry driver stopped me with 'What's the chances boss?' About one o'clock on the Wednesday night I reckoned we could do without the services of my love lorn friend. I put it to the ministry man who said it was up to me. 'The pleasure's yours.' I thought it might be. The driver was having a quiet drag and I said to him, 'Well chum, off you go to your wife.' 'Bloody hell! No!' he replied, 'What good's a woman half asleep to a bloke at 1.30 in the morning. Book me for Glasgow!' he bellowed. He obviously had not read Talleyrand who said that the next best thing to a beautiful woman is sleep.

The unescorted warship did get to India in time and while this changeover was not one of our biggest achievements in production, it was perhaps one of the most satisfying as witnessed by this letter from Trooper Henderson No. 14282588 of the 14th Army which I quote in full, as written, with no apologies.

Defence Platoon

2 Div HQ

SEAC

May I, as an ordinary soldier, on behalf of our own section, thank you with all our hearts, for the way in which you produced more parachutes, and also the cash some of 200 guineas, No doubt our Supreme Commander has thanked you, but I know that you would like to hear the thanks of the, other ranks, of the 14th Army. I can personaly say that your parachutes are doing the job they are supposed to do, while I was with my unit, (The Reconnaissance Corp) in a town which the roads leading to it, was unfit for heavy trucks, and we had to be supplied by air, your parachutes brought our water, food, and other important supplies, down from the planes to us safe and sound, and with out them we could never have advanced so far, they were used mostly in the area of Kohima, perhaps you have heard of Parachute hill? It was called that because of the numbers of them dropped to our troops. Even today I can see the planes go over to drop their loads to the front line troops, and if they get torn they also can be used to keep the hot sun off the lads in their trenches. The most of them though are folded on the spot, and sent back for re-use. During the Monsoon time we had to depend on being kept by air drops and never once have we been disappointed, or have to go short, and we have lost very little of the supplies, I have only seen four chutes which have failed to open, and I believe that it could not be helped they were just beginning to open when they hit the ground, perhaps if they had been dropped from a little higher they would have opened in time.

There is some chaps here, who know some of you personally and they, when they come home, will probably thank you personally and I from Scotland, will also convey our thanks, with the, Irish, Welsh, and other countries who are dependant on your output of parachutes, even the Yanks, who are with us praise you and the work you are doing. We are going on, to push the Japs right out of Burma, and also to help throw them out of China, and even Japan itself and with your help behind us we can, and will do it soon. Well workers, I hope this little note, helps you to picture in your minds how you are playing a big part in this war effort, and that you will continue to do your best, to help deliver the goods and I am sure victory shall be ours in the next year. Good luck to you all, and may God bless you all, once again we thank you.

for the Other Ranks of 14th

I remain

R. G. Henderson

* * *

Early in 1945 the terrible war was coming to an end and our main job now was to repair parachutes recovered from the battlefields. German cities had been subjected to the most intensive bombing and were little more than heaps of rubble. Hitler was dead; his generals and admirals were arrested; others in authority had just vanished. Victory or VE Day belonged to the Allies. It was a victory which revealed the horrors of the German concentration camps, the starvation and ultimate annihilation of a large part of the European Jewish community, a stain as black as any in the history of mankind.

In the quiet countryside Victory Day was a day of relief, but not of great jubilation. The Japanese had still be be defeated. At home my wife and I got busy making flags for our five year old son. He wanted American, British and Russian flags and insisted that we had a little celebration. All three of us marched up and down that remote country lane with our home-made flags. It marked the beginning of the end, and now that the war in Europe was over it would not be long before all war work was a thing of the past. In the factories we now had a heavy responsibility to try and provide work for men and women who had served us so well. It was an exciting yet daunting thought to change over a number of factories to civilian work. It was daunting because raw materials for civilian goods were not available, and all types of clothing and most basic goods were still rationed. Yet clothing was most suitable work for parachute workers.

The government had long before decided that when the boys left the armed forces they were to be provided with a civilian outfit, suit, raincoat, etc, this was quite a human touch in an almost inhuman world. The men returning home would be unlike men from the 1914-18 war who had to cadge anything around. It was good to have a kit that really fitted, for often contours had altered as my father's did after the First World War.

We approached the Ministry of Supply for contracts for any part of the demob kits. They rejected us on the basis that we were not recognised clothing manufacturers. This was a strange point for we used exactly the same machines to manufacture flying suits, a great variety of parachutes, millions of them, to very tight specifications. We urged that there was little difference between making a raincoat or a flying suit, except that flying suits were more complicated. I have argued throughout my life that the difference between managing a fried fish shop and a huge mass production plant was very small, provided the basic rules were observed. However none of our arguments prevailed, just as in the early days of parachute production. We just had not got the right *tag* on our name.

My memory recalled a passage in the speech Sir Stafford Cripps (later President of the Board of Trade) made to our workers in 1944. He said:

> I think you have got together here an excellent team and I would not like to see that team broken up and that team spirit lost, and I am sure that just as in the war, you have, each one of you, made your own individual contribution to the war effort, some of you for several years and some of you for shorter periods of time, so you will all be able to make an equally great contribution to building up that happy and more prosperous country that we want to see.

I entirely agreed, and thought the staff that had slogged so hard and so long should have some little priority when it came to continuity of work. I wrote to Sir Stafford and reminded him of his wish, difficult as I understood it would be to achieve. We got action and quickly. We eventually produced large quantities of clothing for the returning men, not only in our Manchester factories but in Northern Ireland too.

I also pressed the Board of Trade for permission to use the scraps of parachute fabric (there was an embargo on the main fabric and we had no coupons anyway). The scraps we could make into children's clothing, which was in very short supply. The very tiny bits we figured could be made into bras and we eventually made many thousands. I was also anxious to restore our rightful allocation of fabric for our quilt or *comforter* production, which we suspended to concentrate on parachutes but that was not very easy either.

We visited the offices of the Board of Trade and again met a stubborn resistance. The objections were twofold; firstly, that we had no experience in making children's clothing or ladies' lingerie; secondly we were out to supply our own stores. The first point was quickly disposed of; we had experience, and indeed we had a most distinguished children's wear designer, Miss M. Keyes, a relative of the great admiral. Yes, we would if necessary supply our own stores, provided they accepted the articles, but we would supply other traders too. I pleaded, surely it would be far, far better (taking their argument of experience) if we supplied our own stores and got our kicks, congratulations or criticism 'nearer home'.

I repeated I did not want a ration of fabric. I was not looking for coupons because progress in that direction would come as we generated demands for articles we produced from the scraps which would normally have gone to 'the rag man'. Anyway the country was desperate for consumer goods after years of privation, and in our opinion the operation was plain common sense.

I wrote to Sir Stafford again and told him that we had been turned down flatly by the Board of Trade and it to me seemed quite crazy. Next day I had a phone call from one of the heads of the Board of Trade inviting me to London that very afternoon as he had to report back to the President within hours. He did not seem very pleased—he wasn't. 'Have you been in touch with the President?' 'You know I have,' I laughingly answered, and I firmly re-stated I did not write to the President until I had exhausted all other avenues. He stammered 'You could have got what you wanted or partly what you wanted without going to the President.' 'Not so,' I replied, 'Otherwise I wouldn't be here today and neither would you have to report back to the President.'

I was closely questioned as to the feasibility of making articles of clothing from the tiny bits of scrap nylon. From my bag came samples of ladies' bras, babies' frocks and so on. Our ability to make bras could not be questioned for we had used the same machines on parachute production. I was offered a cup of tea which was encouraging. I felt we were on the way; we were, for action followed very quickly.

* * *

During the war Littlewoods had collected quite a few additional companies of varying size and type, together with buildings. Each made a contribution to the war effort and they could play a part in providing merchandise to the trading side of the business; as this bold stroke developed more units were acquired so a very wide range of goods became available covering men's, women's and children's clothing, stockings, mattresses, furniture, quilts, bedspreads, kitchen cabinets, oil fires, even clocks, although this last item was a bit of a damp squib.

One of our bigger efforts was to build a large furniture and bedding factory on a green field in Aspatria, Cumberland. It was here I met the energetic and colourful Jack Adams, for whom I had the greatest regard. He had risen from an unemployed miner to be a powerful influence in industry in that desperately difficult part of the country. Government help in development areas was one thing but it could be otherwise elsewhere. I recalled John Moores telling me the result of a visit to the Board of Trade to obtain permission for the building of new stores. He received the uncompromising answer 'After the dog biscuit manufacturers have been satisfied, it will probably be your turn' — not a very handsome bouquet.

We all realised that one day supplies would become easier and the factories would become vulnerable. In times of shortage the entire production would be demanded by the retail side, while in times of plenty the factories would have a thin time. I almost forgot to mention that in the meantime the company acquired two hotels in Harrogate.

In general life was very enjoyable. We were not only negotiating supplies of raw materials for our factories, but through the contacts we had developed during the war we now had the ability to supply fabrics, etc to other manufacturers for the benefit of the group as a whole. Eric Sawyer and I worked very well together; with one on the retail side of the company, the other on supply, and together accepting joint responsibility, we made very rapid progress. Times were happy. True we had our differences but never ran foul of one another, following a policy that was fair but firm. That lasted a long time but for various reasons it was not for ever.

* * *

Immediately the European war was over, everyone was a Churchill fan — or were they? The grand old man received a tumultuous reception in almost every town and city he visited. I was present at the huge enthusiastic reception he received in Manchester. Came the election and with it a great shock — Churchill was deposed and Labour took control.

In 1954 I had the honour of being present in the Great Hall at Westminster on a memorable occasion. The grand old man, still chubby, and again Prime Minister, walked down the ancient steps to be presented with a birthday gift. The Graham Sutherland portrait was to be his. From his grimaces he obviously did not like the portrait; the thrusting head, the jutting chin confirmed it, despite the assembly of the famous — and a few others like me — he made his dislikes obvious. The picture no longer exists, Lady Churchill saw to that.

After VE day the war in the Far East with Japan had still to be won, a war that had started with a terrible naval defeat for the USA at Pearl Harbour though that defeat I must confess was a great relief for we realised that America was now with us.

Labour was now in power in England; Roosevelt was dead and in the USA Harry Truman was President. The final conflict with Japan was on and many thought it was likely to last for a long time. The end came with dramatic suddenness in August 1945 and the surrender followed the amazing news released early one morning that atom bombs had been dropped on the Japanese cities of Nagasaki and Hiroshima, resulting in the most appalling damage, destruction and deaths ever known.

But to the people of Britain who had suffered many days, months and years of dark despair and long nights of terror, it was, finally, victory.

Reflecting on the use of atomic bombs, it seems strange that the two great allies, USA and Britain—both had pacifist ruling parties at that time, and yet they would together release the most horrific weapon of destruction then known to man. A strange thought that perhaps the ultimate end did justify the means, and it took peace loving parties to do it!

In the post war years of Socialist rule I met many interesting personalities. One minister put out 'a feeler' to me, only a feeler he repeated, but he was impressed by our success in organising production for the war effort. He said these were just his ramblings but there was a rush job to be done at Remploy, the organisation with many factories employing disabled or partly disabled people. He wondered—no commitment (he always put things like that)—how, as a company, we would react if say John Moores became the titular head and I became the managing director.

He thought there was a great opportunity that should not be missed because he reckoned Littlewoods would prove an immediate outlet for much of the Remploy production, and we could inject our organising ability. It was a fascinating and brilliant feeler, with many attractions; it would be an important public act right up our street. The company could easily provide the organisation, could have absorbed some of their production and lastly and very important, we could advise Remploy on the best range of lines to produce.

Unfortunately we did not take up the challenge. I thought it would have been an excellent follow-up to Littlewoods' substantial war effort. I was happy to see thirty-five years after the war ended that John Moores received what many thought a long overdue knighthood.

* * *

In 1946 I visited America to search out new ideas for our factories—for new merchandise we might sell and produce, new production methods and also fresh ideas for decor, shop fronts, presentation and display for our chain stores.

Reservations on ships were difficult. I had accommodation on the *Scythia*, sailing to Halifax, Nova Scotia, continuing by train to Canada and America.

My wife has kept all the letters I wrote to her and it is from these that most of the story of that journey to the New World is told.

To my wife

27th September 1946

The time of sailing has not been announced although it is rumoured that she sails tonight either at 6 pm or 9 pm. Conditions on the ship are not too bad, in fact if we hadn't seen better it might be considered first class.

I have got a cabin on the 'Boat deck A' shared of course with 5 other chaps, very nice fellows — two from a London engineering company, Mr Day, chairman of the Crusader Insurance Co, a Harley Street specialist and a Rolls Royce designer. It is quite a good room, fair size with plenty of ventilation — windows — not portholes. The Harbour Master introduced me to the chief Cunard man. I was carefully ushered through the Customs and introduced to the Staff Captain.

I had lunch at 1.30, not 'super' but quite good — soup, salmon mayonnaise, lemon sponge (Roger would have liked it), coffee.

The ship is carrying a number of Canadian brides with their babies and there is a fully equipped nursery — complete with toys, cots and so on, very tastefully decorated.

As I look through the window I can see Birkenhead and New Brighton; just at this moment the ferry is crossing the river to Liverpool. The sun is shining brightly, the river is gleaming like silver.

28th September 1946

We eventually moved off from the Princes Landing Stage at 9 pm on Friday (note: a day late). The heartstrings were certainly tugged as the ship moved away. We steamed very slowly down the river with a funny little tug giving us an extra bit of help. The lights of New Brighton, Liverpool and Southport twinkled and then quietly died away as we moved to the open sea.

About 12 noon the last outline of the coast melted away — we had covered 138 miles in the first twelve hours (N. Ireland). I was introduced to Captain Francis Drake, invited to his cabin for cocktails and to share his table at meals, which has certainly made the journey more interesting and pleasant.

Two pastimes are indulged in, one table tennis, the other shuffleboard. Can hold my own at both games.

My cabin colleague Day and I struck up a close friendship during the next weeks. Discipline was very strict. Representatives of various arms of the service saw to security and the ever helpful social services tried to keep up with the needs of sorely tried young mothers and their offspring. While men of the merchant navy were in their own words 'seeing that all rules and regulations were very properly observed.'

The NAAFI store sold sweets and chocolates to those who waited and barely a soul failed to queue, for two reasons: no coupons were needed, and some of the extras would be sent back home where they were still rationed. Most of us arranged with deckhands to post our purchases to our families when they got back to Britain. Some of the sweetmeats arrived, others didn't.

The ship was obviously economising on everything but that was nothing new for most of us. The economy on lighting did surprise me, and it gave a feeling of gloom though the general spirit was quite the opposite.

28th/30th September 1946

The day broke clear — church service at 10.30 am, very impressive, very simple — the lounge was converted by means of re-arranging the furniture, an altar table was provided by covering up a writing table with the Union Jack—a very simple lectern of polished oak completed the setting. The sunlight filtered through the windows, glinting on the Captain's gold braid—who needless to say took the service, having as assistants the Staff Captain, Chaplain and Purser. The officers stood at the rear of the altar table— in front the congregation gathered. As I looked across that room it seemed that almost every type and nationality was represented. Canadians, Americans, French, Irish, Newfoundlanders, Indians, etc. A large battalion of St John Ambulance men formed up on one side of the room and was balanced on the other side by a group of naval men.

The whole service was so simple as to be very sincere and as the clear voices rang out in singing *The King of Love my Shepherd is,* one wondered why the churches have to be so full of trappings and the prayers so set and formal. After Church, lunch, the weather changed, a thick fog closed in, the sirens kept up a perpetual scream. One nervous woman took up her lifebelt and perched herself immediately below the lifeboats— no need really because the ship is fitted with radar.

Imagine 1,000 miles from you and our little cottage—you can have the biggest liner in the world—all the skyscrapers in New York, but give me the little cottage in Nether Alderley, I'll not ask for more.

2nd October 1946

I am writing the journal sitting on the Promenade Deck, having just finished lunch. It has been announced that we covered 379 miles from 12 noon yesterday until the same hour today so that you will gather we are well over half way to Halifax.

The sea is calm or to use the nautical expression, slight; very few passengers have been sick except the GI brides—with whom I sympathise, many of them are little more than kids, all seem to possess at least one offspring. They are housed 22 to a room—complete with babies—so using a Pools 'permutation' the odds on them getting sleep is pretty remote. Many of these girls (I am sorry to say many of them are below par) still think the whole thing is a joyride—some of them are so young—they were playing tick [otherwise known as tag] and skipping on the decks—what an awakening for them when they get to the other side.

The news has just come over the loudspeakers that Goering and company are to die, Schact innocent—most people feel the lot should die. Canadians are particularly tough about it.

2nd October 1946

At dinner, we have at table Captain Drake, Captain Fleming, Fleet Air Arm, a Lt Commander (the latter's ADC) on their way to UNO.

You have to make your own fun—this is still a government ship—working under plenty of red tape—you are just 'one body'—rich or poor alike. We are carrying just over a thousand passengers.

Standing on the deck one day, I reflected on the crowded conditions, first of all the civilians such as ourselves, six to a cabin seemed a lot, but we could get to sleep. Then I thought of the naval chaps with next to no privacy except their great coats, with howling children next door. Then the troops, the serving chaps. It was at this time that a young mother obviously very tired ambled along with two kids. She smiled wanly, I went across the deck to speak to her. I asked if all was well, if the children were OK and had the sweets. That point was quickly put right. I said, 'How do you go on for sleep?' She smiled again. 'That's the point, we have up to 22 mothers all with kids, it's impossible. The noise comes through from other rooms too. With every whimper or cry from each child there's barely a moment of quiet.'

As the sun crossed her young face she said, 'Yes, but still I'm one of the lucky ones, off to a new country and my husband.'

Quite apart from sleeping all other accommodation was very basic. The ablution block was spartan. There were no doors on the entrances and exits—doors were only present for the one final act of privacy and then there were no locks. I think both of these restrictions ensured that you didn't linger about. For a ship to function properly conveying such a large number of people, a perpetual queue was the necessary ingredient.

The captain explained to me one day how they carried 5,000 troops at a time (heaven help them) on this comparatively small trooper. 'Come round after lunch and I will show you how we did it,' said Captain Francis Drake (what better name). We started below. On each stanchion, a hammock apart, were welded hooks, three to each stanchion, so that the whole of what would normally be cargo decks would be covered with hammocks, floor to ceiling. The troops (in their jargon) 'slept warm', for as one lot gave up the hammocks another lot took over.

After sleeping the queuing started—first for the lavatory, then for shaving and ablutions, then for breakfast. Next for exercise, then for the eternal broth, then for games. Next for lunch or dinner, for the NAAFI and the fags, yet another queue for tea, so it went on; the snake system kept everyone on the move, this coupled with the ever present threat of submarines.

Regulations for all on the *Scythia* were pretty strict. All women were instructed by loudspeakers to leave the promenade decks at 9 pm. On one occasion after dinner, just a moment before 9 pm I stepped on the deck. Immediately the loudspeakers blared forth 'All women are now instructed to leave the outer decks immediately.' My little group pulled my leg about this for quite a time.

As we approached Halifax, the sea seemed to take on an angry, grey look. The waves rose higher, the sky was overcast, the children cried a little more, the NAAFI was no longer supported. But the brave little brides overcame their boredom, anxiously, yet with a sense of excited anticipation, only to be dashed by the next announcement that the ship would arrive at least one day late.

* * *

3rd/4th October 1946

You must have gathered from the cable that we have made good progress so much so that I have had to alter arrangements again, go first to Montreal and go to New York on the 9th. Last night we saw the lightship off Cape Race. The meals have improved considerably since we started—might now be considered very good.

On the night before docking at Halifax the crew arranged for a little farewell dance. The music was provided by a concertina. Everything was on a make do and mend basis, but the spirit was there and everyone joined in. We were carrying a famous ballet company and the ladies did not look so elegant in their long skirts and drab stockings, but they were very cheery; I am sure they shared my wife's view of my dancing. She says I dance the same to all tunes, but in some I walk faster. For my part I much prefer to see those ballet dancers glide across the stage. This then was the last night aboard the ship — tomorrow would be a new day, a new country and a new way of life. It was.

After a hurried breakfast we went aloft as the ship nudged its way in on a brilliant early autumn morning with the sun shining and the sea blue. The trees wore an exciting variety of brilliant red and gold leaves against a dramatic back-drop of the dark and mysterious evergreens. Perhaps this was just a reminder that summer was over.

5th October 1946

The ship gradually came along the coast of Nova Scotia to the harbour at Halifax — the journey slightly up river was very interesting, the banks are lined with woods consisting mainly of conifers and the water was a brilliant blue.

The pilot took charge about five miles off Halifax, then with the aid of four tugs we gradually drew alongside the landing stage — a magnificent piece of construction work of tremendous length.

As the gangway was hoisted a military band blared forth the national anthem — followed by 'Here comes the Bride' on behalf of the GI brides. Day comments that the real object was sex stimulation — Canada, he says, needs population.

The brides were cheering, and on terra firma so were their relatives. The brass bands struck up, the gangways were in position — the ship was cleared quickly.

I had a stroll around the dock area of Halifax which provided a fine array of painted clapboard houses with deep sloping roofs, narrow roads and high footpaths reminiscent of Norway.

Eventually it was time to board the train on which my friend Day of the Crusader Insurance Co and I had a suite. I asked some of the friends from the ship to meet us there for a drink in the rest and quiet of that little darkened sitting room, to look at the beautiful moonlit countryside. We changed our suits for the occasion.

Although we were all travelling on a very keen budget, that journey proved unforgettable. We had come from a war-torn Britain, a Liverpool that had more than its share of scars, a Manchester that had not suffered lightly, a country that was still rationed severely, to a land filled with nylons — seemingly a woman's best friend, just as they had assured a good introduction for a lot of American GIs to their lady friends. We had been on a ship carrying the maximum number of passengers with minimum comforts to a land where everything seemed fresh and clean, while goods, particularly in the food line, were in plentiful supply and only our restricted money supply curbed our appetites.

Many times I have recalled that wonderful journey and thirty-five years afterwards when my wife and I did the journey together, the beauty and the thrills were still there.

5th October 1946

After being checked by British, Canadian and American officials we eventually got ashore and up to the Nova Scotian — the big hotel for a drink — (non-alcoholic) this about 4 pm — we had to be on the train at 6 pm for Montreal.

Oh! By the way, Day and I cabled for a suite on the train and by the luck of the gods we got one.

Old Parkinson (the Doc) said he has never seen a group of men act so well together to make things enjoyable—he said what is so extraordinary you tolerate an old man like me.

Well, to hark back, we made for the train at 5.30 pm, a tremendously long train, over twenty coaches pulled by an enormous engine—the coloured attendants in smart grey uniforms with their bright yellow footstools, standing guard at their own particular coach. Each coach is named, Lakehurst, Lakeview, etc; we move to Montreal.

The train pulled out dead on time in the gathering twilight (it gets dark at 6.30 pm); as we gathered speed we left the town behind.

We put the light out in the compartment and sat and gulped in the view. The moon shone right across the rivers—the track twisted again, and the moon came through the clouds, chased the pine trees—caught here and there the bark of a silver birch (yes, it is true, silver birches do grow in great numbers), splashed across a lake and died away as we plunged through a cutting. Out of the cutting—a little hamlet—all the houses built of wood—bright windows aglow with light—now the moon shining brilliantly on the walls—now on the green roofs, now on the silver spire of the little wooden church—out again into the open country—more moon—more rivers—more beauty.

About nine o'clock we had dinner—all five of us—very good menu—and coffee—with loads of cream.

I often vividly recall that first moonlight night in Canada, the train rushing through the countryside; the brilliant moonbeams flashing on the silver coloured steeples of the little white churches standing like mothers brooding over the villages of white clapboard houses; pools, some as big as lakes, shimmering in the glistening brilliance of an early autumn night. Lights burning in the farmhouse windows and cottages, this in itself seemed strange after our years of blackouts and fears. As the train whooped and whistled along, the drinks seemed extra refreshing. It was then we noticed that heaps of stones, cleared by the early settlers and neatly piled in the corners of fields, now gave way to reasonably neat piles all around the fields. Finally the neatness was no longer there. The stones, no longer in heaps, were scattered across the grassland at irregular intervals: tired arms must have given way. I wondered that the early settlers, venturing into this new land, vigorous and full of hope, had lost some of their vigour as the years wore on and the stones mirrored their struggle, so that in the end it was the stones and not the fields that became the playground of the moonbeams.

Those uneven piles of stones perhaps mirrored our lives individually and collectively: youthful endeavour, strengthening in maturer years, only to slow down again as indeed we have as a nation.

Back in my sleeper I slipped between the crisp white sheets, with a final look at the countryside as we scurried by, and the stones we left behind.

I suddenly laughed as I recalled the story of a traveller on a long departed railway of the new north west. He was on a sleeper too and in the morning he found that he had at least one extra friend with him for he was covered with pink bites and they were not love bites. He wrote a very stiff letter to the president of the company, telling him in no uncertain terms that he had picked up a bug or two on one of his trains and it was his avowed intention never to travel on his railroad again. Neither would his family or friends.

He received a prompt reply from the railway president. 'Sure I apologise,' he wrote, assuring the passenger that he had never received a complaint like this before and that all steps had been taken to track down the offending bug. It was having priority attention, as was the bedding, the coach and the staff.

He was sad to hear that this kind traveller had decided not to use his railroad again; would the traveller do him one final favour by using the enclosed vouchers; would he take his family on the railroad for a long trip just once more? Honour seemed to have been satisfied and a passenger won back.

The traveller tore again the now empty envelope ready for the waste basket — and out dropped a little slip of paper with the words, 'Send this guy the bug letter.' My sleep that night though was undisturbed.

6th October 1946.

Woke to a view that made me sigh — sigh for you all to be with me to enjoy it. The St Lawrence first, icy blue with the early light, now pink, now red, as the dawn opened — then trees, maple, red and gold, mountain ash with berries a deep red, leaves crimson, ready to fall — the pines and firs, dark and sombre — forming a frame to the mighty — it is a mighty river.

Daylight came full and sure, the sun shone brilliantly — the tints in the field and forest changed with the light — the blue of the sky deepened, an almost artificial blue — the colour we see in films. The little hamlets as we dashed past, crept to life — you could almost trace the progression in the daily round, the old chap with the cattle at this place, the wife getting wood for the fire. Then the children, still in night clothes poking heads through the windows.

* * *

We arrived for breakfast, the steward rattled off a bewildering choice to our then rationed minds. Cereals, grapefruit, fruit juices in variety, oranges, fish of all kinds, a main dish of a mixed grill, cheese. 'Or will you,' the steward queried, 'as you are English, have bacon and eggs?' The plural of egg itself was welcome. 'Right!' he grinned, 'Two eggs and bacon for everybody!'

We tucked into the cereals, cream and all, the coffee with a wonderful aroma arrived — then bacon with two eggs. An amazing assortment of bread and rolls reminded us that for many years we had been used to one sort only.

I have travelled many, many thousands of miles by air since those days. None of the fast food offerings, or plasticised package meals have approached that wonderful meal and, even now, it seems funny that tough businessmen should be excited about a breakfast.

7th October 1946

Eventually we arrived at Mont Joli — by the way all the railway stations have French names — all the notices are in two languages, and even the smallest child speaks English and French fluently.

We had recovered from breakfast and made our way for luncheon, again a staggering choice. One course had been served when the train stopped—we were facing Quebec.

6/7th October 1946

The train actually runs along the river bank opposite Quebec and to 'make the city' one has to take a long ferry ride—we didn't have time for this—so we had to be content with a view across the river.

We saw Quebec thirty-four years later, from the same spot in an ethereal apricot dawn.

6/7th October 1946

The waiters on board had served one course, we were urged certainly to see this city (and we didn't get any more service until we did).

7th October 1946

A truly majestic city Quebec—the Chateau Frontenac dominating the scene. The French attendants on board referred in most hushed tones to the various points of interest (including the bridge across the river) the British 'die hard' with these French Canadians—Quebec is their Mecca.

We looked at this wonderful city. It pleased the restaurant staff no end that we left the train and gazed down on what must be one of the loveliest cities in the world, stately, grand and beautiful with noble buildings, the Chateau looking like a great cathedral. From the station platform the panorama appeared to be beyond a gorge, the narrows of the St Lawrence which the explorer Cartier found on his historic voyage four centuries ago. The Chateau Frontenac was not a cathedral but one of the world's great hotels and certainly the most stunning.

I took a long and pensive look at that lovely sight and vowed I would come to Quebec again. We did, and we enjoyed the Chateau.

We expressed our feelings to the crew, resumed our journey, hugging the banks of the St Lawrence river, little inlets and islands, little harbours with a wide selection of pleasure boats dancing in the sparkling water. It certainly looked like a New World.

9th October 1946

Evening is coming on—an evening that doesn't last long in this part of the world—again the glorious tints across the stretches of water that abound—now night—now the moon.

There is a rumble—we are crossing the river St Lawrence—the darkness is broken with the glare of electric signs—the Sun Life Building, twenty-two storeys high—floodlit at its summit—forming a beacon—slowly the train pulls in—red caps dash for the luggage—this is it, the second leg is over—what is more important a day nearer home!

I was in Montreal now. My hotel was listed as 'Core' but the taxi driver had never heard of it. He was right, it did not exist. He was helpful and tried all names and then I suggested hotels with four letter names (I could think of quite a few other four letter words by then). He came up with Ford and to the Ford we went where he dumped the luggage.

I approached the receptionist. 'You have a room booked for me, the name is Cooke. The ship was a day late, I cabled you.' 'Yea!' she chewed, 'We had it, but it's weekend and we let it!'

I was staggered, and said 'Where do we go from here?' 'I wouldn't know,' she drawled. 'It's now six o'clock on Saturday evening, I've come thousands of miles. I must have a room for tonight and tomorrow.' 'Tomorrow OK, a good room.' 'Yes, but what about tonight?' I talked to her about the journey and England; she warmed a little. 'Tell you what,' she said, 'Have a wash and clean up and a meal. I'll try and find somewhere for you here, nothing like the room you booked, but I promise tomorrow will be the original.' I was in a state when anything would do. I followed her suggestion, acquired for her a goodly box of chocolates and returned at 8.30 pm. 'Look!' she always said 'Look'. 'No wan' has cancelled but I found we have a small room at the back of the hotel. It's got a bed and wardrobe — no "bethroom" but you can get a rest.' I didn't argue but I just wondered that if our blood brothers cancelled on you despite a cable, what about New York?

The description of the 'room' was right. It did have a bed, it didn't have a bathroom, it did have an electric light bulb, without a shade. The carpet had seen better days but a long time ago; but far worse, there was a continual noise going on. I seemed to be on top of a bottling plant and the sound of bottles being re-stacked continued the whole night through or rather until the bottles gave out.

Montreal is a city of rising skyscrapers, set against a picturesque French section with the Hotel de Ville and the inevitable rocking chair on the verandah of old homes. This section I ventured was more French than France and Sunday in the city seemed little different to Paris.

One of the great attractions of Montreal is Mount Royal, where pilgrims and those desiring to confess make an obligatory journey to St Joseph's Oratory, progressing up the steep steps on their knees in a manner not unfamiliar on the continent. I mentioned this to one hard headed Canadian and said it was a most impressive sight. 'Oh yea!' he said. 'It is. Did you ever hear the story of the girl who was making her way up the high "peth" on her knees to confession? After climbing on her knees about a dozen steps, the elastic in her knickers snapped and the further she moved up the further her knickers dropped down, first to her knees then to her ankles. She looked over her shoulder, saw a young man, and whispered *sotto voce* "Would you mind slipping off my knickers from around my ankles?" Back from the male of the species came a rapid answer, "Not bloody likely, I'm doing this for that!"' Possible, probable, maybe impossible, but a good story!

Montreal was fascinating but it also seemed brash and not a little brittle like Johannesburg.

It had its own Notre Dame, every bit as lavish as its Paris parent, and not without its worshippers on Sunday afternoon; plenty of lighted candles too.

Today it is populated by tourists — herded around by professional guides — alas this lovely building to the Holy Mother is, like the French quarter, buried in a forest of skyscrapers.

My room next day was certainly up to expectations, beautifully decorated and appointed—in fact I felt somewhat disappointed that I now had only one more day before I departed for Toronto.

This visit to Montreal was intended as a respite after the ship so it did not teach me much in business. It seemed and has since proved to be the financial hub rather than a mass manufacturing base, and its forest of new skyscrapers and its bevy of beautiful hotels today confirms my original thought.

The stores were similar to our own but dominated by the great Eatons. I thought as I looked at that great name, 'There goes one of Hercules' mighty customers.' What was so different was their store lighting, for they had had no need for black-outs. Window displays were compelling by the very intensity of their lighting schemes and that was something to work on. But perhaps the greatest impact was their passion for building; buildings were appearing everywhere and many traces of the old city were being demolished, to be replaced by multi-storeyed monolithic blocks. I recall that taxi driver from the station pointing to the skeleton of a skyscraper-to-be when I was despairing of a room and saying, 'Old hotel gone, building new big hotel.' The old and romantic side seemed about to *go under* and a recent visit proved it did just that.

I met more booking trouble at the rail-road station. On trying to collect the tickets for Toronto the clerk confessed they had been double booked; mine had gone. One hotel and one railway on and I knew for certain that meant 'persuasion of the pocket'. I was right; a few crisp dollars and hey presto the original sleeper was available.

It certainly was a good idea to have a Bell Captain in charge of porters to carry luggage at a fixed rate a piece, but a farce when compared with the extras you were paying at the booking end.

With the tickets in my hand and a few dollars less in my pocket I made for the Toronto sleeper. As far as precious currency was concerned travelling by night train was a great saver, as I had no expensive hotel to pay for but I paid for that in lack of sleep.

* * *

It was a pleasant journey to a somewhat dowdy city of Toronto; fortunately it was only a one day stop. Many of my friends say it is not dowdy. It was then, but I agree it's a sparkling city today, with its huge buildings and towers, and its old town hall overshadowed by a huge new city hall which looks like half a rocket launching base.

During the morning I walked into the offices of the Singer Sewing Machine company (I was to see their president in New York). I asked for their salesman, these chaps always knew the run of things. He was a very kind fellow, and suggested various places that might offer ideas. 'Come again,' he said, 'With what your main interests are in England.' I repeated, 'Mail order, and in this field we are one of the two biggest companies, and chain stores.' The words mail order acted like magic. 'Let's have a cup of coffee,' he suggested. Over coffee he said, 'Yes! Yes! There is one new piece of machinery in this city (it's not made by us) but it is a winner, made especially for padded bedspreads, "comforters" (quilts to us) and very big mail order business. You're bound to be interested.'

He explained that the machine was invented by a guy in New York but he could show me one right there in Toronto. 'I'll take you to a little Italian chap who owns one. He makes about 1,000 comforters a week from one machine, only his wife and kid are helpers.'

Coffee over, and to down-town Toronto, to a scruffy looking building, a shop in the not too distant past. There was just enough room for the machine and the two humans to work it. I was told with great pride how much it had cost, and what it produced in a week. They mentioned the snags, they were very few, and finally they gave me the telephone number of the inventor. I whipped off a cable suggesting a meeting, and lunched with my friend from Singers but truth to tell I just could not get to New York quickly enough. If I found nothing else but new lighting, new displays and now this machine it would be a successful trip. The machine did prove to be very successful, and put us ahead in this field bringing many large contracts even from our competitors.

After that little episode, trouble again at rail-road. No tickets available—the same dollar note procedure—but results not so good. This time at some price I was offered and accepted a bunk, this meant I slept with the train, head to the engine, feet to the rear. At every station I suffered the tortures of the rack. My head shook in one direction my feet in the other. We were to travel near Niagara Falls; I could not get enthusiastic. I might have been right for many years ago on the Zambesi the story was told of the American who, seeing the huge Victoria Falls, cabled back home, 'Sell Niagara.' I knew little about selling Niagara but I do wish they had sold those appalling sleepers.

So I arrived in New York. The hotel problem was far worse than anywhere else. I had a reservation at a leading hotel; my luggage was curtly taken by the porter—not a good start, I thought. The smartly attired reception clerk took a look at me and obviously he did not like what he saw for I certainly looked British. I explained again Canadian style that the ship was late. 'I have a room booked for several days, the name is Cooke.' 'No room,' he bellowed. 'Just a moment,' I offered, 'I did send a cable.' 'No room.' His voice went higher. 'Next please.' 'Where the hell do I go then?' 'Ask the porter. Next!'

I spoke to the porter, and mentioned three leading hotels. 'I have a friend at . . .' I obviously omit the name. 'I speak with him.' He returned all triumphant. 'I have fixed it. Very difficult. You speak to porter at hotel, yes!' he winked. He opened the cab door with one hand, while the other reached for the tip.

At that hotel I got the lousiest room ever, complete with an old pair of boots under the bed. It accommodated a singular single bed, a tiny wardrobe, a bathroom of sorts—it could only be used if the member next door was not using it, and there was a contraption connecting both doors, that regulated that. Noise and the ever present laughter through the paper thin walls, was always present.

Having surveyed my corner of New York's garden paradise, I kept my promise and rang my friend Day who was staying with friends (the Armstrongs) across the river. The general idea was to fix a luncheon appointment next day but I was subjected to a cross examination of my new abode. He did not like it and neither did I; we agreed to meet next morning. The phone was barely back on the hook when it rang like a wild thing—it was Day's hostess, Doris Armstrong. 'Here,' she cried, 'Don't you know what kind of bad woman's place you're in? Come over right away and stay with us.' I protested that I had got the message all right about the hotel and had altered my plans and was off to Grand Rapids next morning but I would gratefully accept her invitation to stay with them on my return.

She was right about the hotel of course. The coffee room was awful, hardly as good a some transport cafes, and the bar was something of a tarts' paradise.

In New York, the rail-road ticket problem was still with me. The porter settled it as usual while the rail clerk deftly put the dollars to one side and enquired whether there was anything he could do. An American friend said, 'That's how things went, that's probably why some of the rail-roads went.'

* * *

Letters to my wife on arrival in New York and just after.

AMERICA

13th October 1946

Well I know you would like to know something about New York. It is a great city—but that remark applies to construction only—it is also a city in my experience without a soul or character—'Manchester with all thy filth—I love thee still.'—No joking! On one side, after spending a few days in New York—you realise that the American way of life is not the British way—can you imagine practically every restaurant opened all night—shops open all night (I only know because of the signs and the noise). Sunday morning papers being read at *6.30* on Saturday evening.—Advertisements promise the wearer of 'Slip on Slips'—Love at the first wear.—The cabbies smoking big cigars—Sunday, and I think this is what I have noticed most—quite different to Britain and Canada—Sunday exactly the same as any other days—radios and shops at it from the break of dawn. New York (and I am talking now of the many not of the exclusive few) is a great hustle, in an 'over enlarged' Bank Holiday Blackpool.

Now that all sounds very critical—turning to the more majestic side—Park Avenue and so on—the Great River Hudson—the splendid wide streets, the marvellous buildings and they have to be seen to be believed.—There you have something. If all New York was like that then it would indeed be the finest city in the world.

Some of these enormous structures are breathtaking—I went to Radio City this morning—with the chap who went with us to the Waldorf—this enormous structure goes up over seventy storeys—that of course is small compared with the Empire State Building 102 storeys. The docks too are well laid out, with the old Statue of Liberty mounting guard.

Harlem, well I would need a book to describe it—it is really a community all on its own—with the rich blacks and the poor, each living in their various quarters.

Now yesterday I got a taxi and went all round the city—covering poor and rich districts alike.—I was deeply impressed by the new expensive apartment houses flanking the river.—I was sickened by the squalid poverty of the Bowery and Brooklyn. 'Tis true a tree might have grown in Brooklyn. I couldn't find it. Now today I decided (on one's own it's pretty long) to go on a coach ride through New Jersey and into West Point — the Army College. — Here was something different, we went over the Great George Washington Bridge, then along the banks of the Hudson, climbing, climbing, all the time the Hudson still mighty beneath us — whilst on the other side great stretches of rolling forest land went away to the distant hills.

Still upwards the old coach rattled past scattered groups of white timbered houses, very much like the Canadian — no fences — no hedges — lawns just to the edge of the road. Down again we plunged — sign said 'to Albany' the river at this point was full of ships, quite big ones too, on the far side of the river bank loomed up the craggy cliffs, glistening in the sun, contrasted by the dark green of the trees.

Still onwards we come to one of the National Parks, Great Mountain Park, really very beautiful — imagine a big armchair, the back joined by a mountain closing in on three sides, covered with dark green firs, etc — then a plateau — a startling green (mainly because it was I suppose the only grass about) — then a cliff dropping down to the Hudson, at the bottom, the Hudson calm, clear and very blue. On for a few miles to West Point — quite a nice college!!

Well laid out with grey granite buildings set on a very high point at a bend of the Hudson. — I got out of the bus 3.15 pm. 'Supper time at home now and Podge asleep.'

I walked back to the Highland Falls — then on to the bus and here I am now back in New York. But one glorious view I must mention — sunset over the Hudson from the Bridge — New York Skyscrapers on the one side merging into a soft pink mist — the roads of New Jersey on the other side, wearing a veil of pinky grey and in the centre the Hudson merging with the sky into mother of pearl.

Tell RC I did not have to go through Ellis Island coming in from Canada, the train stops at Niagara Falls and the customs and immigration officers check all your papers just before you get into bed.

I did see a report of Churchill's speech in the Canadian papers, they are very pro-Churchill and strangely enough so are the Americans.

Tried to change my hotel today without success — this is not one of the best — but the hotel position is critical; UNO has upset everybody's calculations and even the mighty (including Chairmen of oil companies) and your humble servant are grateful for what they can get.

New York again

15th October 1946

I seem to have written so much about scenery and so on that I have not told you much up to date how I have been going on as far as work is concerned. Well first and foremost strange this will seem — generally speaking we have them beaten for organisation.

They have some very fine machines and know how to use them — as regards welfare, except in the very big plants it just doesn't exist. Canteens are unknown and so are rest rooms.

I have bought quite a lot of machine parts (fitments) and quite a few machines — some very clever machines for automatically sewing quilts — will effect a tremendous saving. — Have visited quite a few clothing factories — two very good mattress firms — most business seems to be in the hand of Jews.

By the by Truman is regarded as much dead mutton over here — New stuff — office girls at Makins Store — parading in front of the stores with picket cards 'Please don't patronize'.

Tomorrow I am off to Grand Rapids from there on to Chicago (and Louisville) from Chicago to New York.

I have been to two shows. *Ice Time* and *Ballet Russe*. The latter at the Metropolitan Opera House — a fine theatre — all to match. Numerous busts of the great artists who have performed there give cultural effect. Magnificent Symphony Orchestra and the Ballet is

101

first class — Saw Anton Dolin and Markova, being British they didn't get the hand they deserved.

Do you know that off Park Avenue there is a swell, yes swell open air skating rink — French cafe one end and English the other — all the skaters were of top class.

The distances here are so great — you really have to be here to appreciate the time it takes to get from one city to another — received invitations to visit two factories, one in Vermont the other in the South — both out at least three days — imagine six days for two calls.

The sun is just beginning to set, the lights are beginning to twinkle on Broadway — soon it will be a blaze of light, twisting, whirling, cascading, sparkling — reds, blues and gold — it's a spectacle — especially from the high ground looks like a fairyland from a distance — a distance, I said.

Tonight I am having dinner with the British Vice Consul.

Last night I had dinner with Day at the Plaza, a swell place, they had a floor show — very select — for Wall Street bankers and so on. But here's the point — a girl sings a funny song — she is applauded, sings as an encore — another verse — obviously written specially welcoming the Republicans — Mud in yer eye to the Democrats, loud applause — this political business is certainly a racket.

I was asked out for this coming weekend to Dr Armstrong — unfortunately I can't go, shall be in Chicago, trying to arrange to see them before I go back.

Well you can't imagine a city with more to sell than this place. I was going to say that I sigh for England, that's putting it mildly — Both in Canada and USA food in particular and other things in general are so plentiful as to be vulgar, and I mean that — what the English lack in worldly goods they make up for in spirit and in their bearing, more than ever I am proud to be English.

There is a seamen's strike on here — pretty serious — so today the seamen parade with thousands of banners round the city — finally make a concentrated band around 'Times Building' simply because a column writer called them a few names and spoke the truth. In all the thousands marching, only a mere handful were whites — what a problem this is going to be in the years to come.

What seems to be lacking on both sides is tolerance and understanding — both sides apparently refuse even to try and understand the other.

Today on the Irish question both sides seem to lack the same vision of tolerance here at home.

* * *

I met the inventor and placed the orders. We had breakfast at the Waldorf Astoria and he tried the dollar game to get me a room but we lost the dollars and did not get the room. He was very helpful with introductions to other bright inventors who were full of new ideas.

I visited all the big departmental stores, the larger chain stores and did a complete round up of the retailing element, particularly the purveying of food, the business I felt they did so very well.

Some parts of New York downtown were both filthy and depressing, and were a complete write off, indeed the back-cloth of the musical *Irene* gives a fair idea of what it really looked like. I said earlier to me Harlem was depressing, but was glad to see it. I wondered why the Americans were so critical of South Africa and Rhodesia when they had such appalling conditions on their own doorstep. I found it hard to believe this unbelievable squalor and poverty, rotting property and shocking overcrowding, was only a few blocks away from the finest hotels and stores. I thought we had our problems but the slums of Birmingham seemed like a Sunday School outing.

I am sure that Times Square and Broadway often evoke the thought that this is a little bit of heaven. I thought it a bit of hell. I have seen our Piccadilly looking pretty awful with waste paper blowing around and Coca Cola tins littering the gutters, sex shops within spitting distance and the girls to go with them. On Broadway I saw the only stage show that had tickets available (I wasn't surprised); the cast was entirely made up of very, very fat women — high kicking, revealing great rolls of human fat — leaving you with the truism 'that the mouse in his trap loses his taste for cheese.'

I studied all the big stores on Fifth Avenue and went over the chain stores and some of the smaller units again. Three things impressed me: the very high prices, their decor and thirdly, and this most dramatically, the lighting of their windows and displays.

I pondered on this lighting business; it was perhaps the Candy Stores Group (Lofts) that made me think yet again for I was shaken by the impact of light. I asked myself why it should all look so different? The penny dropped; the answer was simple. We had suffered many years of black-outs and lack of pennies with no opportunity to experiment. Our friends across the water had taken full advantage of their access to both power and light.

The impact prompted me to do yet another tour of the stores which confirmed that it was the light and colour that was so different. I translated this into what might be achieved by our own chain stores and one thing stood out: our name or fascia boards were red with gold lettering just like Woolworths or BHS. Only Marks and Spencer were different with green and gold. I felt Littlewoods should be different. Taking the colours from some of the American stores, I concluded that Littlewoods' fascia boards should be in blue with gold lettering, something all of their own — distinctive yet not blatant, continuing the Littlewood philosophy story of so many years before.

* * *

The alteration was not to be. When I got back and for many years afterwards I argued this point. Some may think it a simple point but it was not. Long after I left them I noticed that at least some of the Littlewoods' fascia boards had been altered to blue and gold, so while that was a plus from the American scene, it was not in my time. I was consoled that at least it had happened.

So many ladies' shops were selling nylons and I raided my cash reserves, to bring back a few extra pairs. They were tucked safely in my luggage and gave great delight.

In wartime a pair of nylon stockings was an instant introduction for a GI to girls over here yet the impact of nylons was terrific on most ladies, and that may be difficult for the girls of today to understand. It sprang I suppose from the fashion starvation of the long suffering female of the species and it is amusingly summed up in a A. P. Herbert's *The Nylon Light*.

> I bring you nylons from across the seas,
> And learn how pleasant it can be to please,
> Not gold, not diamonds — no other prize
> Could light, I swear, such beacons in your eyes.
>
> These two additions to your shapely legs
> You would not barter for a thousand eggs!
> While I, poor fellow that I am,
> Would gladly give my trousers for a ham.
> Poor men, unthrilled by anything we wear,
> Would that new socks could make us tread on air!

I was off to Grand Rapids. The New York rail-road termini were different to ours then, with a large departure hall with destination gates, very much like Euston is today, for we have caught up. Their layout provided another big economy for the departure gates led directly to the track. There were no extensive covered platforms so consequently less labour was required. The train was comfortable and the black attendant very courteous.

I was awakened with a refreshing tray of coffee, then a substantial breakfast and here I was in Grand Rapids. There seemed to be a country atmosphere about it, quiet, like a county town in England, not nearly half as brittle as New York. I was to learn later that that was just what Americans thought too.

Grand Rapids

17th October 1946

At Grand Rapids a step further on the journey and a day nearer home; at this time in fourteen days the shores of dear old England will be looming up out of the mist.

I had quite a good journey down, an excellent train equipped with dining car, lounges and buffet car and of course sleeping compartment. The black attendant is part of the stock in trade in every coach. Mine was very good and got a beautiful shine on my shoes. Started off from New York at 6.05 pm, arrived at Grand Rapids 12 noon, an eighteen hours' run. That's the whole point — to visit one centre of industry from another is more than a day's run.

The countryside outside Detroit through which the train passed early this morning is very pretty. It is extraordinary, as soon as the train leaves the city, the houses are no longer made of bricks. Up spring these little clusters of white wooden houses, usually with long casement windows, tiny verandahs and always, always, little white wooden steps leading to the front door, with the ever present white wooden balustrade. These little groups are usually set among the trees, which at this time of the year are looking at their best in their coats of yellow, orange, lilac and gold.

Grand Rapids is a town of some 200,000 souls, yet it does not look like a big town. It sprawls, but the atmosphere is more to my liking than New York. It's cool and open. It is raining but it is pleasant; the whole tenor is calmer and more friendly.

I phoned my contact, the president of a large furniture manufacturing company and received a wonderful welcome. 'You're here then! And you're coming over here right now, no excuses,' he said. On arrival I was greeted like a long lost son. It seemed here was a way of life rather than a way of money. I was questioned about the effects of war, of rationing, of bombing and destruction. I spared nothing but said we were fighting back and things were improving, but Britain had suffered much for its principles.

We were in the president's suite. 'Come let's have lunch and talk about you and your family.' They had their own kitchens and cook, and I was asked to select my own steak. The fridge was of outsize proportions and I had never seen so many steaks, really like a butcher's shop. At table everything for the appetite was there, a feast not only of food but of kindness too.

The plant was most interesting and the planning was first class with specialised machines installed in just the right positions to ensure the minimum of transportation. The machine was the work horse. My host volunteered, 'Really you want to spend some of your time in Kentucky. They have a plant there that's claimed to be the best furniture factory in America. It is all go, go! We will fill you in with the level of life thereabouts and of business, the racial problems too.' They kindly phoned the appointment and we talked far into the night. I learned much there in a quiet happy way.

Grand Rapids

17th October 1946

That means *another night* going to Louisville (Kentucky) but I shan't mind that, because I have a daylight journey back through, I believe, beautiful country, so I am scrapping most of the other plans and going all out for this one call.

'Tomorrow starts our weekend,' was their goodnight. 'We will collect you about mid-day; forget all about work, for the day tomorrow, my son, is yours.' I remember the words well, and so they planned to show me their countryside.

Grand Rapids

17th October 1946

Night has just fallen here, the lights are on in the village, rather the town. Oh! it is so much more peaceful than New York. Do you know that the trains cross the main streets in most of these American towns — old bells clanging away.

The president and his colleague who happened to be a lady financier on Wall Street went out of their way to make me at home. Luncheon, dinner in their suites, and some meals out at the club, country club, Lake Michigan. In the car I said to the old girl (she is over 60), 'I feel awfully embarrassed being taken around like this.' 'Why should you,' she snapped. 'The pleasure is ours and don't take it away.'

We had a wonderful tour. Beautiful little inlets with a colourful variety of weekend boats and pretty chalets, clustered the lakeside. We had real fun with everything to make me feel at home; they were anxious to show me the various types of village life around their part of Lake Michigan and I was taken to one exciting place after another. Lastly we arrived at Zeeland which was as Dutch as the name. The windmills, architecure, clogs, clothing, even the flowers, bulbs, vegetables, fruit, blossom trees and the inevitable celery all reminded me of Holland.

My hostess took us to a little hotel that served tea. 'Now!' she said, 'You're English so you like tea.' She hailed the waiter and commanded, 'My friend is from Britain, and he would like tea, not your bag tea, one or two to the pot. We want real tea, let the spoon stand up in it.' The tea arrived, not quite with the spoon standing up, but very nearly. We wound our way to my hotel for more talks after a memorable afternoon.

Anyhow this old girl, tough in business, but extremely, extremely kind, almost wept on my shoulder on Saturday evening. I bought and sent to her room a large bunch of English type roses. She was delighted.

The time came to say our good-byes. My hostess insisted that if ever I went to America again she would do all the arranging, we could even have her flat in New York. We visited America again but alas, I am afraid, too late for them.

* * *

Chicago

10 pm, 20th October 1946

I felt I just had to ring you up this morning—it was so nice to hear all the voices again.

When I entered my room early this morning (I came off the sleeper from Grand Rapids) the scene was so beautiful that I felt I had to share it. This is a crack hotel—God bless Thomas Cook! I have a front bedroom on the eleventh floor overlooking Lake Michigan. The room is marvellously appointed. Well now—the scene that took my breath as I entered—the venetian blinds were down. Porter said, 'Shall I draw them sir?' Then, the sun rising over the lake, this great mass of water, just dull, then misty, then a flash of brilliance as the sun broke through in strength that turned the lake into a mass of boiling silver, the light so intense that I blinked as it reflected well into the room. Then little blots in the scene emerged as small fishing boats and yachts, the bigger ones as steamers.

The hotel is quite close to the lake about 200/300 yards away across motor roads, boulevards, lawns and railroad track. This water front is well laid out; the city of Chicago I prefer to New York.

I had a pretty poor view of Americans just by the precepts of New York, but the quiet rural surroundings and almost English attitudes of Grand Rapids took a lot of the hardness away.

Am closing now to catch the *Kentuckian* to take me to Louisville.

I was off to Louisville via Chicago.

* * *

I was now in Louisville, Kentucky, and the first thing that struck me was the very clear division between blacks and whites, particularly the divides at railway stations and in street cars—blacks in one section, whites in the other. That is different now.

I rang up the company vice president the night before I left Chicago and asked if he would be around at 8.00 to 8.30 am. 'I'll be there at 7.30 am,' he boomed. After a hurried breakfast I was off to the appointment at 8.30. It was some plant. My host was there, sleeves rolled up, tense, quivering with the sheer joy of production.

We talked over general production methods and he emphasised with vigour their positive approach to all new labour saving machinery. With this philosophy in mind they solved the problem of producing high quality furniture at a price the masses could afford. It had been achieved in an effective way, with a big sophisticated plant, brilliantly planned, with specialised machines in operation sequence, demonstrating a determination to contain or reduce by every possible means the labour element and yet at the same time maintain high wages. My friend the energetic vice-president emphasised they had no desire for old practices and no space for old machines, no time for long arguments and above all no desire or capacity for wasting such a valuable commodity as time. He knew the philosophy of Henry Ford.

It was interesting to observe that the enthusiasm of the chief had rubbed off on the work force; they too were production conscious. Maybe it was for real, maybe it was the fear of losing a good job. The co-operation was there nevertheless.

He was not a man of many spare words yet he took me on a verbal visit from the veneer cutting operation to their fascinating packing section. After that short period of pleasantries, we were on our way around the entire plant, with the interjection, 'Ask any questions you like; talk to the operators if you care.'

Very many of their ideas were original and sound. They had studied the work flow problem intensively. One operation was sited very much like the early Hercules efforts with their huge plating plant sited on the top storey of the building. Here it was even more unusual, for part of the large sawmill was sited on their top storey. It started the production flow and the offcuts of timber were fed via chutes down to the boiler house.

I was deeply impressed to see their attention to the work study of even the smallest operation and the willingness of operators to try this or that. In one unit they were producing bedroom suites and at the time of my visit were installing a new continuous spraying plant with very few operators about, everything moving mechanically. The spray guns were sited at the right level, varying in position with that part of the furniture that required spraying. This was impressive and demonstrated a dedication to making even the tiniest operation as near perfection as possible. There seemed to be more time study engineers than operators, which is of course the proper approach to modern mass production; for planners and timers should set up the perfect job, involving the minimum of manual work. They were determined to increase the size of the cake, with little or probably no increase in the total labour charge; that way all could have a bigger worthwhile slice. If only we here could understand the lesson of the bigger cake and the bigger slice!

I was very much taken with the production flow and speed of their packing section which was not very big on space, but the output was unbelievable. The layout was very much a real Charlie Chaplin *Modern Times* set, with many conveyors converging like streams of lava, discharging various units of furniture. Packing tools of every description hung from the ceiling or protruded through the floors; gadgets of all kinds were always near at hand.

The protective packing material was made from old newspapers, shredded and used as filling for 'newspaper quilts' — even the coverings were made from other editions. Packing a chest of drawers was simple: a quilt over the top, fastened underneath, another wrapped around the front, stapled automatically round the back and then on to the conveyor; a speedy, efficient, and economic production. This method of filling quilted envelopes, pads and the like with shredded paper or other material is rapidly gaining ground here as a packing medium. This very simple operation mirrored so well their philosophy on costs and production. I learned much here.

At coffee I posed a question on works canteen facilities. My friend didn't understand canteens and thought they were only for the army. I tried cafeterias; he looked at me, fixed his eye and said, 'You mean here in this factory?' 'Yes,' I replied, 'Do you for example serve meals?' He was quite stupified. 'In here?' he exclaimed. 'No!' He got up from his chair, walked to the window, pointed to a quadrangle between the buildings and said, 'See there, hot dogs, hamburgers if you like, frankfurters, coffee and sandwiches. These chaps come up at break times with their tricycles and sell their food. Our employees buy right there! 'No doubt things have changed now, but they probably had a point then.

I did not agree with the no facilities theme, but it made me think very deeply of our struggle to compete in world trade. For here we were in a war torn Britain and virtually broke, providing not only good canteen meals but subsidising them too, facing ever increasing demands for shorter hours and higher wages, while trying to compete with a country who made not only a study but virtually a religion of keeping the labour content to a minimum, with production the dominant feature, and facilities an also ran.

After my final questions, my vice-president friend reiterated if there was a better way to do a job, a quicker way or a better product to be produced, it had to be found. He remembered his Emerson very well.

Chicago

11.15 pm, 21st October 1946

Have just arrived in from Louisville, most interesting day, but very tiring — am completely exhausted so I am going to close this letter quickly in order that I can post it in the morning. I'm afraid it will only just catch you — if I am lucky.

This is the last letter then on to New York, the Queen Elizabeth and home.

I made my way back by train to New York, this time to wind up my visit, staying with the Armstrongs.

I would still have time to do more important calls — a visit to a lingerie and corsetry company. There nothing was hidden, not even the nude model. I spent much time around the factory where every machine seemed to be fitted with a labour saving gadget, and all sections laid out in streamlined order, avoiding cost of movement. Again there was the same application of the science of reducing the labour or time content to the minimum, creating more work and more wealth, and better shares for all. It was the devotion of the application and the splendid results which drove home the point.

* * *

Back in New York I had an early dinner with my friend Day, we made our way across the Hudson to Scarboro on a warm evening in early autumn. The hot explosive noise of New York was left behind, and with a lighthearted spirit we arrived at a charming home among friends. The lovely house welcomed us, its charming gardens ablaze with tiny chrysanthemums was a reminder of home.

Mrs Armstrong greeted me like a long lost friend. 'Sit down with a drink, tell me about that god-damned hotel. What about the women there?' she enquired. 'I didn't see any,' I continued, 'I was too busy.' 'If you're here for long you had better grow up quickly,' she added.

Her three sons had all left home by now. Each had been baptised with a name of a president of the States and I was to have Lincoln's beautiful room overlooking the gardens. After changing we resumed our talk. She asked, 'Do you know any of the tunes from *Oklahoma?*' At that time the show had not arrived in England and months afterwards we saw the first performance at the Opera House in Manchester with Bill Johnson in the lead. She had a selection of the songs at the ready, including the memorable 'Doing what comes naturally'. She played them to us well into the night.

She regarded us as boys — 'Boys we best do this, we best do that, we best go in the garden, we best call on the neighbours and introduce you.' It was just like home to me.

In Lincoln's bedroom there were many poems and quotations obviously reprinted with loving care — one impressed me so much that I sat at the dressing table and copied it, there and then.

> Let me do my work each day,
> And if the darkened hours of despair overcome me
> May I not forget the strength that comforted me
> In the desolation of other times;
> May I still remember the bright hours that found me
> Walking over the silent hills of my childhood,
> Or dreaming by the margin of a quiet river,
> When a light glowed within me
> And I promised my early God to have courage,
> Amid the tempest of the changing years
> May I not forget that poverty and riches
> Are of the spirit though the world know me not
> May my thoughts and actions be such
> As shall keep me friendly within myself;
> Lift mine eyes from the earth
> And let me not forget the usage of the stars;
> Forbid that I should judge others lest I condemn myself,
> Give me a few friends who love me for what I am,
> The kindly light of hope,
> And though age and infirmity overtake me
> And I come not within sight of the castle of my dreams,
> Teach me still to be thankful for life
> And for life's golden memories, that are good and sweet,
> And may the evening twilight find me still.

I have tried to trace the author of these lines for many years without result; if any reader knows I would love to hear. Sentimental some may say, but that verse is surely filled with many of our intimate thoughts. I read that thousands of miles away from home, in the quiet of a boy's bedroom on the banks of the Hudson river; I did not hear it again for over twenty years until the captain of the *Windsor Castle* on a Sunday morning in the South Atlantic offered it as a prayer at sea. The late Lady Stamp said to my wife, 'What a beautiful prayer, I wish I had a copy.' My wife replied, 'Would you like a copy, I will send you one.' So that wonderful verse now spans many more thousands of miles.

Continuing my story, next morning I went to see one of the great bedding manufacturers. The journey alongside Jameston Avenue is perhaps best forgotten, where the trains went down the middle of the long, long road on an elevated track. It seemed to me that the track had been sited just at first floor level where the filth and noise belched into the rooms of the poor; there was no escaping it.

The reception, whilst courteous, was not as open as it had been elsewhere. Many of the operations were *verboten,* but again there was the same fanaticism to obtain the highest output from minimal labour, not by brow beating, but by careful study, and the use of any mechanical aid. No, I did not really like that area at all.

A final flip around the stores—I counted my pennies and collected—food parcels—who would dream today about food parcels for England? And sweets for the kids.

My friend and I wanted to offer some hospitality to the Armstrongs but they had so much of what this world could give. We decided to pool our resources and give them a night out at the Ritz Carlton. The hotel was a swish affair; the drinks too were of the outsize variety and unaccustomed as we were to much hard liquor through the war years, those gin slings soon told me to go quietly. It was a marvellous evening, men well groomed, women beautifully dressed, so dramatically different to what I had left in England. Rationing at home meant a woman was very lucky to have a new dress once a year; despite it all, I badly wanted to go home. Late that night we finished with a brief spell of peaceful, unspoiled, homely life, so different to ours in wartime, but happy, enjoyable, and lovable.

* * *

The following day I was on the way back to England on the return maiden voyage of the *Queen Elizabeth*, that huge ship of which we were so rightly proud. We had a good send off with the ship beflagged (not on my account). There was a strike on in New York so the huge craft made her way out of the harbour with virtually no help. She turned in the river and faced that wonderful New York waterfront, a futuristic skyline of towering skyscapers, windows beginning to twinkle here and there with early lights. The sirens of the tugs that were working, screamed, the smaller craft squeaked farewell, whilst the other liners gave a stately hoot worthy of their size.

I stayed on deck for a long time watching the skyline of the New World fade in the autumn light and I thought of my experiences.

110

Looking back, one thing that horrified me in New York was the press attacks on the British about what was then called Palestine and now Israel. Some of the newspapers carried double page spreads of sponsored advertisements, urging this action or that, with suggestions of how to deal with our troops; ploys such as 'string them up' — and they did in the silence of the orange groves. Hardly the press treatment one would expect from an ally of our comparatively small country who had found itself twice in modern history fighting for the cause of freedom.

I quote from a friend of mine who was in Palestine about this time.

30th June 1946

I am having an intensely busy time just now as I expect you will be reading in the papers. We have just got to stamp out the terrorist elements here in Palestine.

I think we have made a good start. It is a wretched sort of business. Our soldiers are called Huns, Germans, Fascists and many extremely insulting things. The bearing and discipline of troops are just beyond all praise; they are always restrained and by jove they have every reason to be otherwise.

One longs to be home again.

I was disappointed with the journey home. There was nothing wrong with the luxury of the ship in accommodation, food, entertainment or service — the essence of all that made British cruising ships the envy of the world. As a piece of ship building and engineering she was righly called The Queen, let us not forget that like that other great ship the *Queen Mary*, she was conceived in deep economic distress and had seen service in the war as a troop carrier (indeed one or two bits of graffiti still remained). She was a mighty floating advertisement for all that was great in British vision, ingenuity, craftsmanship and grace.

So, if it was an interesting, indeed memorable trip, what was wrong with it for me? To me the great ship was just too large to be friendly, too grand to muck about in, even the very homely housey-housey or bingo was like a fashionable visit to the racecourse. I devoted most of my time to playing deck tennis (for which I later paid the price with a dose of pleurisy). The weather was anything but kind but we arrived on time at Southampton on a grey day.

I was quickly off the ship and through Customs who were very understanding with only a nominal charge on the nylons, etc. Mabel met me, then on to the train, a stop over at Grosvenor House (then in its hey day) and home.

So my first visit to the New World ended. It was a trip from which I learned much, found some things curious, had some of my own views confirmed. Above all I met many friends; what more could I ask!

* * *

As 1946 drew to a close all divisions of the company were working well and together. John Moores seemed tired after the strain of the war years, and was taking things a little easier; Eric Sawyer and I virtually ran the mail order, chain stores and factories (the non-pools division). Eric and I were friends as well as colleagues, so working together was a pleasure. It was indeed a happy time with heady progress. The new year entered to a whole round of conferences, chain store, mail order and

111

buyers — all were helpful, some were very good, most of them entertaining, but a minority could be abrupt and to the point.

There seemed to be progress in all directions and if I had been asked then if I would finish my business years with Littlewoods, the answer would have been yes, and an emphatic yes at that.

Later that year John Moores phoned, telling me he was very happy with the way everything was going and proposed that my colleague Eric Sawyer and I should become executive directors of the group — the first non-family members. A dinner for all the directors and senior executives together with their wives was arranged at the Adelphi Hotel in Liverpool. It was a breakthrough, and a celebration, for it was at this dinner John Moores announced the executive director appointments.

These director appointments were obviously important to the two of us, but they were also excellent for the business, for the message was now clear that you did not have to be a family member to be a director. It was perhaps the most important decision made in a great number of years. Until the events of 1956 it had the effect of welding everyone together with one purpose only, the continued advancement of the business. We had many entertaining diversions like Miss Littlewood (an early version of Miss UK), Littlewoods Choir, Sports Day, Grand National Day. The Grand National was quite an affair and hard work at times for we entertained the chiefs of some of our largest suppliers which was helpful. It was also good that the wives met together for all mixed so very well.

There were some exciting Grand Nationals; on one historic occasion we were in seats next to the Russian Vice Premier Malenkov. He was an imposing sight, a big man with a very long 1909-type overcoat, crepe soled shoes and with him the ever present bodyguards.

Then there was the Queen Mother's horse, Devon Loch, collapsing virtually at the winning post, well ahead of its rivals, only to lose the National to the great sigh of the crowds, and the brave smile of its owner. There were the game losers too, who would never have had a chance to win if the best horses did not fall. Sometimes all the best horses did fall and that was a bonus for the bookies. These Grand Nationals, with lavish luncheon parties were times to remember as were the dinners at the Adelphi afterwards. No matter how poor Merseyside seemed to be, there was always a goodly crowd of all sorts at Aintree which is not a place where the poor can live cheaply, or bet with no money. Over the years with the advent of television, the crowds declined. The cameras could capture the thrill of most of the jumps while those customers in the stands, on the straight or at the winning post had to put up with the nearby views and a running commentary. But there is no substitute for the National in the flesh.

Boxing was a great evening pastime and I met many of the big names and saw some great fights in both Liverpool and London.

* * *

In the town of Aspatria we were developing a large bedding and furniture manufacturing complex with its own railway sidings. The area was a sad district, indeed all that part of Cumberland seemed to be. It had been sickened by chronic unemployment, both before and after the war. Many said the war was a blessed relief.

When I first visited Maryport and Aspatria, I was shown around by the general manager of the West Cumberland Development Corporation, none other than Jack Adams (later Lord Adams). As we passed through Maryport he said, 'You know Cooke, the biggest pastime here is spitting. Watch the *fether* and son on the kerbstone, just seeing who can spit *farest*.' At many street corners it was there to see. Jack himself had a story to tell; he was a miner's son and one of the very many childers as he called them. Before they were grown up dad was killed in a mining accident. 'Poverty! You don't know what it is. Thy house full of kids, no money and a dead *fether*.' He married before he was 21 and just before the wedding he got the sack for being a union official. He tramped the coalfields for work, was barred, but survived. Jack was a wonderful example of how quickly power, and he had real power, can change the outlook of a person. He was a perfect capitalist in most of his affairs (although he would not admit it!). He boasted of his little terraced house and said he wanted no more, even with a coronet. He could certainly get government departments moving and his memory was prodigious.

It was in Cumberland that I first met Mr Harold Wilson, then President of the Board of Trade. Whatever else may be said of that government it did bring work to areas which had seldom known work.

On one occasion Harold Wilson and his wife were staying at Armathwaite Hall on Basenthwaite Lake. Mabel, our eight-year-old son Roger and I were there. Roger was missing from his room and as it was near time for dinner, I went looking for him, finding a joyful little figure coming up the baronial style staircase. I anxiously enquired, 'Where have you been all this time?' 'Oh! I've just been having a talk with the Wilsons.' Such is a little boy's attitude to even a future Prime Minister of England.

I met Harold Wilson again many years later, I was in the foyer of the Adelphi Hotel, when his hand clapped on my shoulder. 'How are you Cooke, how's Aspatria, how's everything?' He must have had an excellent system for jolting his memory, and if action was needed, particularly on a Government issue, he was prompt, precise, courteous and well informed. His public relations were excellent, even to his envelopes—on the front 'From the Prime Minister', on the back '10 Downing Street'.

Despite problems here and there, we got our factory built in Aspatria, production started, and working conditions were superb. The choice of products was good for here again with luck, or rather good judgement, the new factory was producing bedding and furniture, the very items which were in short supply and from a mail order and chain store angle, the railway siding was an asset for quick despatch—and no stock problems.

I mention here the little story of Aspatria's Jack Adams and the celebration of his well deserved peerage.

A party was organised at Armathwaite Hall and the Mayor of Maryport proposed his health to an almost continual metallic jingle. He had known Jack when they were little lads. *Jingle.* 'Always knew 'e would do well! *Jingle.* A great son of Cumberland.' *A very big jingle.* Finally loud applause, to the loudest *jingle* of all as he released his hand from the precious coins in his pocket and made way for Jack.

Lord Adams rose, spoke of his gratitude to all those who had helped him to bring so much work to this stricken area. He went on, 'Some say this is the "hend" of Jack Hadams. Nay I say I'm just at the beginning. I tell you I was a seven months babe and I've been in a 'urry ever since.'

Dinner ended and he said to me, 'Look, Cookie, I've been asked to autograph these menus. How do I sign them?' I said, 'Jack, either sign Adams of Ennerdale or Ennerdale.' 'What,' he exploded. 'Not Jack Adams or Lord Adams?' 'Afraid not,' I countered. 'You really mean just Ennerdale or Adams of Ennerdale?' 'Just that.' 'Bloody hell,' he gasped. 'Don't seem right to me, but I suppose I'll settle for Adams of Ennerdale. But what about the missus?' he enquired. I suggested, 'Agnes of Ennerdale or Agnes Adams of Ennerdale.' 'Not Lady Adams?' he nearly exploded. 'Can't understand it!'

It was difficult to believe that Jack had been elevated to the peerage for without warning he would launch sudden attacks on this or that branch of society. His particular target was the coal owners. He blamed one in particular, rightly or wrongly you could never tell, for spoiling what was once a beautiful countryside.

He took me to see the town of Whitehaven, originally designed by Christopher Wren. The splendid and beautiful layouts were there, despite the slums which had been built in the remains of once lovely gardens. The basic plan of straight streets, well placed churches and the remains of delightful dwellings were all so obvious. I took his point. It must have been a gem, but time and industrialisation had taken its toll, and what remained was grimy. Jack took this very much to heart, let fly with various expletives and sighed, 'How beautiful it could have been had it not been exploited.' He claimed (and true or false he believed it) coal owners took as much from each ton of coal as the miners did, they probably did for seams were pushed out further and further, even under the sea and that cost a great deal of money. Sometimes these costly explorations failed, then wages and conditions felt the pinch and near poverty became poverty for real. Socialist propaganda maybe, perhaps some of it was. One day he thumped the table with passion and said, 'Do you know Cooke, I was asked to attend a coal owner's funeral.' 'You didn't go of course,' I countered. 'I bloody well did—I just wanted to make sure the old . . . was safely under the ground.' He never mentioned them, but the tell tale blue scars on his face and the deep wound on his soul bore eloquence to his testimony of hardship.

Lord Adams was not only in the big business of manufacturing, he was still a radical at heart (so he said). He was a keen observer of his 'native heath', particularly village life, which in the days of hardship and isolation he said made for communal happiness despite the poverty and it had a sort of communal control, that was an example particularly to the young—he called them 'the people of the future'. My wife recalls vividly Jack Adams sitting next to her and brooding that with the advent of modern transport with bus services plying between the villages

114

and centres of amusement, the modern cinema, the dance halls, the bigger and brighter pubs, there had been a sad decline in family and particularly village life.

The young people drifted away from home and left the simple yet healthy family village life, its quiet ways and perhaps restrictions. The village communities suffered numerically and so did its remaining occupants in many other ways. The comparatively harmless healthy and sometimes restrictive pastimes declined and died — until there was no longer a community life, the village died too. He pondered this deeply, and sadly. In short the wheels of the bus had put the skids under the closely knit communities.

* * *

The Group was growing rapidly and making great progress; as the years went by life was heady, very happy and lucrative. The new vision of non-family executive directors gave great encouragement to the many.

As time went by I could detect a resurgence of the old politics, at the beginning 'no bigger than a man's hand'. Perhaps it was natural that the very success and growth of the enterprise was a breeding ground for the problems, for we had recruited many top level management staff and some had been head-hunted (that is encouraged to join us by someone who 'knew' somebody else who was 'always good' so the hunter thereby had a commitment to protect his introduction). This system is in my opinion a fertile ground for dissension at best, and politics at worst. It certainly seemed to happen that way for it seemed to me that happiness and total dedication seemed to drift away. On the other hand it was no surprise, indeed it was only human for merchandisers to want to show their paces (although sometimes it was not always good for the business). I am not suggesting it only affected us, and the head-hunting business is pretty widespread now.

A fire in one of our furniture factories brought matters to a head — I only mention this as I contemplate that it was a fire at Hercules which gave me my first opportunity — it was this last fire that started problems and caused me to think about the future and what turned out to be my greatest chance in business.

I obviously cared very much for the factories and our workforce; I cared even more for a merchandise policy which would use our own factories to produce basic items not as stop gaps, for there is no future in that — I saw the system as blood in the veins. There could be impelling advantages if the whole of the retail outlets were fed very large quantities of 'bread and butter lines' from the company factories at cost prices with the ability to operate on low stocks. However some wanted the best of both worlds with the ability to switch demand on and off; this though, in my opinion, was hardly a strategy in the world of reality.

Welding a basic part of a retailing outlet to a manufacturing partner was exciting and worked very efficiently when Eric Sawyer and I operated it, but finally it was not to be. However I readily admit that there is far more glamour and a better financial return in retailing than there is in manufacturing, for I have experienced both in a big way.

However in big business you do not scratch the sores — you lick the wounds and get on with the business. Personally though — I began to think deeply.

I well realise that today the strategy I have outlined is followed in some concerns by taking financial stakes in manufacturing businesses. I am not so sure that is good for either side.

Obviously no company large or small, manufacturer or merchant, publishing or printer can ever be without problems on integration — indeed these problems are like a recurrent theme. But to obtain maximum harmony I feel a conglomerate has to insist that between its components there must be either a very close integration or a very tight rein in order to maximise efficiency on all sides.

* * *

I said earlier that among Littlewoods' other interests were two hotels in Harrogate. Before the war it had been a lovely spa, but its former glory had faded a little, for during the war it had been an evacuation centre for several government departments.

After the war the hotel business changed violently; hunt balls, elegant dinner parties and the wealth to seek the cure of healing springs and wells were no more, so hotels turned to catering for trade fairs, conferences, and package tours. It was a pity, for Harrogate with its beautiful Stray, lovely gardens and attractive civic hall is still a delightful place.

One of our hotels was near the town centre and continued to do well, catering for the commercial business and conferences. This hotel, together with the second one, became my responsibility.

The Prince of Wales Hotel was at the right end of the Stray and in course of rehabilitation. Costly refurbishing was falling behind and this had to be put right, together with a face lift to the gardens. Confidence exuded from everyone. We were told it was the right place for hunt balls but unfortunately there didn't seem to be much hunting. We were concerned about its eventual success, but were willing to try.

The job was done in style. On opening night it looked sparkling and we engaged a big London band (alas no more). There was a full house and as an event it was highly successful, but even to the optimist, the palmy and horsey days were no more.

However the company had a happy knack of somehow turning even minor problems to its advantage; so it was with the hotels. The group was growing fast and we were deeply aware that close relations with our suppliers of goods, equipment or services were of prime importance; how better to talk with them than during a golf weekend or to relax with those who didn't play golf? So it was a pleasant and happy time, providing the opportunity to discuss big business in a civilised way. Harrogate has at least one great golf course and at the Littlewoods weekends we always had a guest pro on hand, and twice we had the great Henry Cotton with us, who could tell after dinner stories as well as he could play golf.

John Moores himself believed in relaxation and he often had a piano in his room for the odd tinkle. I recall one Sunday when he said to me, 'Cookie, what are you doing this afternoon?' I replied, 'Sleeping.' He said, 'Good, give me a knock when you are about again.' I did, just as he was making his own yoghourt and was walking around in his shirt and socks. It seemed a bit of a shock to see a multi-millionaire walking around like that — perhaps I expected to see him in gold lamé pants and vest! The yoghourt looked awful. John Moores proclaimed its aid to longevity. 'Try some,' he urged. I did and it tasted worse than it looked, but his claim regarding longevity appears to work. He is over eighty-six now.

Harrogate has recently opened a fine new entertainment centre and is right back in the news in a different world.

* * *

I never lacked variety in my life and for good measure I had a new experience in 1951. After the war Littlewoods made a very modest investment in South Africa.

This African interlude covers visits between 1951 and 1957. This is more of a story of journeys to Africa, in the days of the early big aircraft, nearly thirty years ago. The letters and my comments particularly on Southern Africa give a traveller's impression. I have modified many of my views with more recent visits with my family. I have seen what Africa was, I have seen how much has been done.

It is not a story of a big business as the business had no chance of being big. In the end no money would be lost; at worst, a few dreams just died away.

The enterprise was a small motor body and trailer business in Cape Town. One of our executives went out to buy it; his journey in those days was a flight by seaplane with a landing on the Zambesi. I found it a doubtful proposition though it did have a valuable piece of land and any sale would show a profit, but not of Littlewoods proportions.

It was not doing well, and the job came my way. I flew out to try and put things right, if that were possible. The journeys I made to and from Africa were exciting, and the violent changes in that continent are etched on my mind.

My first journey there was in the autumn of 1951. I took Mac, a member of our firm of accountants with me; when Mac was jolly he was very jolly, but at other times he was almost a nervous wreck.

We landed at Schipol Airport, Amsterdam on a bright Saturday afternoon. Mac was floored when the receptionist asked him for details of his next of kin. 'God! Do they think we are going to die?' he said. Nevertheless travelling by air was then both exciting and inviting.

We departed for Johannesburg as dusk fell. As the power of the engines increased the nacelles appeared to get white hot. My colleague gasped, 'We must be on fire! The engines will burst!' They did not, and we rose toward the setting sun; our first stop was Rome.

Extracts from letters to my wife.

6.15 pm, 13th October 1951

I have not been in the slightest affected by the flight although concentration is difficult, the take off and descent was little different to being in the old Morris on a fast journey up Bradford Lane.

Shall have to get ready for a meal now and then read the booklet (given to me) entitled *To Africa, Stanley and You.*

Just for a few seconds we had a glimpse of Heald Green, then into the clouds until we were within a few miles of Holland. Then the sky cleared and we were over canals, farms and windmills — very well kept, and on to the aerodrome at Amsterdam.

The airport was first class, all food and drinks were free in the restaurant. The plane was an hour late in leaving due to a spot of engine trouble.

Now we are high above the clouds, a few minutes ago we passed over Philips Town, the town built by the great electrical company. What a patchwork of lights — it looked rather like a great Xmas tree against the scarlet red backcloth of the sunset. We passed over Rome in moonlight. St Peter's stood out on the horizon as also did the 'wedding cake' (the tomb of King Victor Emmanuel); it really was a magnificent sight.

A real dinner was served on proper plates with first class champagne too; the plane carried a super cocktail bar at the rear and you could lean on the bar or sit and drink. As we approached Rome, St Peter's was aglow with light. My colleague was a Catholic and this was a bonus for him, but you do not have to be a Catholic to appreciate St Peter's. The note of the engines changed as the undercarriage jerked free and we glided down the runway at Rome. The plane was led to a parking space by a jeep carrying the sign 'Follow me!' There are still a few of these about in the more remote African countries, but they have long since disappeared from most big airports.

Then into the night across the Mediterranean Sea. In those days there were elaborate instructions on survival drill should we ditch in the sea; comforting from one point of view, a bit disturbing if you felt queasy.

13th October 1951

We left Rome at 11 pm — over Anzio, the sea in a very few minutes — fell asleep — awoke to find myself over the Sahara.

We flew many, many miles over the Sahara. The desert gave way to thin scrub where in the distant past trees blossomed. A lush-looking oasis here, a deserted village there, then narrow tracks got wider becoming narrow roads, then real roads with a few mud huts here and there. The trees suddenly became dense. The plane dipped and in the distance appeared a long sandy airstrip, with what looked like heaps of small pebbles around, which turned out to be mounds of monkey or ground nuts.

14th October 1951

Kano is a city of mud huts, everyone, apart from the British, is black. You are sprayed with disinfectant before you leave the plane and again when you return.

The plane bumped down; it was about six o'clock in the morning and already hot

118

as we passengers emerged. Trucks conveyed us to the airport building somewhere in the bush, for the road had been slashed through the forest.

At the side of the track families were making breakfast over open fires using the traditional three legged 'missionary' cooking pot. Many of the natives were as naked as mother nature delivered them.

Kano airport was obviously a government issue prefabricated hut and it wasn't new. Customs notices were printed on paper now turning yellow and curling at the edges with heat and age; the ceiling fans were turning idly, ready for the real heat of day which came all too quickly. Breakfast served in the small room next door on that very hot morning was memorable — cereal or orange juice, followed by a plate of small rashers of bacon with chicken's liver (maybe it was leather) and two of the tiniest eggs I have ever seen — swilled down with luke warm coffee. It was exciting considering where we were and when.

It is so different today, the airport is a huge building, the latest in chrome and concrete and the romance has all gone.

Refreshed we trucked back to the plane, leaving a world we will never see again. I shall always remember the smell of the warm damp earth — the scent of Africa. Vultures, an unwelcome sight, were everywhere, on the hut, the wings of the plane and the trucks. We boarded and the plane taxied to the end of the airstrip. The captain's voice boomed, 'Sorry ladies and gentlemen, there will be a delay; we have slight engine trouble.' Slowly we taxied back, the vultures quickly settled again on the wings. With a look of horror my companion turned to me and said, 'My God, can't they wait?'

We left the plane again. The red-headed Scottish engineer got to work, dismantled a pipe, blew through it and called out, 'Aye! That's it.' It was and we were off, leaving the vultures behind.

14th October 1951

We left Kano at 9 am in terrific heat, the stewardess came round and sprayed everyone with eau-de-cologne.

Onwards from Kano to Brazzaville over the mountains through storms and eventually the mighty River Congo. Brazzaville still is a native settlement rather like the picture books with straw huts, mud huts, all the primitive instruments, even to the hand milling of corn.

We flew to Brazzaville over the great forests, over bleak, deserted wasteland, the setting of some future bloody battles. Eventually we arrived at the old airstrip. A new airstrip was in course of construction. The cement was carried around in skips, and padded down by native feet; the operation was supervised by a 'Sanders of the River' type, complete with khaki shorts and white pith helmet. I felt that without the Sanders type there never would have been an airstrip.

We landed in steaming heat, and were conveyed by truck along a track hacked out of the lush tropical jungle, arriving at a lovely hill-top guest house, the garden already bright with exotic flowers. On the way we had passed a collection of caged and crated wild animals ready for export. Refreshments were served as we viewed the mighty Congo, and the futuristic city of Leopoldville, a city eventually raped and wrecked by so-called freedom fighters. Whatever the type of government that created this great city, it was a monument to vision and endeavour, beside a river explored by Henry Morton Stanley.

Here I recall that on this my first visit to Africa, the speed of the plane was 250 mph; when we we returned on a later journey by Comet, it had increased to 500 mph.

Our next stop was Johannesburg, a flight that took us over the bare and pitiless Kalahari Desert; night fell quickly on a darkened land with just an occasional flicker of light.

14th October 1951

I am writing you now using as a pad, the map which records the fact that the plane is flying over Gangandula, Angola, almost 1,000 miles from Johannesburg. Jungle, dried up river beds, all pass by below at 250 miles an hour.

7 am, 15th October 1951

We had an excellent dinner served about 7 pm — hors d'oeuvres, soup, mutton chops, orange ices, cheese, fruit and champagne. We then settled down to await our approach to Johannesburg.

There really is *nothing* but jungle and desert between the big towns. South Africa is not really a united country, either politically or geographically; it is a collection of a few towns with thousands of miles of land joining them up. [I was to revise my comments on this later.]

A 9.15 pm we had our first glimpse of Johannesburg, a dull glow, then millions of twinkling electric lights, like diamonds on black velvet; then the mark of civilization — neon lights, red, green, blue, all making a colourful picture.

We touched down at 9.47 pm, awaited a further spray of disinfectant, had our medical papers checked and finally went down the gangway at 10 pm on to the tarmac after a wonderful flight — 29½ hours from Manchester, having covered nearly 6,000 miles.

Near midnight we arrived at the old Johannesburg airport. Two years later we took off from the Jan Smuts Airport, with its runway extended for the Comet, the forerunner of all the great jets.

The officials were very strict on documents, particularly those of someone with a good old English name like Cooke. Accommodation in the terminal building was very meagre, no plush seats or hot drinks but if you wanted to sit after all that flying just a few hard-seated chairs were provided. Passengers were called out for attention by name, South Africans first, then Dutch, followed by Scots and so on; last of all the British, Browns, Cookes and Smiths.

Some thirty hours after leaving Holland, I was a little jaded, and felt more so in the customs shed; the officer dealing with me was not pro-British and was anything but polite. He grunted, 'Hev yu anythink to deeclare — jewellery for example?' I said, 'No! I don't wear it.' 'Vat about your vatch then?' 'Oh!' I blurted, 'If you call that jewellery, have a look.' He did and strangely enough put it back on my wrist.

He then barked, 'Noomber of camera, eet's not on your declaration.' 'Camera number? I didn't know there was a number on this old ciné,' I exclaimed. 'Theey is a noomber on everee camera,' he retorted. 'Do find this one for me. I've no idea where to look,' I urged. He took the camera from me and searched for some time, then with obvious glee he said, 'I've found eet ess there on dee back edge of the vinder.' Ciné cameras were not battery operated then. I congratulated him. 'Enee diamonds?' he grinned. 'Why bring diamonds to SA?' 'Well,' he said, 'Thee doo but not the right ones.' Just then a lady was being interrogated; customs officials were demanding the exit permit for the diamonds she was wearing. She could not find it and she had just returned from Amsterdam! I gathered the scheme of diddling was to take abroad very good diamonds in rings or brooches and bring them back set with inferior stones.

Johannesburg

15th October 1951

The airport is roughly four miles from the city centre. In daylight it looked well ordered but not more than twenty-five miles from the city the land became so very barren. Almost at all calls on this journey one is conscious of the enormous number of black and coloured people there are, whites seem to be an exception rather than the rule.

We pass all the usual appurtenances of a big city, the road-houses, flashing signs, the tea bars, the shacks, the gold pit heaps, the outskirts, the slums, then finally the centre.

There are comparatively few big streets, but there are some really fine buildings in the American style.

His Majesty's Theatre is one of them. Roy (my brother) took me in after having the place unlocked; a very fine piece of architecture. The stores are comparatively small, but overall is that American/Jewish influence — flashy signs, flashy ties and so on.

There is an aura of prosperity among the whites. Roy says he would never come back to England (and he never did). An air of resignation on the part of the blacks who are little more than slaves and the victims of a terrible intolerance.

They are a problem no doubt, but they could be a little better than slaves. The car arrived at 6.45 am.

I was to alter so many of these impressions as the years went on and as I got to know all sides. We stayed in Johannesburg just a few hours and flew to Cape Town next morning.

On to Cape Town

16th October 1951

We passed over Kimberley. One wonders how the original prospectors stuck it in that barren land. There are literally no trees for hundreds of miles, the land green with grass in winter and early spring is now scorched either dull red or brown in colour.

The mountains are quite high — barren, full of deep gullies and reputed to be full of minerals. The mountains gave way to hills — the hills to small valleys and then to flat lands at the foot of Table Mountain which stands out majestically, dominating the whole countryside.

The plane touched down at noon — through the officialdom again — Ellis, the general manager is waiting to take us into Cape Town. A good hotel 'Mount Nelson' — I played hell and got a suite which is charming, with magnificent views — apparently the one occupied by Field Marshal Smuts is opposite. I am writing this with Table Mountain virtually overlooking me.

* * *

Cape Town made a great impression on me, a beautiful and stately city with the supreme backcloth of Table Mountain, with an air of quiet confidence and so graceful.

There were then many attractive old colonial style buildings with wrought-iron trimmings and balconies. There are also some very old Dutch buildings too and the Koopmans-de-Wet home is still a jewel with its magnificent display of furniture and Sheffield plate. I will always remember too the flower sellers outside the main post office, a daily flower show for free, now gone for ever among the forests of concrete.

The dedication to work of South African directors, lawyers and executives was outstanding, many of them at their desks by 8.30 am. Lunch breaks were very short, with an equally prompt finish at 5 to 5.30 pm. There is a very good reason for starting and finishing early for the sun sets at the back of the mountain and darkness falls quickly on the other side, so if you want to see anything of your home, best to be home early. We English worked longer hours starting early in the morning till late at night, but working long hours after air trips of 7,000 miles are not recommended.

The business, as I already knew was quite small in a specialist industry, with other competitors all depending on just one big customer, the South African National Railways.

The labour segregation policy made it a very expensive business to run; for example we had to provide separate eating places, wash rooms and lavatories for the various racial groups. Just to add a little extra difficulty, all instructions had to be printed in three different languages, a problem in a business so small.

It was very necessary to have a supply line from England for both trailers and chassis, but the business was not big enough to command a regular flow. It was too risky and the prospect of a very meagre return, apart from land appreciation, made it a business incapable of worthwhile development. I had to decide if the business could be made viable, or rather nearer to the bone, how much we were likely to lose. It was obviously no fortune maker, indeed, it could have been a small fortune loser, however we did make a small profit from time to time.

Import of both material and men was tightly controlled. On the original acquisition we had sent craftsmen out from our factory in Leigh. We had sent a manager too, who was a trier, but not cast in the mould of an entrepreneur and to be fair he was in a business with limited prospects. We had to try and build something from nothing; that would not be easy and there was no promise of ultimate success. Business in Africa would need much thought, much detailed work with little reward, but at least we knew the position.

* * *

Cape Town

17th October 1951

Cape Town is incredibly small, three main streets only, and they are short, certainly not the length of Alderley Edge village. Two of the main streets have mountains at each end. Cape Town is on a peninsula with the mountains in the form of a horse-shoe.

The city is small but where do the 400,000 people live? Half of them are black and live in various colonies in tin shacks, wooden shacks and shacks made of old clothing and other materials in two districts about three to five miles outside the city. They are so poor that they have to walk that distance morning and evening to work, men and women alike.

The whites reside in two areas, one along the peninsula in a seaside district and the others not so well off along fourteen miles of a long straight road to the north. All development which has taken place in the last five years is along this road, with no depth of development at all.

On future visits and after much experience I was sorry I had been so tough and radical in my comments. Such a lot has been achieved by the efforts of whites for the coloured and black people. The white people had vision and set the wealth creation system going; without it the natives would have had a very thin time; back in their kraals it would have been even worse. In short I make apologies for some of my earlier remarks.

17th October 1951

The peninsula itself, which is another way of saying the old town, is very beautiful. Table Mountain, a large mountain with two other mountains attached, the Lion's Head and the Lion's Rump dominate everything. At this moment 8 o'clock in the morning, it is covered in mist (the table cloth) but for the first time since we came the sun is trying to break through. Palm trees abound in the gardens of the hotel and gum trees with beautiful red flowers are everywhere. There is in this hotel and in many buildings the stamp of the wealthy British Colonist, the ornamental façade—the wrought iron balconies, mimosa trees and so on. But you do realise that twenty years ago, when things were good for Britain, Cape Town must have been a lovely place. On reflection and having seen other cities it is still among the great cities, a truly lovely and charming place.

I am not very young (41) but I am the youngest person in the hotel, which gives you an idea of what has happened to the wealthy British. Years ago whole families filled this hotel for the South African spring and summer. The young and not even the middle aged can afford it now.

You asked me to bring back some butter—we ourselves are living on margarine. Notices are displayed 'No Butter', 'Short of Meat'. Perhaps I'll do better at Madeira.

This shortage business is all brought about through the severe restrictions on imports, both of men to do the job and materials to enable them to do it.

The sun is beginning to shine over Table Mountain and it does look beautiful. The birds are beginning to sing and we know where we are going in the business, so my step will be a little lighter.

Cape Town

19th October 1951

The wind is still howling but this morning at 6.30 am as I write this little note in bed the sun has broken through, the sky is blue and the palm trees are waving.

Yes, I can see Table Mountain, the shoulder part just before it slopes down, the pine trees in the lower slopes, the palm trees in the garden—all this as I sit up in bed and write.

I am making this a very short note because I hope to have spoken to you on the phone before you receive it.

Cape Town

20th/22nd October 1951

So far we have had only one fine day and that was on Saturday when it was warm. We took advantage of the weather and went out to the Paarl Mountains (the name Paarl means

Pearl). The mountains are so called because the summit is crowned with great blocks of white granite formations which glisten in the sun.

I had previously asked Ellis to arrange for me to look over a South African farm, so we called on a Boer Afrikaan farmer. He had a beautiful home, built in colonial Dutch style, white walls, crenellated gables, corrugated iron roof (yes, iron roof), overhanging verandah, a beautiful garden and magnificent outbuildings. 'Welcome Mr. Cooke. You must have coffee.' Into the dining room, what a change in temperature! It was so cool inside that one almost required another garment.

The furniture was delightful, made from stinkwood. This wood throws up a two coloured grain, a very dark brown and a very sandy brown. The chairs were in Bergère style except that overall was that robust bulgy effect — rather like their womenfolk.

The farm was of course a fruit farm, 170 acres under grape cultivation together with a large area of peaches, apricots and plums.

The peaches had already set, the plums and apricots were setting while the vines were just sprouting.

On the morning we arrived eighty boys (native men) had just been spreading sulphur on the vines and others were scattering straw to keep the moisture in the ground.

Grapes are subject to pests so this farmer had a big flock of turkeys which roamed through the vineyard taking a tasty grub or two. I saw guinea fowl doing the same thing, but they were wild.

Manure is also another vital necessity to the vine and so two hundred pigs were kept in store and provide bacon as a by-product.

Water is essential so a big reservoir had been built by the farmer at the top of the kloof and pipes laid throughout the vineyard to irrigate the growing plants.

The whole setting was after the style of Treasure Island — mountains at the back studded with great boulders of granite, — protea trees, South African flowers of every description, lizards on the rocks, a stretch of water, the farmhouses, away in the distance a vivid blue sky, great mountains in the background and in the centre this lovely farmhouse.

I could go on for hours but I am due to start a meeting, so I shall have to close.

22nd October 1951

The time is 9 pm and I am in bed — yes in bed. The job is finished — the notes are completed, things have been straightened out quite well — I hope.

I broke off my last letter at the farm. After the tour of inspection we were given directions for the next part of the journey.

The interesting thing about these directions was that quite unconsciously the farmer marked everything by smoke. 'Yes, see that smoke near the kloof, turn right there until you meet that smoke and finally turn off at the smoke at the entrance to the pass in the west.' I suppose this is a reminder of the days long gone by when smoke was the only sign post.

Our next port of call was Worcester with its apple, plum and pear trees, its bowling club (true English Saturday afternoon) and its very poor natives. Then across wild and rugged country to Caledon. The road is unmade and is really only a track of gravel and red earth; — the pot holes and lumps are numerous; we went for about thirty miles under those conditions. There were arum lilies growing wild in the ditches in great profusion.

Eventually we struck the tar road (as they call Macadam roads) to Caledon famous for its wild flowers — and what a sight! The colours and types are indescribable, there are so many varieties and colours. Watsonia is delightful, the wild iris about 9 inches high and so perfect, the proteas and the jacaranda. Purple, yellow, even green flowers I shall not easily forget it. I do wish you could have been with me, maybe one day.

All beautiful things come to an end. Back to the hotel through the native quarters. What appalling sights — there must be twenty children to every house which at best consists of a hut with one division, a fire in the doorway and awful filth all the way round.

Then night came on, Cape Town looked like a sparkling jewel, blue, red and silver lights all twinkling, a very pretty picture. It was this picture I saw when I spoke to you on the phone — that was a pleasure. On Saturday evening we took Ellis and his wife, Mac and one of our customers to the Vineyard which B.G. recommended. It served the only decent food I have tasted in Cape Town. Mac of course wanted beer.

Table Mountain is looking down at me through the window, the sky is vivid blue at 7.30 am.

Arum lilies grow wild in their thousands, along the sides of the road, in fields, woods and ditches. They like to tell the story that a very rich, brittle Johannesburg businessman wanted only the best white flowers for his daughter's wedding and at great expense they were ordered from England and flown out — white flowers as for an English bride. They arrived on time and as you may guess they were arum lilies!

Cape Town

24th October 1951

Although most people say England is finished, let me tell you that the people out here are hanging on its fate.

Today we went to the summit of Table Mountain by the cableway. The excitement as the cage swings to and fro in the high wind added a little fun. The view from the top is magnificent; the whole of the peninsula including the Cape of Good Hope is stretched out before you with beautiful bays, sandy beaches, the industrial smudge, the blue sea, the majestic mountains, and above all the bright blue sky. It's quite a thrill to think that the next stop is Antarctica.

25th/26th October 1951

Another beautiful morning; the sky is so blue, so very blue and the wind has dropped. They depend on a south-easterly to keep the bad weather on the move and even at 7.30 am it is very, very warm. There is barely a movement in the palm trees where the pigeons are calling, another sign of fine weather and Cape Town is waking to life.

The heat has been terrific during the day. The day has ended we have had a little farewell party with our principal customers. This has done a lot of good and now first election results are in from England — no sign of a break yet. And finally it is morning, the sun is brilliant and I have just spoken to you all, what a thrill. In a few hours on to the ship and home, sweet home.

On board RMMV Cape Town Castle

27th/28th October 1951

We made a very prompt start from Cape Town. As the mooring ropes were cast off the crew together with the passengers sprang to attention, the band struck up *God Save the King*, followed by the South African anthem as the ship glided away from the dock with Table Mountain more majestic than ever, quite a spectacle from the sea.

We settled down which did not take much doing for Mac and I have a steward between us. Apart from RAF officers (about twelve) there are only thirty first class passengers on the ship and believe it or not *five* are from Alderley Edge and Wilmslow (our local villages) it is a very small world. Mac has continued to enjoy ill health, has had a bad arm, bad toe, bad foot and now after one game of deck tennis, a bad knee. I am very unsympathetic but he improves with sternness, but he is very kind and guards me like a father — says he has got to, if all these stories of women near the equator are right.

All land faded away the first afternoon — so did the gulls but next morning we saw whale and porpoise and now albatross are circling around the ship. I have just attended Sunday service — as usual very impressive, with at least two favourite hymns *Love Divine* and *Oh God our Help*.

I must look the fatherly type, one little boy came along and asked me if I would play him at deck tennis. He said I played far too fast for him — so he repaid my effort with a compliment, you see, too fast and forty!

31st October 1951

Today is the first fine day since the ship left Cape Town. All other days have been cloudy and sultry, yet occasionally the sun broke through.

Now flying fish appear in their millions skimming the waves, their wings glistening in the sunlight. With a glorious sunset a new moon showing as a thin crescent greeting the evening. We are a bit nearer home; one thinks at times, 'If only a seaplane would land, how much quicker would be the journey!'

We cross the line on Thursday at 9.45 am, and I shall send you a telegram. Also planned to have a cricket team to play the crew, who have the reputation of being first class having beaten the South Africans.

3rd Novemver 1951

Less than a week to go now but first of all back to Thursday. We crossed the line with due ceremony (hope you got the cable). An exceptionally good show was put on by the ship's crew and a few of the more virile passengers.

The procession formed up outside the lounge (Promenade Deck), the orchestra leading, followed by Neptune (bosun) and his queen — nothing was missing, seaweed and all. Then followed Captain Frothblower (none other than the first officer) — the barber (Sweeney Todd) the doctors (deck hands), mermaids, cops and prisoners and of course the prosecutor (assistant purser). The entire company processed around the ship and finally settled down at the swimming bath (king and queen on the thrones) The charges were read out, children first, they were only sprayed and sprinkled with water, their arms being duly marked with rubber stamps. Then the trials — grown ups next — one had to be a good sport to stand it all! The first woman, not young at that, had coloured water down her throat, lathered with a kipper and finally lathered legs and arms and face with flour and water. Then she was plunged backwards (by means of the ducking chair) into the pool. The show continued for at least an hour and a half. In the finale everyone went into the water except Neptune — Roger would have hooted and howled.

Later in the day, the real denizens of the deep gave a display. Barracudas were leaping gracefully out in the air, their silver scales glistening in the sun; porpoises leaping and rolling about and then swarms of flying fish.

The heat has been oppressive. Shirts last no time, and suits are saturated with perspiration.

We have had a little dancing, not much, the choice is extremely limited. Tombola is really the evening pastime which captivates most people. I am on the winning side up to the time of writing.

I have lapsed into evening — what a sunset! All the jungle colours lit the sky, bright orange, flaming red, deep purple and the huge mountainous clouds tinted pink and pale yellow and falling downwards to their own deep blue.

Then a truly marvellous sight from the north, a ship on the horizon. The loud speakers announced, 'Passengers might like to know that in fifteen minutes we shall be passing the *Athlone Castle*.' In the fading light illuminated by the setting sun in the deep purple waters the *Athlone Castle* majestically steamed towards us. It was quite unforgettable; the hull of the ship is pale lilac, the superstructure white, the funnel red, the cabin lights were twinkling and the green and red port and starboard lights blazed out from the bridge, the blinking signal lights. All this bathed in the light of the setting sun.

4th November 1951

The orchestra, or rather the musicians, have passed me on their way to the church service, which is due to begin in a few minutes time and so begins the second Sunday of this long voyage.

After the service I am hoping to go to the bridge. Lusty singing in *Love Divine* and *Eternal Father,* a lesson very poorly read by the chief officer being the only flaw.

I went to the bridge and had a most interesting time. One is very impressed with the clarity of vision and the overall feeling of space. The instruments seem somewhat simple but extremely efficient.

The sea has churned up, it's getting a little rough. I keep awake to see the Canary Islands as we pass through at midnight — just a few lights that is all.

Now it is morning again with very rough seas. Already the dining room has suffered a little. The few passengers are getting yet fewer. In a matter of six hours we shall be in Madeira then for the last leg.

So I close this letter to you; possibly it will arrive after me but then it will serve as a record.

I never did land in Madeira. It was too rough during the various times I went to Africa, We were battened down most times but I did get some marvellous pictures.

* * *

In 1953 I visited South Africa again, with the feeling that we should finally decide to stay in or get out. I felt it was a waste of too much company time — notwithstanding that in common with my colleagues I hated to see anything go down the drain. I thought that the company should get out. To reduce the amount of working time I was away from England I took my annual vacation with my wife and son on the trip.

In early 1954 I reasoned that once again we should reconsider the matter for yet another reason. In Cape Town, our main road site could possibly be acquired by the government. We decided we would stay on and build a new factory with government aid and sell the present site. Everybody tried so very hard to make it a success.

Mount Nelson Hotel, Cape Town

8.30 pm, 25th June 1955

The new church is still without fingers on the clock. The old coloured car-park man with the hobble stick still salutes.

9.30 pm, 28th June 1955

Here we are safe and sound, a little bit tired, in the old room 310.

It is a sense of comfort to know that you and Roddy have both looked out of these windows and seen the same view of Table Mountain, red in the sunset, the mid-day sky a rich blue. One or two things are different, the daffodils are just being planted, the poinsettias are ablaze along the whole drive to Mount Nelson; in fact all Cape Town seems to be one mass of these beautiful flowers.

None of the main streets has altered much, Adderley Street is much tidier near the docks. The grass we saw being planted has taken hold and is quite green.

Belville (the suburb in which we had a factory) is building up fast — Goodwood and Ascot, two Pondoki* suburbs, are scheduled to go under the bulldozer and become native garden suburbs.

Building has already started for the coloured and native population — here and there is the odd car. [On our last visit the whole area had been transformed — a great effort for a comparatively few wealthy producers. Many of the coloureds and the natives had cars.]

The head porter at the Mount Nelson greeted me with outstretched arms as also did the head waiter and valet, and asked after you too — nice to be remembered all those thousands of miles away.

We had a wonderful view of Kimberley and the Karroo as we flew under a clear blue sky — such a surprise after the news headlines had shouted, 'Heavy snowfalls; snow storms threatened.'

Back to the Mount Nelson. It has all been redecorated in the same colours same decor; looks very smart. The two chairs are in the alcove, the bedroom curtains are still pink and I am writing this letter at the little desk in the corner near the window, the lamp is on and the lights are twinkling over Cape Town. The *Old Mutual* sign is still blue and lighting up the sky. The liners, lilac, blue, white and red are in the docks.

1st July 1955

Things are far from good, in fact quite worrying, but I shall stick to it and find the answers. If I had only been listened to in 1954! But I had better not reproach, so will silently plod on.

I went out to lunch yesterday at the Norwegian Club and had a most interesting Javanese dish comprising rice minced with meat and spiced, sardines, waffle, fish roe and two fried eggs with red hot spiced chutney (almost Repton style). There are no preliminary dishes, just coffee at the end.

I am still without news of a plane, but a stay at Victoria Falls or the Park is out of the question.

Eventually I did get a plane with a sleeper at the tail end, and very comfortable with night cap drink and early morning tea. We came over Crete at dawn; it really did look a country of the gods with the ring of pure early morning light over the mountain peaks, and on to land at Athens on a crystal clear early morning.

* * *

In all fairness I must say everybody was trying hard in Africa but the basic problems were always there and even a great company like ours and my own efforts could not alter them.

---

*Pondoki is another word for shanty and shanties they were — little huts made from odd bits of wood and cardboard, flattened out petrol tins and a roof of aged corrugated metal if they were lucky, and if they weren't, it would be twigs and rags or grass. There was a hole in the roof which allowed the damp fumes to escape from the pathetic little fires which provided their only way of heating the shack and of cooking too. But I hope I make the point in these letters that the authorities had all those years ago taken drastic action, but the natives (despite difficulties and crocodile infested rivers) continued to throng in from the bush. Yes, Pondokis were shanties all right.

We were British and among the Nationalists that was not a passport to a successful business interest. The labour segregation, ethically right or wrong, was a drain both on efficiency and costs. We were in a restricted trade, dominated by demands from one nationalised source, South African Railways. We hesitated on a final decision, because we just did not want to lose capital, a point I both respected and agreed. We had real moral and financial obligations to the staff we had sent out there from England. We had in mind the thought that somehow in an outpost we were doing our bit.

I went on my final visit to Cape Town in 1957; the emphasis was now on selling. It was a bit sad opening a new factory, for some employees had left England with high hopes and visions of a bright future, but the end was inevitable for reasons I had put forward many moons before. I wondered if fate had played a hand — two of the first sent out there were Messrs Blood and Mort.

Johannesburg, in bed.

30th July 1957

As you will have gathered from the cable I arrived last night some five hours late after quite a long flight. Nothing wrong with the plane or crew but we had to wait over two hours at Kano for the breakfast to come aboard, even then it was incomplete.

Then we were diverted to Salisbury ostensibly to drop four passengers, in fact I think to drop Oppenheimer (the diamond and gold king) to have a conference, which he immediately did on arrival. He was travelling to Jo'burg with an entourage including children from school and his wife.

As to the flight — we left London promptly, flew over Exeter, turned and flew over France, crossing the Med just west of Marseilles, which was clearly visible in the evening light. The sea was calm and the steamers were gently chugging along (we were doing about 350 mph).

As dinner was being served we made Majorca, which from the air looked very beautiful and most interesting, high cliffs and rocky coasts alternating with sandy shores.

Another hour and a half and we were over Algiers; it looked a radiant jewel from 12,000 feet twinkling lights of all colours. It was very lovely but I don't think it matched the view we had from the sea on the *Chusan* cruise.

Then on into the night to Kano where we arrived well on time, just before two o'clock. How Kano has changed, no longer the wooden huts, the vultures on the roof, but an ultra-modern airport, but lacking ultra modern service; the old individual service had gone to be replaced with a dragooned staff with little or no interest in life, except their wages. Then the long wait for the caterers to bring breakfast aboard. Finally we were off just after four and into the hot tropical night.

At last we were over cultivated country, the tobacco country outside Salisbury, and what a lovely place this city is — from the air *A Town like Alice,* everything so fresh and new, the dark green trees planted by the early settlers giving an almost English look to the whole scene; the roads are broad, the houses varied and interesting and all have much more than a postage stamp for a garden. Yes, I could live in Salisbury.

On then until finally we are over the Limpopo and in to the Transvaal. Pretoria is on our left, the Reef and Johannesburg on our right. As we came into land dusk was falling and the sun was setting deep red and strong at the back of the ilex trees which now hemmed the perimeter.

Ellis was there to meet me and I have a very nice bedroom in a reorganised Langham. Ellis had daffodils put in the room.

Feel fully recovered and am ready for the job in hand. I have sent a cable to our boy in camp.

129

Mount Nelson Hotel

30th July 1957

Had a most interesting day in Pretoria—didn't sell the business but enjoyed the day with the brothers Roole, whose father landed in Pretoria as the war finished in 1902. Saw the church which Paul Kruger attended, together with his house. Discovered that Rooneks (Red Necks) is the name for British soldiers, apparently the red shaved necks of the British soldiers were good targets for the old Boer farmer. Saw the two first jacaranda trees to be planted in Africa; they were actually brought from South America.

Had lunch in the old Pretoria Club which is as English as the RAC in Pall Mall, but striving so hard to prove it was always Afrikaan.

3rd August 1957

It is very cold here with snow on the top of Table Mountain. However this morning has broken beautifully crisp and bright, the sky is pale blue and, the sun is breaking in a golden light over the mountains, which I see from my lazy position in the bed nearest the door, as I lounge before breakfast.

The almond blossom is now out in Cape Town and spring flowers abound everywhere. I have been reading that at home you have been experiencing a heat wave.

I have had Mr Corder (accountant) out to lunch, and am going out with him to the City Club on Monday.

I went to the village of Orchard to visit the home of Jack and Margaret Dicey. I was driven by a coloured boy, Andrew. Perhaps I should tell you that Jack Dicey rang me up and asked who was driving me. I said, 'Andrew, a black boy.' He said, 'Coloured?' 'Yes, he is black,' I said. 'No, is he coloured?' he replied. 'Yes, black.' Then the penny dropped and I said, 'Do you mean is he not quite black?' 'Yes, he is coloured then.' 'OK yes,' I concluded. It was important for him to know this so the right hotel could be booked.

Jack said they might provide sheets but no blankets and it's cold at night. I said I would fix that. I asked for and got a couple of blankets from the hotel. Andrew was to provide his own linen.

We started off. Andrew was a nice boy, thrilled to be entrusted with a long drive. He explained he had to collect his pillowslip and sheets. We pulled up some miles from Cape Town. 'I have to go now and get my linen,' he said . There were no houses in sight. I said, 'Drive the car to your house.' He replied, 'No thanks sir.' I replied, 'Yes do!' He pleaded, 'No sir please; it is not good.' I gathered it was a shack.

[I should explain Orchard is a beautiful place, a valley set among the mountains. Fruit trees everywhere—the very old homestead of the original Diceys presiding over all, the little graveyard and memorials guarding their mortal remains. The roads lined with shade trees and opposite Jack and Margaret's homestead a high and brooding mountain which they had bought.]

As I look through the bedroom window I see the snow-capped mountains dominating the green valley with the young trees springing into life, while in the garden the orange trees are a mass of golden balls.

Opened new works 7th August 1957.

I tried to sell the business. I still felt it was the best way out. I left it ready to sell and it was eventually sold; it was a pity it dragged on.

This affair was never good business but it taught us what not to do, and that can be of importance for it crystallized thinking on many points that could apply elsewhere.

From a personal point of view I had a wonderful experience of Africa that will never be forgotten.

I complete this interlude with comments on my first and latest impressions.

I said on my first visit the natives were little more than slaves. I write now after many visits. I have seen the north, east and south and virtually every country from Egypt to the Cape. I have observed their beauty, and their racial and religious differences, and their miseries too.

There is not one country, despite the massive aid and all their so called freedoms, which has done more for their population than South Africa. Truly it can be said, adapting a famous phrase, 'Never have so few supported so many.'

That of course does not mean I agree with apartheid; we might however ponder on the fact that the Bantu and many other coloureds are no more real natives of the Cape than the Europeans. It was an experience to see the efforts of the many whites who are seldom thanked.

* * *

The factories continued to exhibit at the British Industries Fair, and in 1951 John Moores and I had the honour of being presented to King George VI and Queen Elizabeth. The Queen was delightful, with a voice like tinkling bells; she made you really believe you were the most interesting person present, while the King, wonderfully relaxed, was firing questions right, left and centre and said, 'I don't understand why making millions with the pools, it is necessary for Littlewoods to take on all this extra work and responsibility of chain stores, mail order and this factory group.' 'Your Majesty,' I replied, 'The pools certainly do make a lot of money, and I suppose the answer must be that the money and the making of it wouldn't be worthwhile unless the proceeds were used.' 'Excellent,' he concluded. Previously I had the honour of being presented to Queen Mary, and, ageing though she was, her mind probed enthusiastically. 'How many of these are for export? Where are these sold and for how much?' We had a lovely display of children's wear, designed by Miriam Keyes. The Queen Mother spotted them and followed with a volley of inquiries that might be called in parliamentary jargon 'supplementaries'.

These exhibitions were brilliantly organised and advertised by the authorities, well supported by industry, but above all they were a firm guarantee for real heartaches every Sunday before opening, that day, signalled an outbreak of instant selective strikes. Reading through the newspapers today or looking at television the impression is that selective strikes are a new creation of NUPE, COHSE or ASLEF, etc. It would not be true; for over twenty five years ago electricians, decorators and stand fitters all knew the tricks of selective strikes. The sufferers were exhibitors whose only sin was spending a lot of money on double time to obtain orders to keep their factories busy. The reasons were much the same as today, insufficient soap in the washroom, not enough hot water, tiredness, more being paid for the same work on another stand, and all the other evergreens. However the jobs that would seemingly have taken days to clear were dealt with in a matter of minutes at the sound of crisp five pound notes.

The years 1947 to 1953 were some of the happiest of my life and big business was a happy affair. The top management, John and Cecil Moores, Eric Sawyer and I worked happily together. It had been said in the press that Littlewoods paid its chief executives more than cabinet ministers. I would not have quarrelled with that statement. The business progressed amazingly, differences were few and far between and social events were plenty.

On Coronation Day John Moores gave a marvellous party at Grosvenor House with all the needs of the inner man splendidly attended to, in a real family atmosphere. The viewing points of that majestic royal procession could not have been better. My son, together with two of my executives had been presented with seats near the House of Commons. His mother and I were up at 4 am to see him off; Grosvenor House was still in almost total darkness, yet the streets and Hyde Park outside were already full to overflowing. Bunting and decorations were everywhere, even the stand pipes with drinking water were painted red, white and blue — that was official imagination for real! Rain fell early, but nothing seemed to dampen the enthusiasm of the crowds.

The loudspeakers along the ceremonial route crackled into life with the sensational news that Hilary and Tensing had conquered Everest. When we met Tensing years later in far-away Darjeeling, facing Katchenjunga, in the shadow of Everest, we recalled that coronation morning.

About this time I first met Sir Isaac Wolfson. He phoned John Moores and wanted to try and fix a deal for some part of our quilt production (now made on the American machines). John Moores asked me to deal with it and I went round for a cup of tea and a chat.

He was very jolly. We talked and made tentative contract arrangements. Then he said, his eyes sparkling, 'I've thought about price, if you and I sat down together we could go through the costings and arrive at a fair price.' 'You didn't really think I would sit down with our costings did you,' I replied. 'No, clever boy!' he laughed. We talked for quite a time, then he had to go to the synagogue, but he so wanted to show me his empire of a hundred or so companies. He was about to press a button to reveal all when he suddenly stopped, laughed and said, 'Do you mind stepping back to the edge of the table, you're a competitor, you mustn't see too much!' It was impressive nevertheless.

Later in my business life, though not at Littlewoods, I met Sir Isaac many times. He was always courteous and would display his marvellous collection of paintings by Spencelayh — but as I recall he would always drive a hard bargain.

In July 1953 my wife and I were invited to the Coronation Garden Party at Buckingham Palace. It was both a great honour and experience, unfortunately the weather did not grace the day.

The Mall was crowded with limousines, the men in their morning suits and toppers, with the ladies dressed fit to meet a queen. Progress was very slow, but eventually we were through the Palace gates, then the rains came. For a short period the dignified entrances became almost rugby scrums, ladies with their elegant dresses already spotted by rain, struggled through the door of an ante-room only to emerge on the other side into the rain once more. We ran for cover to one of the splendid marquees; we made it without much damage or lack of dignity. A couple of elderly gentlemen welcomed us with, 'Strawberries and cream are very good in here.' They certainly were. On the way out we observed the notice 'For diplomats only'!

The rain ceased as we strolled across the lawns to await the Queen. The sun came through for a while and we were treated to a close up view of Queen Elizabeth II and her family as they passed through the ranks of people of all denominations and colour. The band played, the rain was forgotten for a moment of relaxed pomp that only the British can lay on. We walked around the gardens which seemed tremendous and so beautiful. It all passed into proud memory as a day that would be hard to forget.

* * *

In 1953 I was asked to deliver a speech to a group of young men in Macclesfield. I chose *Mass Production* as a subject. In 1969 I made the same speech in Manchester. I said, *inter alia:*

First let us deal with the impact of mass production on the worker. Without question mass production has enabled the worker to enjoy a higher standard of living than ever before. This is true in all countries with the possible exception of Russia where the science of mass production seems to have been turned to the weapons of war rather than to the welfare of mankind, but I would have to agree that the Russian worker is somewhat better off than he was before the mass production age. Secondly, I said earlier that a very important impact was that the worker had been deterred from the means of production. This means that the worker no longer has the ability to produce the finished article by himself. In pre mass production society men possessed this — man was able to hunt provided he had a bow and arrow. Today he would at least have to get the permission of the National Trust or some planning committee before he could start.

Let us look at the motor car industry. Take a chap punching holes, or maybe only one hole, in a chassis. In many cases I'll wager he hasn't a clue as to the type of metal he is working on or probably what the hole is for, and you couldn't blame him if he cares less. Follow that on for a moment, without the organisation providing the ways and means for all the other hundreds of jobs that go to make a car, even the hole would be useless. From which you will gather it is the organisation and not the worker, the plant and not the craftsman, that has the ability to produce. Here then is the birth of a social problem, of unemployment, because as the plant is the only means of producing and the worker alone can produce nothing, so it follows that in a time of depression the worker can do nothing to help himself. If the plant stops, he stops.

Now the third point, the question of skill. There is a common thought that mass production has taken the skill out of the job. It depends how you look at it. What it has done is to demand, not the skill of a craftsman, but that of a technician. What is required in industry is not a worker to fashion material with a tool but a technician who can design a tool that will fashion the material and will respond to the press button efficiency of an unskilled worker.

What will be required, is a new type of administrator, a new type of foreman, a new type of operator to plan and control by means of a press button. But here again, whereas the scientist, the technician, the planning engineer create that organisation which in turn creates the product, *the machine minder or the fellow pushing the button has never before had such power in his hands to stop production in such a big way*. With further automation he will be even more powerful, and *it is a paradox in that he, who presses the button but does not himself create, can in fact stop production, but he, who makes production possible, cannot produce*.

So we must endeavour to create a new type of plant operator, and administrator, who with great power in his hands negotiates for his own position through the strength of his own character, *rather than the negative ability to withhold his labour*. A doctor, on assuming his great responsibilities, takes the Hippocratic Oath. Somehow or other, to enjoy the benefits of scientific progress, we will have to introduce, or perhaps I had better say should consider introducing a Hippocratic Oath in industry. Surely if it is wrong for a doctor to withhold the life blood from his patient's body, it is wrong for an operator, administrator or employer to withhold his contribution from the body economic.

My audience was perplexed at my statement that the fellow pushing the button has never had such power in his hands. Few I think would now dispute that statement. Unfortunately the industrial Hippocratic Oath is a lot further away now than it was all those years ago. The need, alas, is even greater. I think it would do most of us no harm to recall the words of Thomas Edison:

'Surely it is not beyond the ability of man to protect and enjoy that which he has created.'

Who would disagree?

* * *

It was apparent during late 1954 that relations were becoming somewhat strained; not much to begin with, for later I had a personal letter from John Moores at Christmas (1955) which concluded:

Once again I want to say thank you for your help during the past twelve months. Your handling of . . . takes quite a load off my shoulders. All the best for 1956 and best wishes for a Happy Xmas to you and yours.'

I felt my thinking was perhaps on the wrong track. Events proved my original thinking was right and we were running into a major merchandise problem, which came to a head at the opening of a new large store. We had a dialogue and treatise on the fine performance of a new recruit. He had shown great ability in obtaining supplies of women's underwear and nightdresses, in fact a whole range of products at really rock bottom prices. The goods were very similar to our own productions and only the buying prices were different, which were about half our own factory costs.

I pinched myself for I could not believe I was the only one to appreciate the problem; it did seem true, that 'there's none so blind as they that won't see.' The adrenalin was flowing as I queried if we would continue to get supplies at these low prices, or was it just a flash in the pan, or even worse? In short were we sooner or later going to be done? (We were.)

It is I think a classic merchandising story. I resumed, 'There is some sort of trick being played on us, either we shall have future deliveries of inferior merchandise or prices will rise, we will have to accept them or search elsewhere with the risk of huge out-of-stocks and of lost goodwill.' The chairman and we directors challenged with similar arguments, but we were reassured that the prices were genuine and supplies would be maintained. I felt this was impossible, but for the moment I was 'wrong'.

Real trouble was not long in coming; all too quickly supplies were very restricted or totally non-existent, except at substantially increased prices.

Shortly afterwards the chairman asked me to see him. It was early evening when I arrived. He was most friendly, perhaps more friendly than usual.

Smiling, he said, 'Well! Well! Promise me you won't hold it over them.' 'Hold what over who?' I said. The coffee arrived. 'Alright, now please tell me what,' I continued. He explained that the possibility of a merchandise debacle argued over at the store opening had turned out as I foreshadowed. The lines were not genuine, they were catchpenny jobs. Worse than that, when it came to repeat business, goods had in fact been ordered at greatly increased prices.

I thought long and hard over our talk, and figured that perhaps the political cells would learn their lesson and relations would improve. I vowed that short of dire complications I would restrain my criticisms because the merchandise or lack of it would eventually tell its own story. I hoped that this might be a new beginning to an old saga.

* * *

I write without any personal hard feeling for I have been very successful. I hope sometime, somewhere, my words might be useful. As I saw it then and even now, it appeared that certain sections of the business had gone in for head hunting at least that is the term we would use today. We would engage so and so, he knew so and so, they were always brilliant and they always knew someone else who could be useful; so eventually a cell of comrade head hunters was born, and the whizz kids were in the ascendancy. The trouble with trying to buy 'loyalty' through this method of recruitment is that you supposedly get loyalty and ability, but of course you cannot buy loyalty. The trouble is that if one person in the cell slips up in a big way, the cell collapses with responsibility going up the line and not down and the domino theory operates.

It was those very early days at Brixton that caused my thinking to be dominated by merchandising and the lines of supply. I felt that with all the goodwill in the world, sooner or later we would have further problems, little were they expected so soon.

I was again asked to a private talk with the chairman, it was shortly after a Harrogate golfing weekend when we entertained many of our main suppliers. I mention this because at these gatherings big slices of our business were mulled over, and even more important, assurances of our continued support were given to the chairmen of our most important suppliers, and vice versa. This particular gathering sticks in my mind because our very biggest suppliers were enjoined to give us their strongest support in the all important section, known as the Manchester goods. I suppose today they would be known as East European, Indian and Korean goods, in short they were textiles.

It appeared that something was amiss from the many complaints received about long delivery delays. (Shades of the Wirral in wartime.) A crisis had developed, so once again I was invited to an evening chat. The chairman explained that something had gone wrong in a big way with the buying and merchandise control systems, and he wanted me to make a full investigation with recommendations.

This assignment was more than touchy, for my main criticisms and opposition had been centred on these very sections, but I agreed to do it; I could not do otherwise, yet I realised the recommendations I might make could well prove not so good for me—if they did, too bad! On the other hand, if accepted they could do a lot of good for everybody. As for me I was eventually ostracised.

Early next morning I went to the head merchandise controller who had worked for me in the early days. I posed a simple question 'Why are Manchester goods in such a perilous position?' Trembling a little he replied, 'I am sorry to say, despite my (his) advice, very large contracts have been reduced by one of the new whizz kids and the supplier quite naturally has sold off his production elsewhere.' This was very serious from two angles; firstly we would in a matter of days be in a desperate position, and secondly this particular company was one whose chairman had received our own chairman's assurance of continuity.

I suggested a chairman to chairman chat. That was successful and whilst we did not get our supplies back entirely, we did get assurances that we would never be allowed to go without; the exercise succeeded and one great pitfall was avoided. Nevertheless it demonstrated the problem and I was pressed to have a detailed and exhaustive survey ready on his return from Bermuda.

This effort in my opinion was as important to the retail side as the early efforts at Brixton and during wartime in the Wirral. The merchandise problem was surveyed in great depth, troubles were revealed, reasons observed, and above all, cures were offered. I thought this must for all time put things straight, for personalities, both in the company and with me. I delivered the survey with assurances that it would be at his home awaiting his return. On that Sunday I stayed at home, awaiting a phone call I felt certain was sure to come.

That day went and the next and the next, eventually I rang up and enquired if he had received my survey. The reception was not friendly. At first I thought he might be pulling my leg so I said, 'But you asked for the survey, it was you who instigated it, you who asked for detail and remedies. If there is any credit due, it's due to you.'

It seemed to me the report must somehow have been leaked and an incorrect construction put on it, but it was obvious to me the analysis was right and my original fears correct.

It was some little time afterwards that heads began to fall, unfortunately in my opinion not always the right ones. In that great and successful organisation we had so many very good men, excellent chaps, well versed and very knowledgeable, some indeed had been passed by during a period of head hunting and that was sad.

For myself, enough was enough, I had spent nearly twenty years of my life with Littlewoods, notwithstanding the very tough and hard days at the beginning and the war years, but life up to the last three years had been very happy and rewarding. True we had our disagreements, even arguments, but up to this time my personal relations with John and Cecil Moores and Eric Sawyer, my colleague, had been excellent, friendly and always exciting.

J M phoned me at home one Sunday evening and suggested I might like to take a very long holiday or even think of retiring early, which was very fair but of no interest to me; I said I would carry on. It could have been that he thought that over a period problems would sort themselves out. As events turned out he might well have been right. I pondered deeply on all these matters and felt it was no good hopping from one complicated position to another.

However things did not improve and in the summer of 1956 I had made up my mind, and my wife agreed, that I should sever relations whatever the cost. I told John Moores it saddened me that after twenty years with him and ten years as an executive director, I would be leaving in a year's time and I would do one more journey to South Africa.

In my opinion the reasons for the break in a happy family were rooted in a deep philosophy, involving my hatred for head hunting and a fundamental difference on merchandise policy. I repeat my feeling that sound merchandising is blood in the veins of any retail business.

* * *

Social events continued and my wife and I were invited to our final Grand National gathering at Aintree. As usual we were very well received, the atmosphere was happy.

Some time before the great race J M took me by the arm and said, 'Cookie, let's have a look at the course.' We went down to the sacred turf and the formidable jumps. 'Cookie, we have been together how long?' he asked. 'Over 20 years,' I replied. He continued, 'That's a long time in any business, we have had our ups and downs, surely there is no problem we can't overcome.' I listened as I had always, it was an emotional moment in my life. We talked and walked for a while. After many more questions and many more silences he enquired, 'Don't you think we could?' I replied, 'Yes, I think we could, but there's one possible problem. May I ask you a question, a very personal one?' 'Yes, carry on,' he replied. I said 'It's very simple but very serious. Will you tell me if blood is thicker than water?' 'You have a point. Let's go back to the others,' he replied. The point of no return had been reached, many said a pity. In later years on some accounts I could say so too, but it was the right decision, for me and my family.

I made my final business journey to South Africa and tied up the ends. I then said goodbye to John Moores, a very important part of my business life journey was over.

I tell this story without any feeling of grievance or any sense of injury, for after all I was to meet another challenge and make a fortune. No, I tell it to illustrate the enormous problems and tensions that occur through internal politics and head hunting, the excitement of life in Big Business, the thrills and happiness and sometimes disappointments. I am still a firm believer in the philosophy that politics in business is a killer not only of ambitions but of company progress.

However it is certainly true that a human being in the form of a catalyst is extremely useful to have about as I hope to reveal later. I received very many letters from staff, suppliers and friends, who could not believe that this chain of events could ever arise. The feelings were perhaps best expressed in a letter from a business associate (outside the company) who in a farewell missive wrote:

> Sorry I could not talk freely the other day, but I do want to wish you real happiness and pleasure in whatever sphere you eventually decide to enter.
>
> Was it not the Prisoner of Chillon (Byron) who said 'I welcome freedom with a sigh!' and that is how I imagine you feel now but freedom it is, freedom of thought, freedom from politics and freedom to become an individual again. Freedom which I sincerely hope you will be able to enjoy for many years to come. . .

That feeling has, I am sure, been expressed many, many times relative to life in big business.

The fateful day came. I left, with a swift shake of the hands and off I went to Lime Street Station and back home to Alderley.

Here I jump the story a little. Not so many years after the successful public flotation of the big John Myers company which had been built from nothing, I met John Moores in Manchester Airport. My wife and I were off to a function in London. On that Saturday morning I heard a voice call out, 'Yes, it is Cookie; my god, you have done well, I'm very proud. I hope everybody is looking after you, you deserve it.' Those words certainly made up a bit for the frugal parting. We all travelled up to London; we parted there, we to meet our son, and J M with a little box containing his luncheon salad to follow his beloved football team to Norwich.

* * *

The story that I was leaving got around after a leak in February of 1957. It had been kept secret for over six months and that was not bad. I was approached by companies with great reputations; one an electrical company of international standing had expressed a wish to see me and we seriously discussed a position, which unfortunately would involve considerable travelling around the world. The interview was kindly, courteous and exciting, but not around the world again for me. I saw another great American company who had interests in Great Britain, again most courteous and lengthy, we agreed the job was not big enough. A friend then approached me, whose company was of national standing, he foresaw that in the future the textile game in Great Britain would be dicey; that was an understatement. He offered me a seat on their board and said, 'We have money—have you any ideas?' I replied, 'Don't let's beat about the bush, Eric, I presume you want to get in to the mail order business.' He replied, 'Yes, if you will have a try, it could be a bonanza; our shares are standing at under par.' I told him that a lot of money would be required and hearts could be in mouths quite frequently.

'A lot of money,' I continued, 'And that for a period of possibly three years it would mean sacrifices by all concerned, and an extraordinary effort profitwise from the textile side before such an operation would or could be brought to fruition.'

I promised to think seriously about the proposition, but certainly I would not do anything about it whilst at Littlewoods, notwithstanding that my contract was more than already exhausted. I did suggest they test the market, by advertising for a small company to see what the temperature was like. In any event on my return from South Africa, my family were going for a holiday, I promised them a reply before then. I was forty-seven years old, I had a family, my wife had stood staunchly by me through one traumatic and risky change—was it fair? I knew that in the early days my friends or their company certainly could not match my Littlewoods salary standard. Would they get cold feet when the pressure was on? (Indeed they did.) Could I personally stand the strain of competing virtually alone? I did not have to do that as I will explain later.

They advertised for a small mail order company and had a few replies and all but two were consigned to the waste bin. The second was interesting only from the point of view of what people think they can get away with. Therefore there was one left to buy and it was bought with never, no never, any financial regrets.

My wife said if I thought I should have a go after twenty years of strain I should try it, for I would never forgive myself if I didn't. So I decided to have a go if other things could be agreed. I finally reviewed the matter: there was now a fragile company to develop. I said I would take half my salary, and as I revealed that amount, it seemed that their hearts nearly stopped beating; it was the amount that did the shocking. The chairman had to have an immediate increase. I would have to cover both my pension rights and insurance from my own funds, for any disclosure might have wrecked the whole thing. I was assured that I would be recompensed.

Finally and of great importance I detailed the financial side. I explained that agents (customers) would have to be obtained and very quickly; advertising would eventually have to be as big or bigger than that of our competitors, to the point of domination; we would have to create very rapidly a catalogue of 400 pages, rising to 800 or more (my own secret wish was for a 1,000 page effort). Lastly we would have to face a big financial loss on bad debts until the weeding out process was completed and our number of agents reached the budget figure.

I repeated, 'In short, you must be prepared in the first twelve months to *lose* £750,000, not working capital, but a *loss* which will to some extent be covered by the goodwill element for many years to come. In this game you will be buying immediate goodwill at a high cost, a high cost it must be, which will ensure big profits in the coming years. Can you get that sort of money?' 'Oh, yes, the £750,000 is fine.' I continued, 'That is not all, if we do well we might need another million.' 'We can get it' was the answer. Finally, I said I would not be doing this for nothing and immediately we were paying our way I would expect both my salary and other considerations restored. I would want a block of shares in the parent company at that day's price (that is what I paid). I would expect to be chairman and managing director of this subsidiary and vice chairman of the holding company though I insisted that this latter appointment should be deferred so as to avoid publication of my involvement.

My points were agreed. The chairman (Eric Cartwright) and I were friends and remained so until his death. I make these comparatively detailed points to show in all fairness that the arrangements were not one-sided but acceptable to all.

I have been asked many times why I gave up a big position in a great company for a salary that was less than half the previous one, doing in many instances work which previously had been delegated to junior executives. I hope I have made the point that it was not for money alone, I personally lost a lot of money in the first two years of the new adventure. It was not for position, for apart from being the parent of a virtually unborn babe, or grandson of a dying grandpa, I refused all else until the new venture was established and making money, I would be working twice as hard and I would put my family at some risk. It was not for money, standing or recognition, I suppose it was simply to prove a point — that I could do it.

Silence was imperative, we could not break through without stealth, for the big boys could and no doubt would have crushed us, so although we were of necessity in a hurry, we had to endure twelve months of quiet but very fast preparation, and very few people, indeed apart from Mabel, *only two* knew the details of the operation. It meant working almost day and night.

CHAPTER SIX

John Myers

This part of the story deals with my final years in big business.

The daunting task was to build John Myers, virtually a worthless company, into a leader in the mail order field. Barlow & Jones of Manchester and Bolton was an old and respected group in the textile trade prepared to act as step parents in the exercise and to risk £750,000, which says much for their courage and convictions.

The dying company, John Myers, was in Westminster Bridge Road, London, with old offices and warehouse so proudly acquired over the years standing then amid the wasteland awaiting eventual demolition.

This very old company was formed in the reign of King George III (many of the old papers quote 1817). The family had been in business even earlier. I should be doing less than justice to the very old family of Myers if I did not dwell on them for a little while — after all, in addition to being clock-makers of repute they were early pioneers of the mail order business in this country.

To John Myers the founder, his son, grandsons, great-grandsons, and his relative Henry, clocks and watches must have been their first and greatest love. John's and Henry's names both appear in *Watch Makers and Clock Makers of the World* — indeed a long case clock reputedly by John Myers is in the Victoria and Albert Museum. Their clientele was both wide and somewhat exalted. On the other hand they had an eye to bigger business, and they sold a great number of clocks and watches to the ever growing railroads of the day, and until a few years ago many of their clocks could be found in the waiting rooms of the once countryside stations. They were not without pride and wit and I quote from their early catalogues.

As to the pride:

> Among the relics of the Franklin expedition, discovered in the Arctic regions by Captain McClintock, and brought to England in 1859, were two pocket chronometers (in excellent preservation), one of which had stopped at four o'clock; also a small silver watch by 'Myers, London'.

I should mention that Myers thereafter carried a range of Franklin watches. Then there is the wit:

> JOHN MYERS & Co have repaired, for many years past, a gold watch of considerable value belonging to the Rev R_____, Chaplain of one of HM's prisons. A short time since we were surprised to find a handsome inscription engraved inside, stating that it was presented to the Rev R_____ in consideration of his great kindness to the prisoners in Her Majesty's _____ Prison. On asking our customer's explanation of the inscription, which was not previously on the watch, he informed us that, a short time previous, his watch, much to his annoyance, was stolen from him; but, singular to relate, it was returned to

him in a few days, by post, with the above-named inscription engraved on it, evidently having been stolen by one of the former inmates of the prison, who had benefited by the reverend gentleman's kindness, and who wished to mark his appreciation of the same.

Lastly there is evidence of their business methods which has certainly stood the test of time.

25th May 1893

Dear Miss Sutherland

In reply to your letter, I should like to remove from your mind the idea that your watch is not worth the money I asked you for it, and with that object, I have been making enquiries this morning and find that this same watch is supplied to the Goldsmiths and Silversmiths Company of Regent St by the dozen and they charge £11.10.0d for them. They are also supplied to Dents, the Queens Watchmakers and they charge 10/-d less. These statements which I can prove should satisfy you that £9.9.0d was not too much to charge, and that the persons who valued your watch were not like myself — practical watchmakers. I am perfectly willing to send your watch to Switzerland and have a new movement put in — of the same quality as the present one — but it would take about six weeks. However, I would lend you one in the meantime.

They started the mail order business nearly 170 years ago; for quite a time they were successful. The catalogue idea was new; they took advantage of the improving delivery system of the railways and the emergence of the national parcels system. After World War One, and indeed more so after World War Two, they failed to appreciate two points. Firstly the power of advertising and secondly that mail order on credit was big business. It was a pity. On the other hand, I am sure that in many parts of the world their beloved clocks mark the hours and that's probably how they would have preferred to be remembered.

When I came on the scene all but two of the clocks (and they were in bits) had departed; the clock and watch business was no more, and the mail order business was in its death throes.

But to us it was different with the thrill and challenge of reviving that defunct concern; building a very big business with a first ever 1,000 page catalogue. The creation of a huge merchandise warehouse, a large office organisation, the formation of a public company with all the mystique and traditions involved and how we managed to keep the build-up secret almost to the time of the flotation is a story in itself.

I recall those first few desperate years when my wife and I, our family, friends and associates all held our breath until success came in an amazingly short time, that is if you measure years in days and not in heart beats!

The story tells of threatened take overs and a real take over, and my departure from the scene. For ourselves, we achieved what we set out to do in record time, one can't ask for more, and I still find the story fascinating! Finally, it reveals how nine years after we had left the scene on a take over, that very prosperous business collapsed. I found it unbelievable and still do. It was a pity after it had done so well.

* * *

From time to time and with threats of war the old Myers were forced to look for further outlets for their wares.

It is said by some that Sears of the huge USA mail order firm of Sears-Roebuck had the same idea of offering clocks and watches down the emerging railroads of the USA, just as Myers did in England. Sears too, it is said, also had a brilliant mail order idea for the giant catalogue was printed on very thin paper, and stories have it, perhaps rightly, that his catalogue was, and possibly still is, the biggest combined catalogue/toilet roll in the world, and that very many of his orders emanated from moments of solitude.

There was of course a connection between selling watches and clocks down the railroads in both countries, for the age of steam was opening trade over vast territories. It was a pity that the Myers family did not achieve the fabulous success of Sears but neither has anyone else.

In sifting the rubbish and old papers when B & J and I acquired Myers, we found a little book published by John Myers in 1876 entitled, *A Few Words about Watches and Clocks*. It is a concise and interesting story of 'our time' starting with the sundial of King Ahaz who lived about 742 BC, the water clock of Ctesibus of Alexandria in 145 BC, the taper time-piece of King Alfred and so the history proceeds through the years, finishing with John Myers, who proclaimed 'the most extensive retail establishment in the Trade.' No doubt it helped his business and makes excellent reading to both the expert or those just interested.

I also found some very early catalogues, tattered and torn. I quote from the collection of letters of which old Myers was justly proud and we put to good use.

SURBITON, *March 10th*, 1888.

MESSRS. JOHN MYERS & COMPANY.

Gentlemen, — Referring to your letter, I have great pleasure in stating that during the Firty years that I have done business with you I have always found your goods of the best quality, and the greatest satisfaction has always been given. You are at perfect liberty to make whatever use you like of this letter. I should be pleased to know that the already large number of S. W. employees who deal at your establishment was still further increased, and that a firm whose reputation for fair dealing, extending over so many years, should receive the support they deserve.

I remain, dear Sirs, yours faithfully,

W. DYSON.

GOODS DEPÔT, NINE ELMS.

Gentlemen, — Please send me one of your Watches at £5 5s., also cards and circulars for the purpose of forming a club. I bought my Watch of you Thirty-eight years ago, it has been a first-class timekeeper, and is as good now as when I had it; and as your clubs allow men to obtain them in such an easy manner, all those who have not got one should join at once.

Yours sincerely,

JAMES LAKE, *Inspector*,

Nine Elms.

RETURNED LETTER OFFICE, LONDON,

July 30th, 1888.

MESSRS. JOHN MYERS & COMPANY, London.

Dear Sirs, — The Marble Clock is safely to hand, and gives immense satisfaction, so that now the whole of the members have received something from your establishment. You will be pleased to hear that one and all are perfectly satisfied, and that I start another Club next week with a larger number of members than I have ever had before.

Yours obediently,

F. J. PENDRY.

GROVE'S TAILORING & OUTFITTING ESTABLISHMENTS,
EDGWARE ROAD & LAMBETH, LONDON,

August 1st, 1888.

Gentlemen, — I have great pleasure in stating that the Thirty-shilling Prize Medal Watches supplied by you to the members of my Club at this establishment have given universal satisfaction, by comparison with others and from practical experience we consider them equal to any other Watch sold at double the price.

Yours respectfully,

C. RANDALL.

INDIA OFFICE,

WHITEHALL, S.W.

Having had personal transactions with MESSRS. MYERS & CO. in many branches of their business for upwards of Twenty years, I have much pleasure in being able to bear testimony to the excellent quality of their goods, and to the superior manner in which they execute all work entrusted to them. I have at all times found MESSRS. MYERS & CO. very reasonable in their charges, and most attentive and desirous of carrying out my wishes.

J. F. NURSEY,

Financial Department,

India Office, Whitehall.

LAMBETH PALACE, S.E.

August, 1888.

MESSRS. MYERS & CO.

Gentlemen, — I have much pleasure in stating that during the Twenty years you have done the work at the Lambeth Palace, both in Clocks and Watches, you have given satisfaction, and I shall continue recommending my friends to your establishment.

I am, yours very truly,

W. NEWBURY.

Steward to the Archbishop of Canterbury.

HER MAJESTYS OFFICE OF WORKS, WHITEHALL,

August 16th, 1888.

MESSRS. J. MYERS & CO.

I have no hesitation in bearing testimony to the excellence of your Watches. I have had one for more than Thirty Years constantly going, and my constant companion, it goes as well now as when I first bought it from you. Of course you know that I have had it cleaned at your establishment regularly every two years, and it has never been in any other Watchmaker's hands.

Faithfully yours,

T. A. DASH.

Land Surveyor, H. M. Office of Works.

144

Another couple of letters I rescued from the debris illustrates the point that even in those far off days they had problems with catalogue printing.

11th April, 1890

Dear Charlie,

I want to remind you that I am still without any catalogues and that is *two months* on Monday since it was first put in your hands, in consequence of which I have been compelled to discharge a traveller who has been with me eleven months as I cannot afford to keep him in idleness.

In respect to a proof, of course you must take the responsibility if my instructions have not been carried out.

Yours truly,

J. Myers.

14th April, 1890

Dear Charlie,

I am in receipt of a dozen catalogues which I am not at all pleased with and have just sent you a wire stating, 'Marble Clock pages printed very badly, cannot pass them.' I am surprised that you allowed them to be sent in that state as I shall certainly never sell any clocks from a catalogue printed in that style. All I ask you to do is to compare the old one with the present one and give me your candid opinion as to how the two books have been turned out.

The watch headings are not all the same now, for instance Pages 17, 24, 25, 26, 28, 62, 63, 64, 65, 66, 67 and 69 are all badly printed.

The paper is very inferior to the previous book, although the estimate is for the same quality, however I suppose I may pass it, although I cannot pass the clock pages. You have not returned the last proof so cannot see if all my corrections have been made. I am heartily sick of the whole thing as I do not think you have acted fairly towards me, first in not completing it sooner, causing me a very serious loss and now sending it on inferior paper, badly printed.

Yours truly,

J. Myers.

* * *

With their early ideas of this new type of trading in the eighteen and nineteen hundreds they obviously succeeded and at one time they increased their range of goods dramatically. But they failed to appreciate the great growth of this type of retailing and the power of national advertising, coloured illustrations and the extension of credit. They obviously believed in the money motive and paid their agents the highest commission in the trade; but that alone was not enough.

Reading through the letters, it seems that the family were somewhat divided between their reputation as clock and watch makers and their position as traders. After being bang up-to-date with their ideas and the latest methods of trading in the early days of the rail-road, they failed to notice that the novelty of convenience of trading by post was wearing off; they didn't realise that to sell their goods in this new way of trading, they had to improve their catalogue by means of photography; and later full colour illustrations.

Others were now pushing forward in the mail order business and spending vast sums on promotion. It seems at that moment Myers made a vital mistake, instead of putting money in they took it out.

Members of the family in the early days owned quite a bit of property in what might to us today seem to be the seedy districts of London. They were respected and certainly not on the bread line. The old letters reveal they were tough negotiators. Looking back again at those old catalogues and correspondence I had the feeling that one part of the family fancied mail order trading, another jewellery, and another property deals; but above all 'they liked clocks'.

I repeat, for it is very important in the story that follows; they were right on one point—paying the highest commission. They were wrong not to use national advertising and dominate with a very large coloured catalogue and push in more money. They failed to notice the importance of credit.

So the writing was on the wall and the sand drained from the hour glass.

In 1957, the company was in utter decline, the staff was old, tired and underpaid, though they had been very loyal. They really didn't want change, they were awaiting the end. Advertising was non-existent, the catalogue and the selection declined, no new staff with up-to-date ideas were recruited. The field was now wide open to competition, the grave for Myers.

So having bought them out what did we get? First we had a building, true it was scheduled for demolition, but we would have breathing time. It had a good address and we were out of the main mail order belt; that was important. On the other hand the building was depressing, standing alone in acres of devastation, the result of war and clearance.

There was the trading record. Only once in a period of five years to 1957 had a profit been made. The turnover had fallen from £165,000 in 1931 to £59,000 in 1956 and was down still further in 1957, or to illustrate the decay, in 1919 they were doing nearly three times as much trade as they were in 1956, despite years of inflation—so we could not do much worse. There was a tax loss which we could use against profits when we made them!

There was a workforce of fourteen full-time and sixteen part-time people, a mere handful, paid at pitifully low wages, and many of them old and tired of struggling. It had a catalogue of sorts, a very small affair with its illustrations drawn from newspaper clippings, poor in price and presentation, and, having being prepared against an ever decreasing budget, it had even smaller choice.

On the other hand it was a very old established company, in the business since 1817—*nearly 150 years of service—Established in the reign of George III, service through seven reigns.* This was a great advertising plus of which we made great use.

As a business Myers had very few plus points in its favour, but it had one which was virtually priceless—the company was incorporated in 1899 and was therefore not subject to later legislation which required companies registered after 23rd November 1916 to show directors' names on business stationery. Being exempt from this requirement provided us with the secrecy that was vital to our success. If my identity had leaked out we might well have been smothered at birth.

146

Yet again, we had to face things squarely, the business was dying, new staff would have to be sought—the task of building a company with a pathetic annual turnover of just over £50,000 to a multi-million concern was daunting to say the least of it—thinking of the time scale it was horrendous.

I can imagine my friends saying 'and you thought you were lucky'—I agree some of the points I have called a plus were fragile. No, I didn't think I was lucky, but they were points on which I was determined to build. Of course there was the other side of hard detailed, even menial work, which I must admit made me wonder at times why I really did it. I recall a member of staff, the packer, and surely the most poorly paid; I was told he was quite mentally unstable and I was warned that as he used a big knife for cutting his packing cord, I best walk at the back of him. Yet I am convinced that the staff thought it was I that was 'crackers'.

* * *

For the benefit of those who may not have read the thousands of words written about the fascinating method of mail order trading, in the popular and financial press or in the many stockbrokers circulars, I should explain mail order is divided into three main sections.

Agency Mail Order
This covers the major part of the trade. It operates in the main through spare-time agents. They are armed with the main tool of the trade, a truly massive and fascinating catalogue, compiled with brilliant illustrations mostly in colour. Merely to browse through a large catalogue is an experience, and there is a built-in guarantee of quality and value with goods sent on approval (appro). In practical terms this means if you do not like what you get, or the colour or size does not suit, the goods can be returned, and no charge is made; surely a guarantee of confidence and quality second to none.

The agent is a key figure, obtaining orders from relatives, friends and workmates or neighbours, orders are sent in weekly (now with heavy postage charges fortnightly is very popular). Goods generally are despatched in one to three days after ordering, and commission, calculated on payments, is paid to the agents.

There are some who still wonder as to the real attraction. To me and many millions it is fairly obvious. The agents and customers have virtually a huge store in picture form (the illustrations are very good) and shopping is at the fireside, in the kitchen or the works canteen. With a huge buying potential, prices are very competitive, selections are dramatically wide and there is no carrying to be done; goods are delivered to the door. Payments may be spread over periods varying from 20-38 weeks, all without credit charge; some companies offer even longer terms. Above all there is that guarantee which is so jealously guarded.

Direct Mail Order

This is exactly as the title suggests. The catalogue is very much smaller, but still well illustrated. No agency is involved and therefore no commission is paid. This method appeals to customers in rather higher income brackets or of independent persuasion—loners to some extent.

The same guarantees are usually given as to quality and approval before payment. Credit instalments are also available, usually at no charge. It should, and one day will have in one form or another, a big future.

Saturday or Sunday Squares

These only account for a very tiny amount of the mail order business. The title means what it says, goods are offered through small advertisements in the bargain pages of the popular press, mainly at weekends.

Usually the offer is for one off items, and there is little, if any, continuity of business. Catalogues are not used and credit seldom given. Such bargain offers cover things for the house or garden. I take a few at random—hand-woven shawls, burglar alarms, light fittings and bean bags. I remember well one regular advert from the now departed Headquarters and General Supplies Company for 'ex WAAF bloomers (knickers)'. Judging from the number of advertisements for this item, either there were many WAAF's without bloomers, or many thousands had been over-produced.

* * *

So in the autumn of 1957 we faced the big task. I had with me just one other person who knew the intricacies and opportunities involved. Freda Adderley had been my personal assistant in earlier days and joined me now at Myers as my deputy.

I shall not easily forget the original Myers boardroom. The table was covered with green baize, beneath which were the tell-tale rings of tea stains from countless thousands of saucerless cups of tea. The carpet and curtains were threadbare and only an occasional light worked. Frowning down on the scene was the painting of one authoritative John Myers—more sorrowful though were the lovely remains of an old Myers' clock that alas ticked no more.

I gave the picture of old John Myers to the oldest Myers' employee. She told me afterwards that she had taken the picture home and hung it above her bed. Adding that old John Myers, such a lovely gentleman, would always look down on her.

The stockroom had an air of 'search me to see if you can find anything good'. I can remember picking up several pairs of boots and pulling the laces which snapped, rotten with age. All the stock seemed to have the same life expectancy; it had to go. Bad stock is a deterrent to any business; to mail order it is a killer.

As we looked around it was surprising how many curious things emerged. In a locked room of valuables there were numerous boxes of Brasso used for cleaning the one solitary name plate, which had over the years proudly proclaimed the name Myers — it was almost obliterated then. It was probably correct to have the stock of Brasso in the valuables room as it was the only item of good stock. One item I have never been able to fathom was a huge stock of red, blue and white rubber rings for preserving jars, I could understand the rings but not the colours.

We interviewed the staff. They were waiting for the end; some were too old or not mentally alert enough to face a future. They just wanted to give up but stayed on as long as the old firm existed; we offered them continuity of jobs until we found other premises, and we would at least wait for them to try and improve the present position. At best we thought they might do this with fresh merchandise and a new look to the advertisements. They accepted with resignation that the last little catalogue planned for the autumn was going to be late from the printers; but we dealt with that.

It was not surprising that few of them could possibly believe the organisation would be made to blossom; there was certainly a death wish around and the pathetic little pensions which had been promised were their private Koh-i-noor diamond.

Having made a full survey of the possibility and the problems and agreed the vital access to finance, we took the first steps to build up the moribund concern into a leader.

We had a plan — an impelling one — and the brunt had to be taken in the beginning by Freda Adderley and me. It was a tough plan for even a big organisation to fulfil but for an organisation where publicity of the company progress, particularly at a personal level was dynamite, the burden was very heavy with the days long and hard.

To my family, who gave sustenance and inspiration, and to my wife in particular, I owe a great debt for love, tolerance, forebearance and understanding.

Our plan of action was based on six main points.

1. Catalogue

Our idea was to create in rapid stages a 1,000 page catalogue (at this time it had only 100). The theory behind this was that we could then offer the widest possible choice of merchandise. But more important by far — we would then be able to advertise it as the biggest catalogue and that was a cornerstone of our policy.

As we approached the 1,000 page stage we had our critics, but it was interesting over the years to watch our competitors fall in with the big catalogue idea; it was an advertising must. At this point I jump many years. After we left Myers the new owners reversed the policy and actually reduced the number of pages in the catalogue which in my opinion was a fatal error, and time confirmed this.

2. Quick Recruitment

The idea was to recruit agents/customers over the widest shopping spread and in the shortest possible time. We would, as part of this aggressive policy, continue to pay our agents 12½% commission against the normal 10% in the trade for we wanted the best agents. That this was the right way was confirmed when the managing director of a very large concern phoned me in what he called a friendly threatening way, stating, 'You pay higher commission than is general and you advertise car competitions as rewards to better agents.' Obviously something was beginning to hurt. 'Now take my advice and stop it,' he continued. I replied with a chuckle, 'Sure, we will if you agree to advertise no more than us and not to increase the size of your catalogue.' He did not change, and neither did we.

3. *Advertising by Domination*
This was a crucial decision and once we had a presentable catalogue we decided that to succeed we had to *dominate* our competitors, not only in space and colour but in offers such as our higher commission and car awards. This was brilliantly carried out by my colleague and Jimmy Sherring.

4. *Timing*
This was vital, the time to begin had to be just then, not twelve months later, for then it would have been too late. It would have been easier if it had been twelve months earlier; I made a big mistake in giving Littlewoods an extra year. I forecast that should we be successful we would be the last sizeable concern to enter this type of mail order business and time has proved this correct.

5. *Profits*
We planned to make heavy losses over a period of three years to ensure a quick build up. After that we would make reasonable profits for a couple of years, then good, very good, profits (they were achieved).

6. *The Individuals*
Because of the need for secrecy the principal load fell on the shoulders of just two people, and much later on three or four, for when we moved to Manchester we immediately recruited a few more staff we could intimately trust, but the great work burden in creating a catalogue from virtually nothing, writing the copy and planning an entirely new advertising policy fell on just two. Later of course we had great help from a marvellous and devoted staff, but that was seemingly light years away.

Having decided on the plan and the cash position we turned to the all important catalogue. We made a dummy catalogue by pasting the illustrations from various publications on to blank pieces of paper to represent our vision of an improved and larger version and the result was encouraging. The 1,000 page catalogue was always in our mind.

With the dummy finished there came the vital job of selecting the merchandise, and we had to cut corners. We each made selections for one half, there was no time for checking, and we relied on our judgement, but there was one exception to this, that of women's fashions; at the best of times this is a problem, so we checked each other. We had only a limited amount of photography, knowing full well it is a must in a good catalogue, and again held our breath; for the rest we used drawings and art work. Time being of the essence it meant that the copy and all printing had to be completed in a month, to be ready by January 1958.

Office space was limited as the samples rolled in and, we assembled them into ranges. Dresses, blouses, skirts, jumpers and coats, were hung from picture rails, pictures and doors. We did our selecting in a little office attached to the boardroom, which had two doors, these were an advantage, goods for selection were on one door and those selected on the other. This worked well until someone with a message pushed a door open too far, and the lot came tumbling down. We brought into use two very ancient coat stands (customers and staff in years gone by must have hung their hats and coats on them) and to some extent we hung our own futures on them.

We emptied the stock room racks of old goods and filled them with more selections, each bin representing one page; a far cry from the sophisticated selection rooms in the palmy days of Littlewoods. As we were determined to win, the facilities would follow later.

Each item was selected and listed with meticulous care. Manufacturers were advised and requested to send a merchandise description form (to meet the Merchandise Marks Act) and, to avoid wrong or misleading descriptions, the copy was compiled from the details provided which proved quite a task. Often the evening was the only available time to write copy, which had to read attractively and contain all the essential matter, be correct, yet flow easily. Even the first tiny catalogue meant the writing and checking of 40,000 words by two people in their spare time.

In London we had a small studio which submitted layouts as soon as selections were finished; these were then approved or otherwise in a matter of minutes.

In those early days the printing order was not large enough for the less costly and more attractive photogravure method, but using the old-fashioned setting had an advantage, for we could leave pricing to the very last moment and take advantage of any reductions. We did, believe it or not, have price reductions then, and as we began to get time to argue we obtained an ever increasing number. We were inured to take advantage of any setbacks, trials or tribulations—I believe firmly that you must live like it at some time in your life if you want to succeed.

I have been through some sticky times in my business life and some tough arguments but the job at Myers beat them all. Though I had accepted the challenge, I must confess there were many moments when I wondered why but eventually the results justified the efforts.

I was now working terribly long hours (which most unions would define as slavery) at half salary, nearly two hundred miles from home, in a decaying old building with a pervading atmosphere of gloom, dust and decay.

For sustenance we had a couple of sandwiches brought in daily from a café, and saucerless cups of tea. We did not have time for an evening meal; all we had were packets of biscuits until about ten o'clock. It is surprising what the human body can take for we arrived at the office at 8.30 am each morning with eagerness and renewed strength.

I do not pretend it was exciting, exhilarating or even tolerable, to come down from a top executive position with plenty of off-duty activity, a family at home, the clean and pleasant, indeed humane, way of eating one's meals, and many times I asked myself why hustle from the north to London and back again to work in conditions which I would have condemned for the lowest labourer even as far back as 1931, doing jobs so menial that I would have apologised to the workers before I had asked them to do it. But we did not flag for I honestly believe tasks undertaken should be completed. Justification of oneself was important, and the belief that new ideas and concepts of business could and would pay off. The money and all that I personally was sacrificing was of little account.

I didn't mind the fight, but the soul destroying feeling was the overwhelming sense of abject defeat that possessed the staff. Despite that we looked to the future and a few extra weeks in London brought us nearer to getting premises in Manchester for the second stage of our expansion. Our usual working hours were 8.30 am till 10.30 pm and in those long days among everything else we produced the layout and illustrations for a new and more attractive catalogue for the spring and summer of the next year.

Those first four months of perpetual strain, long hours, the travelling times to and from Manchester and the anxiety for other people's welfare took a toll on my reserves. Fortunately at home I was tended by my understanding wife and family and set off to London refreshed each Monday morning to take yet another dose.

Our policy of domination in advertising could not be achieved for at least eighteen months, as it would take three issues to create a catalogue to back up the big campaign we had planned.

As I sit in my study writing these notes I look at the twenty-seven catalogues produced during the period of re-building Myers, and I almost wince at the thought of the toil, sweat, brains and anxiety that went into their production. Nevertheless I feel some pride at the millions of sales they created and the satisfaction they gave.

In the initial period of the new Myers, it was not only a matter of catalogue and advertising planning; our printers had to be convinced of our ability both to produce the correct copy and pay for the paper and the printing. As their invoices were getting much bigger, we always paid our bills on time. I cannot speak too highly of the understanding shown by the head of Knapp Drewett, the late Tony Baynham who later joined our board, and his ever faithful assistant, Maurice Barfield.

In the winter of 1957 we obtained premises in Manchester for Barlow & Jones had a liability of an old but substantial building in the centre of Manchester which we took over.

Much work had to be done but in the end we would have offices and a small warehouse. We needed furniture, but the budget which we had set, was small, so we hired most of our furnishings. I left this part of the job to my colleague who set about furnishing at least one office with carpet, desk, two chairs, and a typewriter, all on rental. I recall being in London and my colleague in Manchester, with a meeting previously arranged for the early afternoon in London. During the morning she had tramped the streets of Manchester looking for equipment, and a violent storm broke out with torrential rain. She rang from a call box, and said, 'I'm soaked and I haven't got a dry thing on me and water is pouring out of my shoes. I shall have to go home and change.' She did, and the meeting in London was held just a little behind time.

* * *

In early 1958 I brought three of the senior staff from London to look over our new building. They were deeply impressed and yet aghast. Impressed with the space, aghast at what we could ever do with it. What plans had we for letting off the surplus space? We had none because we were already thinking of the next quarter of a million square feet we would need.

Our job now was to plan a much bigger catalogue, and two people had to deal with that too. It was quite a task to jump from the original 100 page catalogue to a 400 page catalogue in less than twelve months; this new one was to be in full colour, and the break-through was achieved. With all the photography, studio work and colour processing that was necessary it was a man sized job — it turned out eventually to be a woman sized job.

The year 1958 blustered in with a long bleak winter. Early replies came in to our advertisements which appeared in leading newspapers and women's journals. The replies were down on target and the quality unbelievably poor; this did not really surprise us for when a new company advertises, particularly offering credit, crafty would-be agents attempt to cash in with quick applications, creating a trail of bad debts.

So we were prepared for the first big advance, the premises in Manchester were ready for a fair sized office staff, and could also function as a warehouse. Early in 1958 we, a buyer, a secretary, and a supervisor, were installed in Manchester; I remember that devoted staff so well. There was our first buyer Bob Coghlan; Hilda Painter, our general supervisor and future employee manager, and old Mrs Walker, our first secretary and general factotum. We had more room in which to manoeuvre so that samples could be unpacked, listed and submitted, selected or rejected and passed back at great speed to another room; we were set to double the size of our catalogue for the autumn and winter of 1958.

Pagination is all important. For example, in the spring and summer catalogue ladies' fashions were displayed in the opening section with the low sales takers coming towards the end, while the final pages, particularly in the winter, closed with very attractive merchandise such as toys, Christmas fare and gifts. Nor was the catalogue constructed just by whim or fancy. We studied catalogues from all over the world, fashion and trade publications, ideas from designers and *price*. Above all we studied the government forecasts and statistics, and the likely effect of tax adjustments on various types of merchandise. Looking over those forecasts and prices now, one gets a shock as to how far we have slipped. Casting an eye over those earlier statistics, they included the details of both people in employment, and those without a job, the effect of increasing wage rates, levels of taxation, total national income, percentage spent on clothing (a very big factor in mail order trading).

The final and important consideration was how the great body of the working population was likely to spend its earnings, bearing in mind the movement in wealth. Later there was the dramatic effect of four colour illustrations on the sales of various types of merchandise and the exact position on a catalogue page.

* * *

Samples for the autumn catalogue of 1958 came racing in, shortly to be followed by the ever watchful suppliers' representatives, with important information, help and even concessions.

At times this could be very strenuous because we were selecting on the third floor while the reception room (one chair, one table and one bell) was on the ground floor; we did not go to the expense of proper security then because there was nothing to steal except samples, all our statistics, hopes and fears were carried around in our brief cases.

Copy was still as difficult a job as ever, especially if the merchandise forms were not completed properly. The goods were laid on the floor and we worked on our knees; that was perhaps appropriate! We used the biggest floor as a dummy page. The forms for boots and shoes always seemed to omit the details of materials used which meant a quick conference. A scrape of the soles, and the shoes passed around for a smell: leather or what? Leather was fairly easily recognised, therefore the copy would read, *Finest Quality Leather Oxford. A product of superior shoe craftsmanship!* or *The quality leather uppers are moulded on a medium fitting last to ensure comfort and smartness. Wear tested sole and heel of selected bond leather.*

If any missing details did not arrive on time and we were only certain that part of the material was leather, the description would read, *Brogue Court, a supreme shoe masterpiece in quality calf side leather uppers with admirable gilt buckle, vamp trim and comfortable built heel and hard wearing sole;* (the missing piece of information was the material from which the sole and heel were made). On some things you could let yourself go, for example, describing a nightdress in bold print, *Sheer Enchantment—this gossamer nightie in 50 denier nylon jersey bodice and shoulder straps in ruched nylon finished with a rayon satin bow,* etc. Then your mind had to switch to an urgent discussion perhaps about Wellington boots.

Instead of sketching almost everything we were now photographing large sections of merchandise, and this gave a definite lift to the catalogue, but it was not until the 1959 spring and summer catalogue that we were photographing a part of our fashion section using live models—another breakthrough, for these better illustrations increased sales and obtained advertising allowances from our suppliers.

The spring and summer catalogue of 1958, small though it was compared to our competitors, produced much bigger sales. One month's sales were now equal to six months of the old Myers business of 1957, still small but an advance. Our advertising was still restrained until we could produce a really big catalogue. In Manchester we were increasing our staff and by the end of 1958 we had a small, efficient, and above all enthusiastic buying team and credit office; with all the other ancillary posts filled, we aspired to two secretaries. We now had an efficient warehouse, pitifully small, yet a great improvement compared with anything Myers had experienced before, with business above target and losses below our plan.

* * *

We now delegated quite a bit of work—but five jobs were never entirely delegated. The first was selection. The buyers prepared their suggested ranges with a big supply of reserve samples and the final selections were always made by the top two.

Secondly we always checked the final catalogue copy, for 'material description' as this was a mirror of the company's integrity. The detailed supervision of copy had a spin off in that accumulated knowledge was passed on to the executives concerned—an important step in a simple but efficient method of educating them in the overall policy of the company.

Thirdly, either Freda Adderley or I checked all pricing. This ensured that the buying price was reasonable and the selling price competitive, and that the final overall buying price over thousands and thousands of options would work out correctly. It did.

Fourthly we personally passed all our art work or photography. This determined that the overall look was right. Advertising was the final job we would never delegate. The space siting allocated in any particular newspaper had to be right. Wrong locations reduce the number of replies, resulting in a considerable increase in unit costs; they can be very wasteful.

Even today I wince when I see the wrong locations. The space we never wanted and very seldom had in any newspaper was the gutter (the inside fold where the pages joined), replies from these spaces were poor in quantity and quality, again increasing the unit cost. Jimmy Sherring was the front man of our advertising agents, a small, tenacious cockney, full of pluck and pride, who could take an idea, tear it to pieces and have the right job to view before the proverbial words 'Jack Robinson'.

Finally credit sanctioning was very important and started at the very beginning when applications for a catalogue were first received for they were subjected to very severe scrutiny. There were many guide lines, bad credit areas, doubtful credit roads in a good area, the type and style of handwriting (this was also important because we certainly did not want agents who could not write), and for that reason printed names instead of written were always suspect, as was immature or childish writing etc. After discarding the obviously unacceptable, the remaining applications were subject to report from a Credit Status Agency. This may appear costly, in fact it was quite the reverse for it avoided sending an expensive catalogue to an applicant with a bad credit record.

When the status agency suggested a doubt as to the credibility of the applicant, he or she would get an application form only; this was seldom returned. If on the other hand it was finally submitted it provided further information for us to consider; some of these applicants eventually got a catalogue, others did not for a variety of reasons.

Many status reports were sad, amusing or revealing, like the following:

> Blank, married but living with blank. . . Blank has 15 judgment summonses. . . Blank is a kind old lady living in a high rise flat and while she might make a good customer she couldn't carry a catalogue around. . . Blank is unknown, but there are four different families at this address.

Then there was one particular area of London that was very dicey, a district jokingly known to some as Hopping Valley. A frequent reply was, 'It is believed that so and so is about to leave the country.'

When the orders arrived we had another set of sanctioning guide lines.

1. If the application came via a canvasser (we employed some teams of these) and its value was say £5 (1957 value), it would be referred back either for additional orders or cancellation, being considered too small.

2. A guarantor was required for an under age applicant.

3. A guarantor was required for anyone living in unfurnished apartments, if they had been there for under three months. If the apartments were furnished the qualifying time without a guarantor would be six months.

4. Caravan dwellers were dealt with strictly. Everything had to be first class, and the applicant must have been in residence for at least twelve months.

5. In those early days servicemen (because they were mobile) and their wives did not usually get appointed, though later there was much relaxation, as there rightly should be.

6. I know of one company that took the strongest view of some self-employed in certain trades, yet I suppose it is in line with some canvassers who will never go to a house with blue curtains (a so-called bad debt sign). It is awfully hard if your favourite colour is blue.

Looking at things the other way round, if an agency appeared to be developing rapidly and orders were very large, we would send out our special representative, who would weigh up the position, and if he considered the agency was good, every possible assistance would be given, together with additional catalogues.

We did get curious orders (probably not by today's standards), like double beds for single people. Some provided us with laughter, some were incredible, and some even sad. For example:

1. Name: *Ellen Blank.*   Status: *Single/Married.*
2. Address: *As filled in.*
3. Order: *1 Wedding Ring,*
              1 Nightdress,
              1 Layette,
              1 Compendium of Games.

While I could understand the necessity for the first three items, I found the last one difficult to appreciate.

I have found so often that being able to absorb detailed information provides the ability to make big decisions, which in turn makes it easy to read other people's intentions.

* * *

Estimating sales in an ever-growing business was difficult. Christmas of 1958 was no exception. Catalogue appeal is one thing, time of recruitment and therefore sales life of agents is quite another. If agents joined us late in the advertising campaign (as of course a large number did) the amount of repeat orders declined as the season progressed. By early December we were doing much better than I had anticipated, but I had forgotten to make an allowance for the actual day of the week on which Christmas day fell — if this was in the middle of the week sales fell about ten days before, if it fell at the end of the week they declined seven days before. While we had met our schedule I was disappointed and somewhat downcast. I sat and analysed my thoughts, the truth of the few words that had been dropped by our temporary paymasters suddenly dawned on me — the big money was being used very fast and it was a worry to them; for my part I knew money had to be lost both sensibly and fast if we were to achieve our object. That was it!

Barlow & Jones were more than a little nervous and I suppose that rubbed off on me. Nevertheless we were on target, our loss would not be as great in the first year as anticipated, we had cut expenses, we used our own cars, the next catalogue was ready, and stock was coming in fast.

We decided to have a good Christmas and face the new year looking at things through less tired eyes; we had after all increased our turnover to nearly half a million pounds in that first year. It may not seem much now but that leap forward meant a lot then.

The new year arrived and with it some dreadful weather. Replies to our adverts were not good and the quality poor. In early February the snow was falling heavily, and we decided facts had to be faced; if we were worried about money now, what about the future when we would be talking in millions?

Indeed we were thinking of millions now to provide for a full buying team, new warehouse equipment, saturation in advertising and a bigger catalogue for our policy of rapid expansion.

The parents, Barlow & Jones, suddenly woke up to the fact that over half a million pounds would shortly have been used. I had said originally that we should lose £750,000 of their ready money. I concluded they still did not understand the drill of losing money to make money; of course it is not everybody that does.

I said to Eric Cartwright that it was useless huffing and puffing. We had our plan, we knew what cash we wanted, we knew how much we would lose and we intended to lose it intelligently — that way we would succeed. There was no other way.

He countered that he was very worried. I replied, 'So am I, it's snowing, the catalogue is late, the replies are late and of poor quality, but one week of snow won't put us off course.'

I said with some force, 'If you really think enough is enough say so, I certainly don't want to waste any more time or energy. It seems useless to talk about £750,000 when we know that even to get into the first eleven another million must be provided. Let's have a meeting,' 'When, today?' he asked, 'Yes, this afternoon can't be too soon. Have Raymond Baldwin there and ask Sir Thomas to come too,' I replied. (Sir Thomas Barlow was a past chairman of B & J). 'Our house then 3 pm,' he suggested, to which I agreed.

The conversation ranged over the effect on B & J's finances (money would be tight) and they were worried. I said I could be feeling likewise about myself, but it would not do me any good; it never did.

I could not quite understand B & J's problems over figures and neither could Sir Thomas Barlow. It had all been planned. After half-an-hour or so he turned to me and said, 'What's the trouble, Andy?' 'In a word, *money,*' I replied.

'Well, we know don't we, that you have planned for what's required, how much do you want immediately, meaning the next twelve months?' asked Sir Thomas. 'A million, at once,' I replied. 'So what?' The jolly old boy laughed, 'I'm chairman of the bank . . . I can't agree to anything, but, tell you what Andy, if you're free tomorrow we'll see Mitchell, the chief general manager, he has the authority of sanction or veto.'

We arrived at the elegant banking hall, Tommy with his umbrella and I with my documents including the detailed financial plans. We were ushered into the presence of the chief general manager, the redoubtable Mr Mitchell. The two assistant chief general managers were ready on call at the far end of his magnificent office. After we had exchanged a few pleasantries he said, 'Now tell me Mr Cooke, what exactly is meant by mail order trading?' I explained in broad detail. After my explanation he said, 'In short, you have a catalogue and this is advertised through the press, from these replies you appoint agents, applications for appointments are checked for suitability, particularly credit worthiness and they get 12½% commission on all the goods they sell and for which you are paid.' 'Correct,' I commented. 'Now,' he said. 'I gather you have stipulated all along that large sums of money are wanted to finance it, and now so much and only so much is available from Barlow & Jones. Obviously you want more money as you increase the size of your catalogue and the amount you sell on credit. How much do you want made available now?' 'A million,' I replied. 'Have you got your plans and figures available?' he asked. I had indeed, covering the next two to three years.

He pored over the financial plans for a few minutes. — 'It seems a jolly good idea,' he ventured. I thought we were on the way. Looking me straight in the face, he said, 'But I disagree with the amount you want, you say £1,000,000, I reckon it's £2,000,000.' 'I know the difference Mr Mitchell,' I said, 'It's one of time, I am quoting for one year, and you I think, are quoting for two.' 'Yes, that's alright then,' he said cheerfully, and continued, 'I'll wish you all good luck, but I don't think somehow you will want to count on that.' It was a master stroke by old Sir Thomas in arranging that meeting.

Mitchell, smiling and relaxed, said, 'Now that's over, your coffee, how do you like it, with cream or milk?'

It was the fastest financial interview I have ever had; we left that meeting with the firm determination to keep to the ultimate aims of a huge catalogue and a policy of advertising domination.

When I saw that excellent television series on Churchill, *The Wilderness Years episode three,* I was reminded of old Tommy again. When Myers was an assured success Sir Thomas invited me to lunch with him at the Savoy. I was to pick him up at his house at Strand-on-the-Green; he had a delightful place there.

Sir Thomas either did not like buying hats or must have been very fond of the piece of head-gear he always wore. As we left for lunch he picked up this piece of revered clothing, a bowler hat that had seen better days. True, it had a crown, green with age, it was attached by very scanty and wide tacking stitches to a brim of a slightly darker hue, the braid had still a touch of black; at a mere touch the contraption wobbled.

On arrival at the Savoy he gracefully removed it and dropped it on the porter's desk where its crown quivered in the bright light like a green jelly, resting very insecurely on its uncertain brim. The quivering green in the bright light though has always fascinated me. I should add he was a connoisseur of Moselle, it was excellent.

That meeting at the bank was one of the most important meetings in my life. Having settled with the bank, the financial way ahead was clear and a great worry had been lifted from my mind; the task would have been nigh impossible without that backing. So now we were able to think ahead to late 1960, when the catalogue would jump in size very considerably — bringing us in line with some of our competitors; that would be after just two-and-a-half years.

We had a devoted crew who, virtually without exception, put the job before themselves. Here I would emphasise again that an enormous amount of work was carried out in absolute secrecy, without which the task might have been impossible. I doubt if the secrecy act could ever happen again.

But the lifting of the financial burden also gave the heart a lift. On looking at my diary notes I see that in April we had grown from 2,000 agents in 1957 to 18,239 in 1959. Sales were now rather better than anticipated and our targets were being exceeded month by month.

In the meantime we had to devise original and exciting methods of attracting new agents. We knew exactly how we would dominate space and colour in the advertising media; what we had to do in addition was to hit upon original ideas to stimulate interest in our catalogue. Finally we decided to develop in depth the car competition. We awarded a new car for the new agent who did the greatest amount of business over a six month period and one to the existing agent showing the greatest improvement in sales over the same period. The resulting increase in sales was beyond our wildest dreams. Over the years these car competitions proved a tremendous boost to the rapid recruitment of agents.

Good progress was made in those first six months of 1959. Our buying and office organisation were well bedded down, we were employing some 400 people, and enthusiasm in the business was at a very high level. My personal notes at that time read:

> We already have a fully equipped organisation of both inside and outside staff.
> Certain parts of the administration have worked extremely long hours and must be given assistance before long and rewarded accordingly.
> The inside staff is capable (with the exceptions mentioned above) of handling turnover to the extent of £1,500,000 per annum.

* * *

Towards the end of June, dark clouds appeared on the horizon, for a printing strike was forecast and it could have spelt disaster of the first magnitude to us even though we would not be the only mail order company without an autumn and winter catalogue.

The printers certainly did stop work at the right time for themselves, and the wrong time for us. The managing director of our printers was well informed and fortunately Tony Baynham kept us abreast of events. Early on, before the trouble really broke we booked a pull out supplement in the *Weekend Mail* as an insurance. It was a catalogue in miniature with the equivalent of ten pages mostly in full colour, with order and application forms contained in the one presentation. It was a first rate insurance to save something, if the strike went on for only a short time. While it would save the lean of our bacon, it certainly would not save the fat.

This idea in the short term, even if the strike were called off, would mean extra business, and either way we really could not lose. At that time it was the biggest colour advertisement ever carried for a mail order company.

The autumn and winter catalogue was due for delivery in mid-July, but the strike continued; we mailed thousands and thousands of leaflets containing special offers.

We were told that in a matter of days the strike would be over, but with stock pouring in to service the new catalogue the strike went on. One always had an eye to the fact that one day soon the stock would have to be paid for, and without sales this would be inconvenient to say the least.

I asked our printer to find a local printer to produce a complete run on newsprint covering important items which would sell immediately. The snag here, confessed Baynham, was that he had to find a printer who could say with his hand on his heart he could do the whole job himself. At long last he found such a chap and on a fateful Friday morning, I was in the basement stockroom and took the call informing me of the arrangements; the telephone was close to the limewashed walls and without thinking I nervously rubbed my back on the wall as I was speaking, 'Thank God!' I said. I was still not happy, though, as I walked away, one of the warehouse staff said, 'Scuse me sir, on the back you look like the "Abdominable" Snowman!' I felt worse. One of the problems Baynham had was how to smuggle in some black ink via a contact at a meeting place in Regents Park.

Our family was due to go to Scotland that Friday night, but we all decided we would not go while the strike lasted. During that time there were many false reports that the strike would be over that very day. I thought, if the worst comes to the worst, we would at least have the newspaper as a standby.

At 5 pm Baynham rang me to say there was just a chance that the strike would be over on that Friday night, and I left the premises a bit wearily. My son met me half way home — still nothing definite. We reached home, and my wife met us at the gate. 'The strike is over,' she said. Baynham did a quick re-check. Yes! He would start delivery over the weekend. Freda Adderley quickly organised a weekend gang for despatching the catalogue and once more we were on the move. A very relieved family left for Cape Wrath that night.

The reaction was immediate and the monthly sales were many times greater than the annual sales two years before. The organisation was strong and we were preparing to double the size of the catalogue the next year.

Speaking to my son recently about that first weekend in Scotland, he said his outstanding memory was of me phoning Freda Adderley and hearing all the reassuring news. He thought I had bought the freehold of the isolated little phone box in lonely Durness near Cape Wrath — what a name to suit the situation. The annual sales for 1959 were running at just under £2,000,000. The programme for 1960 was £3,000,000. I quote my notes.

The catalogue for this entire year of 1959 (both summer and winter issues) consisted for the first time of 400 pages, admittedly not all first-class, but we were moving fast and we were exceeding all our targets.

As Barlow & Jones was a public company it was vital to have secrecy and anything so radical as their venturing into such a capital orientated business as Mail Order, would without question have brought the financial people down on them. Textile shares were already a very low market and they would most certainly have gone a lot lower if any news got out. It is a strange paradox that companies are very often criticised, condemned indeed, for being woolly, not forward looking enough, or not using assets.

In early summer 1959 we were searching for new merchandise to give an entirely new look to our new and very much bigger catalogue for 1960, and we looked for new lines here, there and everywhere. One idea we had, motivated by personal experience, was a horticultural section, not only bulbs this time, but plants, young trees, roses, azaleas, etc. We decided to obtain first class advice. My deputy flew to Boskoop in Holland and among the many firms and gentlemen she interviewed was a Mr Jongejan, of Charles Mesman and Company. The extract from her notes gives an idea of the care given to selections.

7th/9th July 1959

I saw Mr Jongejan and asked him for a further quotation for roses in quantities of 5,000 and 10,000 and for flowering shrubs in quantities of 100 and 1,000.

I explained that we would require to place bulk orders for roses and flowering shrubs and we would want to call-off on a weekly or fortnightly basis, we would want them to be priced at the bulk rate. Mr Jongejan agreed to this in the case of roses.

In regard to the call-off, they would require at least ten days notice in order to prepare the delivery.

I went through the complete selection of roses and shrubs with Mr Jongejan, cut out some we had named and inserted substitutes which would be popular enough for our market.

I asked Mr Jongejan if he could give us the proportion of sales of one type of rose to another. He told me that up to a few years ago sales of HT roses and polyantha roses was $10-1$, but during the last few years the demand for polyantha roses has grown with the result that the demand is almost $50-50$.

HT Roses: Peace $(2-1)$ to any other roses, Ena Harkness, Sutters Gold.

Polyantha Roses: Masquerade, Fashion, Frensham, etc.

Brooms: I told him that his price was much too high and he confirmed that he had originally quoted for the best pot-grown but his new quotation now covers field brooms. He made the point, however, that he would not be too happy about supplying these.

The illustrations were brilliant, and from a supply point of view it seemed an easy one, at least so we thought.

At home we have for years planted very many thousands of daffodils, narcissi and tulip bulbs in our gardens. We thought if the first bulk orders sold out (which they did) we could fall back on our personal stock. Then orders tailed off and we decided our own bulbs should be planted. Just as the job was finished, demand started again; the weather had been a bit upside down. We could get no further supplies from anywhere and at that stage in our growth we hated the very thought of leaving an order unfulfilled.

I phoned my wife about five o'clock on a late autumn afternoon. Apologizing, I said, 'I just must have 300 to 400 daffodil bulbs to take in tomorrow morning please.' 'They're all planted,' came back the answer. 'Yes I know, couldn't you get Reg (the gardener) to dig up a few and clean them, they can't be growing yet,' I pleaded. Mabel said she would try, but it was getting dark, though fortunately there was a moon and they had torches.

Anyway torches and moon helped a lot and I had my bulbs for next morning. Unfortunately the weather held up and I had to repeat my pleas several times, getting less popular all the time. Then winter came and the exhumation of bulbs by moonlight ceased, with relieved sighs all round.

* * *

Business was growing and in 1959 we realised that within another twelve months we would need much bigger and better premises. We were aided in our search by the depression in the textile trade. It was much deeper than even Barlow & Jones thought at their first fateful (and what later proved to be a very fruitful meeting) with me.

Spinning mills and weaving sheds were closing down at an ever increasing rate; great Victorian mills became ghastly memorials to the great age of cotton, both on rising land or in sheltered valleys. Buildings which were a credit to the architect's vision and the builders' craft, were being offered at prices less than half the value of the land on which they stood. The cry was to get rid of them, and, in the Lancashire jargon, 'bloody quick'. There was no shortage of options.

So in early 1960, we bought from Fine Spinners Ltd a very large cotton mill at Reddish, near Stockport, for a sum in the region of £45,000. I quote from the *Financial Times* when we went public.

> Houldsworth Mill, which was built in 1865, is used as the company's buying office and warehouse. It also accommodates the remainder of the clerical staff. Their freehold premises were acquired in 1960 and the book value at 19th June, 1962 was £62,525. The building stands in just over 5 acres of land, leaving just over 2 acres of land for further development should this be required, although there is at present adequate room for expansion within the existing building. The floor area of the building is 236,000 sq ft on five floors, which is equivalent to 5.4 acres. The interior of the premises has been extensively modernised and the warehouse is well equipped with conveyors and lifts to all floors.
>
> The GPO and British Railways have their own site Post Office and site railway station on the premises to assist in the speedy delivery of merchandise to customers and this is further assisted by proximity of the important Stockport rail junction.

The building itself was an achievement of Sir John Houldsworth in 1865 (witness Houldsworth Square in Reddish). In its day it was one of the most modern industrial buildings in the north with its two huge wings joined by a central section dominated by the tower housing the clock. For even now it is impressive.

I sometimes wonder how many thousands have been sent scurrying to work on time by the gilded fingers of that clock. One can only guess. Certainly that central block, its two small towers and the clock, dominated the countryside.

The two wings each containing five floors, were extremely well planned even by today's standards. The entire floor area was work space; none of it was wasted on lavatories or washrooms, which were sited off the main staircase alongside each floor. The substantial staircases could have withstood the worst of fires as they had withstood nearly a hundred years of clogged feet tramping to the machines —although the steps had worn a bit thin as silent evidence of the human traffic. The centre block was excellent for canteen facilities, again no waste. The mill had its own reservoir, and small gardens outside the main gate. For nearly a century it had been a haven and workshop with a watching spirit of time over the surrounding houses; a vision which in its day must have seemed the ultimate in efficiency.

But time is a spoiler of visions. Came the 1960's and the textile industry and cotton spinning in particular were beating a hasty retreat before loads of cheap fabric produced by low paid labour in the emerging countries—and as I saw in Africa operating in conditions which would hardly qualify for a good health certificate in this country.

When we came on the scene the mill was silent, some of the old hands were sitting on the benches outside, and they seemed to be in almost the same despairing mood as the workers I saw in Maryport years earlier, indulging in that same competitive 'game' of spitting. I talked to some of them. 'Now lad,' they proffered, 'Mill will never work again, no jobs here.' They were quite wrong for in a short time we were employing over a thousand people.

There was little bargaining as the sellers were very willing. The mill had recently been equipped with very modern machinery but to qualify for a government payment under a contraction scheme the machinery had to go. Holes were cut in the floors, chutes fitted and sledge-hammers battered the machinery to bits and it slipped like slaughtered lambs to the waiting lorries beneath. Even the toughest guy could not resist a sigh and utter 'What a waste.' We tried to make up for it, and I hope we did.

The year of 1960 had seen us make very big strides. We had a big catalogue, and we were occupying a very big warehouse. Our agencies and customers grew in strength and we were beginning to dominate the advertising field for mail order agents.

To intensify the penetration of our advertising we continued to extend our car competitions by varying the classifications of competitions and competitors status every season. All competitions were based on improvement because our future as a company depended on just that.

* * *

In the latter half of 1960 we produced our first precious profit. Joyously it was not of the petty cash variety. So after just three years of effort 1960 came to a happy end, and from then onwards we never made a loss.

This profit event was a motivator and the size of our catalogue increased again, as did our advertising and the size of our competitions. Our prize list included a super prize of a house worth £4,000 (which today would not even buy the kitchen), plus eleven new cars and heaps of consolation prizes; all this was to back our biggest catalogue to date — over 900 pages and a winner — and it certainly did charm the ducks off the water earning record sales and profits. We produced our 'killer' catalogue of over 1,000 pages in 1962; we were the very first in the field. Some competitors missed this important point for which we were grateful. This idea could be promoted in simple words, 'The Catalogue with over 1,000 pages.' It was a great success.

Progress continued and the Barlow & Jones share price was moving up; it appeared that things were beginning to leak and it was now very necessary to give some information to their shareholders.

The chairman of Barlow & Jones, Eric Cartwright, and I decided that on this issue we should take the bull by the horns and in the annual company report dated 23rd September, 1961 he stated: —

> The group trading profit is £657,869, a record for the company and compares with £549,147 for the previous period of approximately eighteen months. This figure has been achieved through the excellent contribution made by the mail order group, John Myers, which has provided approximately 30% of the profits. This would be a magnificent effort at any time but it is particularly helpful during this period.
>
> During the year we received compensation for scrapping of machinery from the reorganisation scheme amounting to £89,180. We also received £106,848 for cost of re-equipment and our estimate of the figure outstanding is between £80,000 and £90,000. In the balance sheet we have provided for the lower figure of £80,000. I emphasise the terrible waste that occurred in the destruction of machinery to qualify for the grant.

These remarks written in the autumn of 1961 showed which way we were going; they *also* showed another thing, for which none of us received very much credit — how right it was to switch from textiles.

Be it noted that in that year Barlow & Jones actually received no less than £89,180 for scrapping spinning and weaving machinery while textile machinery was being exported to the third world.

Barlow & Jones — Report to Shareholders

21st September 1962

The group trading profit is £610,350, against £657,869.

John Myers & Company Ltd Mail Order Group contributed £316,000 representing an increase of 64% on their own profits and a contribution of nearly 52% of the total profits.

The excellent increase in profits is a striking tribute to the leadership of Mr S Cooke and the magnificent support of his co-director, Miss Adderley, and also the executives, buyers and staff. We are fortunate in having a very young team of senior executives of great ability which augurs well for the future.

During the whole of the past year textiles have been in a trough from which at present they show no sign of emerging. On the information now available it is quite obvious that the government's policy is to give facilities to the Asian countries at least to maintain their present level of textile exports to this country — it is equally obvious that the members of the six have no intention of allowing low priced imported goods to eliminate their home textile industries.

I pause here to repeat that not only were we allowing these cheap labour textiles into Great Britain to destroy our textile industry, but the government was actually paying textile manufacturers in this country with hard earned cash to smash up machinery. In those last two years Barlow & Jones received over £100,000 through this policy.

Acts like this of allowing almost unrestricted imports from developing countries at great sacrifice to our basic industries and job losses to our people with costly compensations should at times be remembered by our left wing lobbies, and communist countries and the like when they hurl abuse at Britain as a colonial power of the past.

I have quoted these remarks at some length for I consider the decision to sheer off from textiles was vitally important; the swift move made five years before with Myers was to pay off very handsomely.

Barlow & Jones shares advanced and fortunes were made. This was adequately summed up in *The Statist*, 23rd March, 1962.

> Probably the most interesting investment in mail order at the moment is John Myers. This house, which has the largest catalogue in the country, was acquired by the Manchester textile firm of Barlow & Jones together with its subsidiary, Pinnacle Warehouses, in 1957. The company pays its agents 12½ per cent commission, higher than the average, and has the benefit of the expertise of Mr S G Cooke, now vice-chairman and formerly a key executive with Littlewoods. In the year to June 1961 John Myers made a profit of £192,000 against a previous loss of £63,000, a turn round which reflects energetic and skilful management. The mail order business contributed 30 per cent of group trading profits in 1961. The proportion has since risen further, and may now well account for more than 40 per cent.
>
> The striking thing about Barlow & Jones is that the indicated mail order profits of around £240,000 suffice by themselves to give an earnings yield of almost 6 per cent on the present price of 42/3d for the 10s shares.

The shares were below par of 10/- when I joined them and started the Myers venture. In the recent spate of cotton failures one shudders to think of what might have happened to Barlow & Jones.

The press told the story—'Textiles need new approach,' 'Mail order issue,' cried another, 'Manchester brokers consider Barlow & Jones cheap at 46/-.' It will be seen that I had now taken up the position of vice-chairman of Barlow & Jones.

Yet I am sure that had B & J made an announcement that they were about to enter the mail order business or that I was directing the operation, their shares, indeed the whole company, may well have taken a hammering and the venture would have been still-born. The result for the shareholders would have been traumatic, for not only would they have seen their share prices fall, they would have lost the proverbial packet. It is a reminder once again that the company registration prior to 23rd November, 1916 was of the most vital importance.

I am still of the opinion that it is impossible to create a new business like Myers accompanied by a pre-announcement, simply because the plans would have to be disclosed either voluntarily or under pressure. Either way great damage would be done both by competitors and by exposure to the market, which would ultimately destroy the operation itself. I know that many of my friends would argue that without that pre-knowledge of a new venture intelligent comment on the company as a whole would be impossible. This only confirms my feelings that there will never again be another B & J/Myers situation. That is, of course, unless some original thinking in the capital market on new ventures can be brought about.

* * *

By the end of 1962 we knew that we would achieve, indeed even exceed our targets. We had an excellent team of enthusiastic executives and buyers, a first class office, a fully mechanised warehouse organisation, a thousand page plus catalogue, increasing profits and unbounded confidence in the future. We were now planning an 1,100 page catalogue for the autumn and winter of 1963.

In those days the Post Office joined in the spirit and nobly supported our promise that every order received by us, even four days before, would be delivered by Christmas. We worked Saturday and Sunday shifts, executive buyers and controllers would check orders in the warehouse and would prepare them for packing and if necessary pack them for post or rail; all in the farming vernacular, 'mucked in'.

At the end of every season the stock position came under heavy strain; at Christmas time last minute orders always rolled in, but we took the view that it was vital to give customer satisfaction so if no further supplies were available to us on time we had to *sub* (the mail order jargon for substitute), with a similar, or in some cases, a superior item, with no extra charge.

Gifts and toy orders had to be executed at any cost. I remember my son (just home from Oxford) chasing up and down the country for many toy items, especially *Fort Laramie* and *Fort Cheyenne*. We purchased them wholesale, and he even bought them from retail shops, sometimes at a price higher than that in our catalogue. We substituted one for the other as the story of both games was much the same anyway — 'Injuns'.

Our policy was that a few shillings lost on satisfying a customer was a good investment for the company.

Of course we did get our howlers; they were usually thrown out at the inspection stage. I remember a shirt being subbed for pyjamas, and it was rejected with a tired comment, 'Well, it was something to wear.' But again a good substitute in the toy section was a panda for a teddy bear. On men's slippers substitutes were nearly always acceptable, as long as they were better slippers at the same price.

* * *

When we took over Myers I decided that one of our most important aims was to create a catalogue of 1,000 pages, which would provide a wide appeal to agents and customers alike. At the same time it would dominate the advertising programmes . . . It had to be a closely guarded secret known only to a very few, and the work load would be considerable.

I reflect that when we took over Myers in 1957 the catalogue was little more than 100 pages; by 1959 it was 400 pages; by 1960 it was over 800 pages and in 1962 it topped the target of 1,000 pages. The secret had been well kept. Fortunately some of our critics and competitors missed the point and for that we were extremely grateful.

Apart from offering a very wide choice of merchandise, the big catalogue provided us with a ready made advertising slogan, which could be expressed in simple words — 'the catalogue with over 1,000 pages' (it was part of our original thinking). This tremendous advertising pull was part of a well thought-out plan and was a great bonus. Sales leapt by nearly fifty per cent and profits by nearly seventy per cent. In a short period the business had been transformed.

I have often been asked when I thought of the idea for the 1,000 page catalogue; the answer is that it came to me when we started in 1957. Another question invariably followed — how did we know we could do it? Well, in fairness to all and in gratitude, I quote from recollections of others and from the notes I made at a meeting we had with the printers way back in 1959.

Tony Baynham vividly recalled meeting us at London Airport. He wondered what problem we wanted to discuss so urgently. On the way we talked about everything under the sun. On arrival at the Kingston Works we sat around their mass produced canteen-type board table (later to be replaced by a much more elegant one), on chairs of a similar style. He remembers that after a cup of coffee I calmly said, 'Well, the question is can your organisation produce a 1,000 page catalogue?'

Our friend looked astonished, his eyes closed, and he gasped, 'Incredible, when?' I replied, 'By autumn 1961 or spring 1962. What is your answer?'

'Yes!' said Baynham still wagging his head. 'No! You're kidding,' he continued.

'Not so, we are in deadly earnest, it is part of our master plan,' I replied. We said we would produce that 1,000 page catalogue and we did. Eventually the catalogue reached 1,200 pages big.

* * *

We were ever watchful on the financial side as higher sales meant more money to be obtained, and more stock and more debtors.

The financial requirements were finally dealt with in the early summer of 1963. As a preparation, our discussions with Lazards had begun in earnest early in the year; company accounts were prepared for the half year, and were very encouraging. Sales were up by some 30 per cent and profits by a third. The first discussion was on hiving off the baby from the mother with a Stock Exchange quotation for the child, Myers — and the child incredibly would be bigger than the mother.

For the benefit of those who have not been involved in placings, hiving off or flotations I will try and explain the surroundings and some of the traditions and the infinite care involved in the preparation of statements for the investing public by the merchant bankers with contributions from solicitors, accountants, advisers and the company's directors, and all checked and double checked.

Many meetings took place with Lazards in their lovely old offices in Old Broad Street, London. Their old building had a quiet period look with a dignified entrance, a marble reception desk, and was staffed by well trained porters who gave me the impression that I was doing them a great honour in allowing them to take my bowler hat and umbrella.

An official (hardly the right name; perhaps a commercial Jeeves is a better description) ushered us to the board room floor via the private lift, indicating very carefully where our belongings had been deposited by his meticulous and loving hands. A knock at the board room door on arrival was always followed by a pause, then the door was reverently opened and we were ushered in. 'Mr Willis will be with you, gentlemen, in just a moment,' he murmured, bowed, and left.

The period board room was delightful with windows hung with rich velvet curtains matching the exquisite paintwork, a large highly polished board table, chairs in keeping, beautiful cigarette boxes and ash trays, two little alcoves, in which nestled two antique tables to hold the coffee pots and cups, and of course the sherry for celebration when the graduation days were over. I must confess that I rather liked the atmosphere.

At this, our first meeting, Derek Willis appeared, remarked on the weather and in a general light-hearted way let us understand that despite the big fee we would be paying, we were indeed being done a favour or even an honour in having Lazards look after our affairs — that was true!

The conversations started in earnest. There was a quiet knock on the door which opened very slowly, and the butler entered carrying a gleaming coffee pot, delightful china, with first class coffee, making the atmosphere relaxed. Willis talking slightly between his teeth, turned to me and said, 'You were an executive director at Littlewoods and Vice Chairman of Barlow & Jones, you know all about big business, but do you know that when these two companies are separated Myers will be a prize of which to be proud? If the figures that I have seen are correct,' he continued most politely, 'And I don't doubt that they are, the Myers shares, when we eventually go to the market will open at 30/- each.' I must have been deeply impressed for on my doodling sheet as I look at it today, I see in great scrawled figures 30/-. He was a modest man, for the shares eventually opened at 38/-; but that meeting was just a preamble. The later sessions were larger, not only in time but in the number of participants, until at last the table was full to overflowing.

Returning to the first session, which went something like this: —

Please let us fill in the history of the company — how, when and why? What does it do? Why do people buy this way?

Premises — Where are they? What did you pay for them? What are they worth? Who says so? If you expand, have you enough room? What will you do?

169

Management — Where does the power rest? What is the average age of your senior executives? Who has control after you? What happens should you both be killed?

Accounts — To what dates are your accounts produced and when available? When will the latest certified accounts of past profits be available? Reports on prior profits or losses will be required too. Who were the accountants and where are they?

Bankers — Who are they? What are your drawing facilities?

Contracts — What contracts are there with directors and for how long, and in what terms? Senior officers — Who have contracts, for how long, and in what terms?

Solicitors — Who and where are they?

[This is very important. I should explain that when issuing a prospectus the issuing house have their own independent accountants, auditors, and their own solicitors — we on our side had ours.]

The information is vital, for it all serves to protect the investing public, and the number of people increased at meetings as the proposition proceeded to its final conclusion, in the form of a series of national advertisements embodying not only the answers to the points listed above but a great amount of other detail as well. In short a prospectus.

We were asked to approve their advisers to the issue and they likewise approved our company advisers, I was questioned most seriously and in great detail, and earned their thanks for an exposition of the Myers business.

The final decision was that the two businesses should be separated by means of a hiving off operation.

I would give up my seat on the Barlow & Jones board, and Eric Cartwright would do likewise on the Myers board. John Myers would be a separate public company and have a share capital of £1,000,000 split into 5/- shares which would be distributed to present holders of Barlow & Jones shares. Willis concluded in a very solemn voice accompanied by a very wry smile, 'All this is subject of course to our statements being accepted by the Stock Exchange.'

At the next meeting Lazards produced a detailed draft document with full information on the business, premises and management, etc. We and our advisers were asked to check the details. When Freda Adderley came to the meetings, our merchant bankers were somewhat put out as there was no powder room provided, and a secretary was hurriedly detailed to make arrangements. At that time women were not considered to have the stuff of management in them; that view has changed with the years.

Fast progress was made, and more time taken at each meeting. I thought and said *sotto voce*, 'The sherry ritual must be near at hand.' Graduation time arrived, the door opened, the butler entered with clinking glasses and gleaming decanters containing various types of sherry, together with cigarettes for all who wanted them.

A new timetable was agreed and the date set for a further meeting — the final ritual of luncheon was a little nearer.

In the meantime the investigating accountants had begun their work at our premises, meeting a tight schedule, and how they worked!

Things were well organised, everything was coming together and after each meeting it was all carefully sewn up by the experts at Lazards, who would from time to time ask for further information and would recheck anything which was not crystal clear.

The final meeting reached the peak of rituals when we were invited to lunch. With a wide array of drinks it took place on the top floor and it was fitting that the windows revealed a magnificent view of the city. All the directors and managing directors seemed to be there, many of them great names in the financial world. I asked myself how could an issue fail with names and families like those? More so how right it was to have a long-drawn out ritual. The lunch was very good and so was the conversation, everyone seemed to be genuinely interested in us and not in the money or share side. Socialists may well say, what a charade. Until I had been through it all personally, I myself might have expressed similar but not such strong comments. But having sat in on all the major points of policy and disclosures and considered the fine print too, I was impressed, indeed won over, by their sheer professionalism, their uncanny touch and foresight, the unhurried patience and scrutiny of details. This was particularly so in the letter to the shareholders, couched in language that all could understand — no wonder our financial institutions are the envy of the world and our invisible earnings so good!

The documents from the reporting accountants arrived. They confirmed our own checking, and eventually at later meetings we saw the documents move to the final proof stage; included in these was the letter to the shareholders in Barlow & Jones advising them of their good fortune — with respect to the shares in John Myers, and that they were theirs for free!

The newspapers gave banner headlines carrying the message, 'Shares of Barlow & Jones up 13/- to 62/- on Manchester Stock Exchange'. In London they jumped 13/9d to 62/6d following the announcement of the projected rights issue and the proposals for reconstruction of the group to allow shareholders to have a direct interest in the equity of the mail order subsidiary.

The rating of mail order shares on the Stock Exchange was much higher than that of textiles and understandably so.

The financial split was due to take place in June, advertisements were to appear on 19th June 1963, share dealing to commence on the 25th. The letter from Barlow & Jones to the shareholders was despatched, the issue of stock underwritten, and the result a foregone conclusion.

I was at Lazards just before publication and I remember Willis, just like a father, taking me to the second board room, away from all the rest, and he asked me if I was happy about how things had gone. 'Yes,' I replied; 'Very, very happy.' We shook hands for the last time on that deal but we later sought their advice on a number of occasions.

The day of publication arrived and if there is a story anywhere the press will find it; they picked on the following item in the prospectus; I quote their words.

The life of 53-year-old Stanley Cooke, chairman and managing director of the John Myers firm of Manchester, has been insured for £400,000, and a director, Miss Freda Adderley, 39, is insured in the sum of £200,000.

In the event of their death by accident the John Myers company would collect the money.

You may be thinking that £600,000 is a vast value to put on the lives of just two people, but look at the success of this man and woman team. Six years ago the Myers firm traded at a loss of £29,000. Now it was getting a stock market quotation for its shares. Its profit is forecast at £440,000 and its capital is £1,000,000 [later our stock market value was over £10,000,000].

'It's just good business—it's just a matter of good housekeeping' was what the woman who has had her business ability priced at £200,000 said today when I spoke to her. She is 39 year old Miss Freda Adderley, a Director of the Manchester Mail order firm of John Myers, which has insured her life for £200,000. The Chairman of the company, Mr Stanley Cooke, is valued at £400,000. The money goes to the firm in the event of a fatal accident.

The woman who is worth nearly twice as much as Dennis Law told me in crisp and efficient terms that she didn't feel more important after her price tag had been written.

'We regard our Shareholders as a family and like the heads of any family, adequate financial steps have been taken to insure the future of the family. That is why the policies have been taken out.'

Men? She indicated merely, that they treat her as a business equal.

She was appointed deputy managing director in October 1963.

Insurance on the lives of top management is common today but in 1963 was quite new though it was regarded in financial circles as of great value in helping a company to recover from the early death of an executive whose contribution to profitability was crucial. The sums insured seemed large to the press in those days before high inflation overtook the country.

I remember that the night before these press releases I arrived home to find several reporters' cars in the drive. Mabel was quietly but firmly refusing any photographs though they had pleaded for just one. I slipped in via the kitchen. We had a business that lived by publicity but we both hated it on a personal level.

The telephone rang endlessly and the raves went on; the employees and the executives were very proud as they later displayed in a presentation to me. I too had my moments.

On the day dealings were to begin, I met up with Leng Smith of Peat, Marwick, Mitchell & Co, the reporting accountants—I said, 'I'm off to the Centre Court at Wimbledon—do you want to come along?' 'Sure,' he said, 'You could do with a bit of relaxing.' On arrival he said, 'Stay here at the gate—I want to get a newspaper'—he came back flourishing a newspaper, 'Look,' he said and there under the City column in banner headlines 'Myers makes a Happy Debut' and so it was.

Shortly after the launching we published our results for the year ended 30th June, 1963. There were the usual press comments. 'John Myers profits increase'. 'A flying start for John Myers'. 'John Myers beat forecast'. Another read:

John Myers, the Manchester mail order group which has the *biggest catalogue* in the trade, turns in a glowing set of figures today which will please those who bought the company's shares when they came to the market a month ago. The company, which emerged from the Barlow & Jones Textile Group reports a profit of £520,532 for the year ended 15th June, 1963 against £316,014.

The Myers famous catalogue is to get even weightier. The board says the next one will consist of a record 1,100 pages.

Nice as they are and kindly intended the trouble with these press and stockbroker praises is that helpful though they are intended to be, some do put directors on a treadmill. They restrict in more ways than one; they restrict adventure and debase courage — two very necessary requirements for real success — be it in public or private life. We received much help from stockbrokers, particularly Kitcat & Aitken (Kenneth Philpot) in London and Peter Henriques in Manchester; it was they who arranged a meeting in London where I addressed members of the financial world and press — it was a very good idea.

The following is a comment at that time from our principal bankers, a comment containing much truth and wisdom.

> It is probable you may think it rather disappointing that the excellence of your preliminary figures which of course very comfortably exceeded your profit forecast given at the time of introduction should have failed to have lifted your price by any substantial amount. It must however be remembered that there are *fashions in the stock market just as in any other market* and at the moment mail order companies — and there are not very many of them — are highly prized as pre-eminent growth stocks. The present price in effect carries a substantial capitalisation of future growth. It is in a sense capitalisation of a projection forward of your present earnings curve. *I suppose this is something that chief executives in your industry will have to learn to live with, for in effect you are never working on a norm, you are working against a projection that assumes higher efficiency and increased throughput and which does not allow for any setback on economic and political grounds.* I am not suggesting that your industry is the only one to which these conditions apply but I think it is very pronounced in the mail order business because of the very limited number of experienced executives and the relatively small number of companies which have established themselves on any substantial scale in this retail distribution field.

* * *

1964 was another year of excitement, and there were problems with which we had to live. First we had that new phenomenon of the industrial society, the go slow adopted by the Post Office workers; it seemed strange how the cheerful co-operative and often generous postmen could change like the wind at the whim of a vocal shop steward. This is how I recorded that episode in my annual report in that year of 1964:

> We entered our new trading year to the accompaniment of the Post Office 'go slow', and one-day strike, a sad and unfortunate disruption to business. However, like all problems, the trouble it caused was offset by the ingenuity it provoked.

This brought forth a commentary from the press, 'And even the lamentable breakdown of Her Majesty's mail, (which once had to go through at any cost) looks like acting as a stimulus'.

For example we sorted a large number of light parcels down to districts, likewise we delivered our letters by private carriers to the main cities for local delivery, thus cutting out long delays or go slows; in other words leap-frogging the junction centres of distribution and in effect restoring a normal delivery time. Many times we could even do the job cheaper, particularly when we used General Post Offices in other cities for delivery (having thus regained on delivery time by using our own vans) we could get a discount. We used our representatives to deliver at week-ends and despite the brotherhood of the union we used the railways for delivering smaller parcels. This in the future helped our bargaining power with them as the volume grew larger. We invited our agents to order once a fortnight; that was not only a speeding up process, it also effected big economies, for many of the economies would stick; the business transferred from the Post Office (much heavier parcels fortnightly) would be lost for ever and they in turn would be left with a lower volume with a huge staff demanding more money, and a public hell bent on reducing their dependence. They were left then with the three main ingredients to the destruction of any business, falling business, failing services, higher charges and just one other point, the lack of confidence on the part of the public — and so the position of the Post Office still deteriorates and will continue to do so until these points are realised and put right.

Earlier I mentioned postal charges. I quote for the sake of sober thought *delivery times* in 1967:

> *Analysis of parcel despatch, week ending 21st April, 1967*
> A random sample of 1,479 parcel despatch slips sent out during week ending 21st April has been analysed for delivery time. The resultant percentages are as follows:

	Daily	Accumulative	
Next day delivery	26.8%	26.8%	
2 day delivery	24.3%	51.1%	(note more than half delivered in two days)
3 day delivery	24.5%	75.6%	

People unused to this type of parcel delivery service may well think it a fairy story, but even after the huge increase in mechanisation in both post and rail at great cost, together with big price increases the service of our two main carriers, the post office and the rail has declined rapidly.

* * *

Another time consuming problem in 1964 was the abolition of retail price maintenance, RPM for short.

The Act was to abolish what is called price fixing — for many manufacturers at that time dictated the price at which their goods were to be sold, particularly items in the heavy domestic trade, such as washing machines, sewing machines, irons, electric fires, fridges, freezers, radios and the like, although many other goods were affected.

To abolish price fixing seemed fascinating on the face of it, as it seemed an easy way of reducing the cost of modern living. There were many people who had thought deep and long on this subject who realised that the business would go to the big chains, thus to the bigger, 'the mostest', and so it was. True, prices were reduced but so was service; it was a question of balance.

I summed this up in my annual report.

> Re-Sale Price Maintenance
> In this connection I feel the resulting effects on your company of the recent legislation will be minimal. In short I think there will be as many 'opportunities' as there are knocks. What I think has been wrong is the propaganda which has been spread suggesting that there will be huge reductions on a wide front, this will not be so. Reductions there will be at times, and of course there may be upward adjustments too, but it remains to be seen if in the case of reductions they are consistent with the maintenance of quality and service — a point which so far appears to have had too little attention.

Village and small town life altered, the local electrical shop disappeared and with it the local service. The cowboy service sprang up and with real service hard to come by many were the phone calls my wife had at home offering free inspection of the washer or fridge — no charge at all. Of course on the free inspection many serious faults were proclaimed, the service charges were excessive, and as the ardent salesman-cum-serviceman pressed home his point so service charges increased, not only by the cowboys, but quite naturally by the experienced and well trained company experts who became self-employed — for there was no control.

Our 1963/64 profits were up by 41%, and we entered the autumn and winter season with relish. The Reddish premises were extended with an entirely new building, part of which was ready to cope with the increased trade in the autumn and winter. Our expenses on catalogue and advertising now exceeded a million pounds per annum.

I was able to report in the summer of 1965 that the extensions to the Reddish premises were fully equipped and were now amongst the most modern warehouses in Europe.

Thinking of our packing lines reminds me of an amusing incident as one day in a very busy period I did my daily walk through the packing conveyor lines, exchanging a smile here, a word there. I came across a new packer dealing with a large number of small items and said to her, 'Are these out of stocks, Miss?' (We always despatched these items instantly.) She replied in broad Lancashire, 'Ah doon't know luv, I'm new 'ere meeself.'

I remember the little celebration when we made our 'first million' pounds profit in a year. The figures were to be brought out to me at home where Mabel had the drinks at the ready. We all had much to thank Mabel for, help, encouragement and understanding. It was a late summer evening, meaning that it had been wet all day, and, with the rain dying away, the setting sun drenched our lovely garden to welcome this great event. After just over eight years we had a huge catalogue, a turnover of some £12,000,000 and made a trading profit of over £1,000,000 — all in the face of tough competition, and achieved by a small band of dedicated people.

In mid 1965, another problem was the heavy increases in postal charges. Strange, or was it? Following the previous year's go slow almost all expenses seemed to be on the up. I suppose the wags would say, 'What did you expect, the silent reaper of inflation never waits.' I put my thoughts in my report which I quote:

> However I am a great believer that it is not by bemoaning our lot that we make progress, but rather that we concentrate on vigorous action to overcome the problems on hand. Steps to combat the impact of extra postal charges and other like expenses have been taken, for example we are making a very much increased use of bank credit transfers (remittances were paid in to the local banks). The revenue lost on postal and money orders (they were no longer required in big quantities) must have been very considerable. The Post Office lost out for ever.

As we neared the end of another momentous year with all its problems, our draft accounts showed that sales and profits had once again made considerable gains and we were set for a further record in 1966. The spring catalogue would reach a level of 1,200 pages, never attained by any competitor in my time.

The catalogue was brilliant, so was the sales competition. Business was brisk, sales hit another record at over £13½ million, and trading profits reached nearly £1¼ million.

But a General Election took place in March 1966, sweeping Labour to power with a big majority of over a hundred seats, and Labour Governments are not always helpful to big business.

My half yearly report to shareholders read thus:

> The trading period was extremely trying, faced as we were with the Credit squeeze, Selective Employment Tax (a vicious tax if ever there was one), increases in Purchase Tax and Bank Rate and very severe increases in Postal Charges.
>
> We estimate that the increased charges covering purchase tax, postal charges, SET and the like, together with the hundred and one little items all showing increased prices amounted to over £100,000. Fortunately your company, by means of rigid economies, was able to offset some of these increased charges.
>
> Profits were up by some 11 per cent for the period ended 31st December, 1966, against the comparative figure for 1965.
>
> Turning to the future, which as things stand is beset with falling production and rising unemployment, it is difficult to forecast results six months ahead etc, etc, for the next six months we will have to run quite a bit harder to stand still.

The press commented, 'John Myers, profits up 11% with three main points of policy—hold prices, no chasing sales, and, while the trading period remained difficult, to pursue the economy campaign.'

While the *Investors' Chronicle* dealing with the conception of mail order in general stated:

> Mr Stanley Cooke, chairman of John Myers, whose quietly insistent optimism is founded on a sturdy blend of calculation, enterprise and enthusiasm, holds firmly that the more successful the multiple stores and supermarkets become, the more mail order will flourish. It can offer all that these can at less trouble and at comparable cost. He concedes that the best stores put up formidable competition, but shrewdly contrasts the vast acreage and

under-employed staff of the representative store with the automated factory salesmanship and conveyor belt line for selection, packaging and despatch by which mail order firms maintain efficiency and precision with personal control and service.

It must be admitted that the number of ultra profitable break-throughs in mail order have been few and far between. But if genius — even rarely attainable — is needed for pioneer work, it can hardly be doubted that the necessary experience and skills will be found if potential rewards are great enough to attract them.

I never let these friendly comments upset my determination, but the continuing insistent demands for further information from stockbrokers and finance houses were a terrible time consuming operation.

The end of 1966 passed off well with good Christmas business and for the year ended 15th June, 1967, trading profit was at a new high.

In my annual report I stated:

> This is the 150th year of trading of John Myers, the business having been established as early as 1816. However, perhaps of much more importance to shareholders is the fact that we are now approaching the end of the tenth year of business under the present management. During that time (the last two years) sales have multiplied by something like three hundred times. Whilst profits were non-existent in 1957 — in fact there were losses — group pre-tax figures have now risen to the present figure of nearly £1¼ million. I mention these facts merely to indicate the rapid and continuous progress, and at the same time to pay tribute to your executive and management who have made this progress possible.
>
> *New Project*
>
> For quite a long time now we have had under active consideration the possibility of extending our present mail facilities, by offering a service generally known as a direct mail order service. I feel I need hardly mention that both in the financial world and the world of shopping journalism there has been confirmation of our own idea. Indeed some time ago one of your directors, Miss F J Adderley, visited the United States to survey this method of trading and as a result of this visit your directors decided to try and purchase a company at present in this field to handle this extension to your company's business. In the event we were unable to purchase a company at a reasonable price and we therefore decided to create one.
>
> This direct mail order service, under the name of Orbit Mail Order Company Ltd, is quite different from the agency service we now operate and will embrace people not presently served, in areas outside the scope of agents for one reason or another. Let me make it quite clear at the outset that this extension of trading will not affect our spare time agents in any way — it is, I repeat, a mere extension of our trading policy.
>
> I must take this opportunity to advise shareholders that new projects of this kind do not easily get off the ground and are quite costly in the initial stages and indeed you will see that your directors recommend a transfer of £250,000 to a Development Reserve Account. It is considered that this is the best way to indicate to shareholders some idea of extra costs involved. Please, therefore, do not expect quick profits during this year or next year but if we can (and I believe we can) achieve even a fraction of the success enjoyed by your company during the last ten years then these present efforts will have been well worthwhile.

The Press reviews were quite encouraging both to the idea and to me personally; among comments were:

177

The offer of a 500 page catalogue for personal use is dramatically larger than anything that the industry has so far produced for Personal Shoppers. [That was the idea à la Myers.]

Orbit has entered a personal shopping market and even though the success rate in this sector does not appear to be high, the man behind it is not one to accept failure lightly.

What is the prize for Orbit's boldness? If a high purchasing sector of the retail market can be attracted by the industry, a sector which is already familiar with careful budgeting, a sector therefore with a higher turnover even than the current mail order customer, then the prize will be commensurate with the boldness of this venture.

Chairman warns shareholders that the venture will involve considerable sums, and it is not likely to produce quick profit.

Whilst again *(Investors' Chronicle)*

The Manchester-based business of John Myers & Company was first registered as a private company in 1899. Its origins however, go a long way further back, for the concern was engaged in mail order trading (sometimes thought of as a peculiarly modern and, ipso facto, American invention!) almost as far back as the Napoleonic Wars. In fact, 1967 is the 150th anniversary of the business.

What however is important for the present shareholders of the new public company is, as Mr Stanley Cooke comments in opening his statement circulating the accounts, that an initial decade of trading under a new management is coming to an end. It has been a tremendous decade. During it sales have multiplied something like 300 times, and from a nil, or, more accurately, minus position, group pre-tax profits have reached the £1¼ m level.

Indicative of the fact that in the board's view this milestone merely represents the end of a build-up period, is the decision now to engage in direct mail order trading.

Three vital factors prescribe optimism in looking for a continuation of this outstanding performance in 1967/68 (apart that is from the internal influence of the new trading development). These are cited by Mr Cooke as (a) continued rising costs, (b) rumours (it is to be hoped false) of yet more rises in postal charges and (c) the unhappy trend of unemployment figures.

Yet, this was of no avail, the market wanted quick returns. No one can blame them but it isn't always possible.

Despite problems, we came to a happy year ending June 1968 and I reported for that period as follows:

I am therefore pleased to report to you that the Trading Profit of John Myers & Company Ltd, (exclusive of the development charge of Orbit) at £1,388,903 before taxation was the highest in your company's history . . .

I also think shareholders might be interested in the profit record of your company since it became a public company in 1963.

Profit before Taxation	
1963	502,208
1964	711,029
1965	931,109
1966	1,127,138
1967	1,244,874
1968	1,338,903

It is as well to remember that this growth in profits was achieved before the era of high inflation.

But life isn't all unending success. As one of my friends said, "There is a slow movement in every symphony." So next year our profits slumped badly to £719,791 (I suppose to many medium sized companies today, that figure might be even joyful). In that year the Post Office work to rule and strike caused not only serious delays in delivery of our spring and summer catalogue, our very life-blood, but also in the delivery of goods to our agents. (It is surprising how often since the 1960's the Post Office and Railways go slow or strikes have occurred quite regularly but we had to live with them.) The 1968 Purchase Tax increases supplemented by the Chancellor's Budget of 1969 had the inevitable effect of a severe reduction in demand in the electrical, hardware and furniture sections and these were the goods with the highest unit sales value. It was not only this, but margins were further reduced by increased postal charges, National Health Insurance contributions, carriage charges and bank interest — a sizable package. We absorbed these charges pending the issue of the autumn catalogue and the great majority of our agents were faithful.

No, problems never come singly! I tell these not as excuses, but as reminders to any rising young entrepreneur that continued unbroken success can never be guaranteed — as many great companies realise today, no matter how hard they try.

So at the risk of repetition, I turn to the Orbit development and refer to my statement issued the previous year (it was really an appeal for understanding) when I said that:

> I must take this opportunity to advise shareholders that new projects of this kind do not easily get off the ground and are quite costly in the initial stages, etc etc. Please therefore do not expect quick profits . . .

I make these points because within days of issuing my statement I was persistently asked two questions: 'How soon will a profit be made?' 'How much will the development cost in total?'

Yet again, a responsible financial house came out with this:

> The Chairman has warned shareholders not to expect quick profits in the next two years. It has been estimated that it takes £5m to bring a new direct mail from scratch but for a company such as Myers, already firmly established in the mail order field, the cost should be very much less. Even so, the initial losses will put a further strain on the cash flow and may make future dividend increases more difficult.

Of course it would not have cost anything like £5m and that paragraph, particularly the last sentence was damaging. On the other hand it only needed one small addition to the last sentence to be very helpful, such as — *Even if it did cost one or two million out of profits it would be a small price to pay for another Myers story.* It needed just that to encourage another fortune.

I have recalled earlier how we managed at John Myers, by one way or another, with stealth and little or no publicity to rebuild the company to a very profitable position before bearing the full glare of financial analysis and publicity. I still vigorously maintain that had the development become widely known it would have been killed stone dead and Barlow & Jones shareholders would have suffered much; instead they had a bonanza. The problem about early announcements or publicity, then and even more so now, is that you can't avoid notifying your competitors as well as your friends.

I don't blame the 'financial boys' for trying to squeeze out information; it is their job to do so on behalf of their clients, but I wish that there was some answer to the problem, for I feel that many good ideas never see the light of day. The difficulty is how to 'square the circle'.

The new Orbit enterprise started well, and it made a planned initial loss just as Myers did in the early days. We knew it would certainly make a loss in the next year and possibly the year after that. We never got to the third year for we came under pressure from some of the financial people who expected profits immediately. Of course, new ventures do not operate that way, it would be very nice if they did, but I realise that the stock market too had to meet the expectations of its clients. The theme was 'Orbit wasn't making profit' — I said it wouldn't for some time.

But pressure continued, this and a lack of resolution in some quarters made it inevitable that Orbit would go. I must say though, I sighed many times for the secrecy of the early days when we rebuilt Myers. Many years afterwards a stockbroker, Kenneth Philpot, said to me, 'It was a pity about Orbit. You were ten years in front of yourself!' I could hardly have been in front of myself but I knew what he meant.

The Orbit idea was sound as later developments have so vividly proved. It was damned in some quarters because there was no immediate promise of a quick return which gave rise to the inevitable sniffing around and ultimately the take-over crews. This was understandable and I make no protest, for I had done the same myself years before.

It always seemed to me that the Orbit idea was a natural for the future development of mail order business for the following reasons. The field of 'would be' agents is limited and as competition increased for their services there would be a further spread in the number of customer/agents, followed by a dilution in their size. There is no great wisdom in that thought for as more competed for the cake, the slices (the size of agents) would get smaller. We realised that early on when we had the Myers programme of domination in advertisments, catalogues, competitions and commission. Smaller agents are more costly to operate for many reasons. As parcels got smaller they would travel by post which is more costly and the head office cost of operating a smaller agency would be little different to a large agency, and advertising would be less rewarding.

We now see quite a move in home shopping which in short means no agents, therefore existing agencies would in future be smaller and the number of different customers greater.

Indeed only a few months ago I received a circular from one of the big groups on the lines of:

Dear Mr Cooke,
Why not shop in the comfort of your own home? *You do not have to be an agent.*

As I was checking the proof of this page, further confirmation of the switch to direct mail order business appeared in the *Daily Telegraph* of 12th October, 1982 on Grattan, one of the last remaining big companies.

> First-half pre-tax profit of mail order group Grattan slumped from £2.65m to just £1m. Chairman Michael Pickard strikes a very cautious note for prospects in the rest of the year but hopes that benefits from the modernisation programme should show through thereafter.
>
> He is also pinning his hopes on two new direct mail order catalogues going out to customers.

I notice now that many concerns opt for 'home shopping' which is another way of indicating 'the Orbit' idea of direct shopping — yes, I think we have been vindicated.

* * *

In late 1969 I had an urgent telephone call from Lord Poole (Lazards), inviting me to London to meet an important client of theirs about a bid for Myers. I was not very enthusiastic but I went, and met the great American company, ITT (sometimes called the Sovereign State), one of the biggest conglomerates in the world, with interests in insurance, telephones, communications, car hire, bread-making, mail order, you name it, they would have some sort of finger in the pie; they were said to have the highest paid chief executive in the world, one Harold Geneen.

The ITT top brass were there already. Jim Goodson was the big shot, vice president of ITT Europe Inc. Another I remember vividly, P H Spagnoletti, of ITT London was a charmer, mild and quiet in manner. Jim Goodson was just the opposite to Spagnoletti, he was a very big man, thrusting as only an American can be, smoked almost continually the largest line in cigars and wore what seemed to me the biggest line in cuff links, almost gold nuggets.

After the preliminaries we eventually discussed Myers. ITT were more than interested in Myers, and would very much like to be involved in a takeover but above all they wanted the management and they did not say why, that would come later. We pored over figures, theirs and ours.

The haggling went on next day. It was revealed they owned a mail order company in Italy. They admitted it was pitifully small by our standards and losing a lot of money, and what they wanted from us was management. The tentative offer was absurdly low. Goodson suggested he would phone Geneen. I said, 'Surely he will be asleep.' 'No matter, he will always answer the phone,' came the answer.

Their financial experts were called in from their European headquarters in Brussels. They arrived complete with computer information and slide rules; the assembly was two deep around one end of the table. Evening came, and we were getting no further. The currency expert reminded them that they did not have sufficient currency available in Great Britain, that was vital. He put the shortfall at around 7,000,000 dollars. That was brushed aside with, 'What's 7,000,000 dollars to us, why, we are in the course of taking over Harvard, one of the biggest insurance companies in the States.'

We seemed to be getting nowhere, then Lord Poole and I went into another room. He explained that Lazards were advisers to both ITT and Myers, and said, 'Obviously, this can't go on.' I agreed. He continued, 'I should emphasise that what they really want is your management. They have an idea that mail order could be big in Europe and they have in mind that your British management could direct both Myers and their operation.' I considered this and I agreed we should withdraw as the proposition was unattractive.

In December 1970 ITT were back again with another proposal. My notes read, 'The meeting was called to discuss the possibilities of Myers acquiring an interest in "B" of Milan. They were very frank and went on to explain the disastrous postal system in Italy, and implied that Italy was strike ridden.'

While I was keen on getting a toe-hold in Europe I did not fancy doing it this way. ITT had estimated that there was a market potential of some £250m. I had little doubt they were right, however we could not see this badly needed turnover coming from their present system. We advised a much bigger catalogue and an approach to credit sales via the club system. We suggested this method because Italy was family orientated and the possibilities were excellent.

Apparently they had approaches from another (Italian) mail order company and they thought there was scope in creating a consortium of the three companies, that is 'B' (ITT), the other Italian company, and John Myers, who would provide the expertise in exchange for part of the equity.

Finally they sent us further details of the Italian company and shortly afterwards two of Myers directors went to Milan to look over the organisation. Freda Adderley prepared a report, and it was not conducive to further negotiations, indeed the outfit was extremely small and a lot of money had gone down the drain. The second company seemed to consist of a large shop and a small catalogue and this was no good. The detailed report was presented to ITT and we expressed no further interest. The whole thing seemed to me to be peanuts to ITT—but their wider vision was right.

During this period we had two approaches from Sir Isaac Wolfson of GUS. I have already described my earlier meeting with Sir Isaac in my Littlewoods days; meeting him was always an experience. At this first takeover approach he showed me his marvellous collection of paintings by Spencelayh. He said he wanted to take us over, I replied, 'I guess so.' 'Yes,' he continued, 'I have a very big holding of your shares, I could buy more.' I replied, 'No doubt.' He said with a wry smile, 'Do you know Mr Cooke, I could also sell them.' I needed no explanation of the last point. He continued, 'On the other hand I thought perhaps you and I could get round the table and arrange a deal.' I told him I thought not. He went on, 'You see, all agreements would be honoured, the staff would be looked after and so on.' I believe he would have done that too. But back he came on to price. 'I could pay you the present market price, with perhaps 2/- extra or a little more, but I tell you now, I do want the company.' 'Yes, I know,' I replied, 'But you will never get it at that price, and I couldn't go along.' He said, 'Will you think it over? If you are as interested as I think you will be, come and have lunch with me at my home in Worcestershire.' I agreed to think it over on my way back north.

Back home my wife told me that Sir Isaac Wolfson had just phoned and he wanted me to ring him back as soon as possible. I phoned after a good think over things. I was pressed to think again. I said I would consult my colleagues, and in addition I should want to speak with our merchant bankers. I rang off cheerily. Early next morning he was on the phone again. I said we were not really interested but I would be seeing our merchant bankers. I saw Lazards and we agreed to go no further, and they spoke to Sir Isaac immediately; the conversation was short, pleasant and to the point, and Isaac Wolfson, with his usual courtesy, asked if he might have a word with me, he said 'You want to be left alone then? Fair enough.' 'Yes,' I replied, and that seemed to be that.

Later in the year I had a phone call to my office. 'Sir Isaac Wolfson of GUS would like to have a word with you.' I agreed to take the call. He was on the line immediately. 'So nice to speak to you again,' he said genially. 'I was just wondering when you and Miss Adderley would be in town, we would have much to chat about on common ground, just a friendly lunch, the three of us.'

We went to London, Isaac Wolfson met us on the landing outside his office. We were welcomed like long lost friends. As usual he was very polite and kind. 'Do come in right away. I have so looked forward to this little gathering. Oh! I am so sorry I have slipped up, so unusual of me to forget, but we had a board meeting arranged for this morning, so most of the board will be in at lunch, sorry about that, but they are a nice lot of fellows, and they will all like to meet you.'

He was very jolly, saying, 'I'm getting old and want to see everything settled for the boys. I like you! We could do a deal, on a really friendly basis. There would be much to gain.' Once more we mulled things over. He was frank, and said to me personally, 'Of course there wouldn't be room for someone like you in our organisation but we would honour all obligations.' I replied, 'That is the least of my concerns.' He pushed across his desk two ornaments—one marked big deal the other small deal. Quite a novel way to open a discussion.

At lunch he was witty as always, and picking up the cutlery (Mappin and Webb), he exclaimed, 'Good cutlery, specially hired today for you!'

We talked over many things, sales, prospects, margins, the lot. There was no nitty gritty bargaining. He was a very sparse eater and seemed to be like a piece of spring steel, jumping up now and then to take the odd call from Tel Aviv. Luncheon over, he repeated in an aside 'Nice lot of chaps, think about my idea and let me know.' With that, and hands on our shoulders, we walked to the lift. 'And now,' he concluded, 'I must check that my car is ready to take you to Euston.' It was, and the chauffeur. I felt, and still do feel, that however shrewd he was, above all he was friendly, correct and polite, despite his great financial power. It all came to nothing; the offer was not one we could consider.

* * *

We had yet another approach, via a third party, who suggested that a very large concern wanted to get into mail order in a big way, and they had plenty of money! We were always strongly opposed to a takeover, but one cannot refuse to talk without incurring comments, although it is so time consuming.

The suitor now making an approach was another big High Street outfit — United Drapery Stores (UDS). We met on neutral ground at the Midland Hotel, Manchester. Their negotiator was Jacob (Jack) Sampson, their chairman and a big shareholder in UDS.

Mr Sampson (I later knew him as Jack), was small, erudite and likeable, endowed as most Jews are with the ability to take the mickey out of himself. The manoeuvring overtures had gone on long enough. I said, quite bluntly, 'I understand you are interested in our company.' 'Very,' he replied. I continued, 'I understand too, that if a bargain was arranged, and it would have to be very good, you have plenty of ready money to pay for it!' He exploded with mirth, this was part of the act. 'Money!' he cried, 'We haven't got any money.' This was hardly correct but what he was trying to convey was that they did not want to pay out very much money.

This first talk came to no conclusion, but they were in some dilemma. I quote from an article on mail order in the magazine *Business* of March 1965.

> Here, as with the handling of agents and preparation of the catalogue, the new entrant must either spirit away senior executives from existing companies, or buy experience the hard way and at great cost. United Drapery seems to have recognized the dilemma and has bought two tiny agency companies, but problems will remain and UDS shareholders would be unwise to get excited for a few years.

It is a pity they did not appear to heed the warning. I later had a phone call. My notes read:

> They would not bid unless they had 35% secure votes. (I did not reply) — also full figures — promised to speak to board — did so — advised them that not available for talks until September or first week in October.

Again from my notes:

> Our view has always been that the end of September was vital to our shareholders' interests, simply because we have arranged our business flow to this end and as we have to wait until the end of September to really estimate the position for the winter, it follows that on the one hand early settlement is essential, whilst on the other it is not in the best interests of our shareholders unless the price fully covers our future position.

An early settlement was essential to them for they had a catalogue print sharing arrangement with a third company. This arrangement, which seemed to be anything but friendly, was about to come to an end.

They also had merchandise problems, apart from the catalogues; before Jack Sampson left he had his say and made a point which eclipsed all others. I quote:

> That if any deal ever came about one prior condition would have to be met — 100% retention of management by agreement.

184

He recognized that continuity of top management was vital but that failed to mature. A pity and a mistake for which they may have paid very dearly.

I later had another call from UDS with yet another suggestion, an idea which could be developed to deal with the question of timing and also resolve their catalogue sharing problem. My notes read:

> The proposition was to hive off their mail order interests to Myers with the price payable partly in shares and the remainder in loan stock. Indications were that cash would be available for development. Arranged meeting Wednesday, 20th August to discuss viability and instructions to advisers. [The development in my time was of no significant proportion.]

Their three small mail order interests were centred in Manchester (headed by Atlas); the proposition was risky but it had its attractions.

At a meeting the suggestion was discussed in detail, it was agreed that it could be ideal from many angles (providing Atlas was in fact making a profit to the tune of £100,000 per annum).

There were risks of course from Myers point of view, particularly if later on an all out bid was made for the company; but reflecting on our duty to shareholders we felt they could not lose out and they did not.

We discussed the matter with our respective advisers; their correspondence was long, deep and searching.

We always accepted that the quality of their mail order management could not be too dynamic otherwise it would have gone places. There was the quality of agents too, an item which could not be accurately assessed for very many months. If agents did not re-order then they were valueless, on the other hand if they did, they would be very valuable.

Atlas etc. had an overall loss position and therefore accumulated tax losses which could be put to good use by slanting the emphasis of sales to the Atlas group by using Myers expertise and catalogue, which in my view, was very important.

In the early days of 1970 we completed the takeover. The press reaction was very mixed.

We were now free to visit the installations. Even accepting that it would be unfair to compare a highly efficient and large organisation like Myers with this acquisition, we were not happy. The quality of the agents worried me, I just could not see the majority of them lasting very long, which in turn would mean even greater effort to maintain sales, *but it was necessary* for there was still the tax loss we could use and that would be a plus to the Myers' overall position.

So then, it was not a very happy start, but with our usual spirit we decided to make the complete outfit work, whatever our inner feelings and whatever our eventual inheritance.

* * *

We worked with a vengeance and slanted priority of advertising toward Atlas. It was vital that they made a profit, and they did, with the strength of Myers behind them. It was certainly a strain, and the benefit to Myers was hardly commensurate with the effort, but we had extra names to play with in advertising and we gave them the Myers treatment. All things considered it went along quite well; the tax losses were absorbed, stocks were combined to free finance—all very useful. We could utilise little of the management, as it did not exist in quality at most levels.

We now had a mixed board of Myers and one UDS director. It would be untrue if I suggested things were harmonious. What we did have was an enormous increase in paperwork, statistics in short. This I criticised on the basis that extra paperwork tied executives to the desk and did not necessarily improve the business, a point so well illustrated in *The Wild Wheel* by Garet Garrett, Cressett Press, 1952.

> The story goes Ford had a kind of feeling for statistics that most people have for snakes, even friendly snakes. 'Too many figures,' he said, 'Make your head swell up like a drum.' Nevertheless they persuaded him to let them make a few figures just to prove how useful they might be, only a few. He had forgotten all about it, when one day a year later, he stood rigid with bewilderment on the threshold of a large room full of computing machines, tabulating typewriters, mimeograph equipment, people drawing lines on large sheets of quadruled paper, and some coloured charts on the walls. He beckoned to a person who looked up and Ford said to him, 'What's this?' The startled person said, 'This is our statistical department, Mr Ford.'
>
> He stared for a moment with the look of one trying to remember something, then he turned and walked away.
>
> In the yard he found Sorensen [the great production executive of Ford] and said to him, 'Did I hear you needed some space?' Sorensen said, 'I need space like hell.' Ford said, 'In that corner on the second floor where I'm pointing there is a big room. I just happened to look into it. A lot of people making figures. You can have that space if you will go and take it.'

He was right. Financial boys and the whizz kids create paper; the entrepreneur is the catalyst who creates wealth.

Temporarily we were on a treadmill, but with prodigious efforts we fused the companies by the autumn of 1970.

In the early spring of 1971 an all out postal strike was called, this lasted many weeks. In the end it probably did more harm to the country's postal system than it did to its customers. A severe postal stoppage to a mail order business could well have been the kiss of death, at best there was a massive loss of sales and a sharp increase in expenses. The delay in receipt of payments caused a reduction in the money supply, but we got through. I pressed everyone to use all their initiative. We installed groups of answering machines throughout the building, so that orders could be phoned in by our agents day or night; the tapes were transcribed by our staff and a substantial volume of orders was despatched locally by our own transport and to distant destinations by rail or private carrier; very small parcels and envelopes just had to wait.

Throughout the country we organised pick-up points where our agents could deposit their cash and orders and in this we had the tremendous co-operation of two prominent national companies who very generously made facilities available at their numerous premises, for which we were very grateful. Above all, during this disastrous and crippling strike our main job was to keep contact with our agents at all costs, not only because it was a critical time in mail order, but also to ensure the continuity of goodwill and spirit of togetherness which characterised the relationship between agents and the company.

It was no good disguising the fact that sales losses were heavy, the great question was whether the mail order business would flow away for ever to the big stores? We produced sales leaflets (containing very special offers) and they were enclosed with all the thousands of parcels we were able to despatch; and just as important they were enclosed in all the light packets awaiting the end of the strike.

* * *

One question that dominated our thoughts was how best to get the parcels and mailing away once the strike was over? It was essential to do this very quickly.

The local postmaster was not on strike; we obtained from him a copy of the sorting and transfer points, and agreed how the packets could be made ready for immediate delivery once the strike was over. The copy of the 'roads' (the postal trails) as they were called, provided by the thoughtful postmaster, was vital; now we could at least prepare. My deputy organised a complete sorting system; the packing room became a huge sorting office, parcels and packages were sorted down to the tiniest village. When completed each container held the entire mail for one *main road*, the letters and parcels in each main road were sorted down to bundles for lesser routes within the road system. In the lesser bundles were smaller bundles and so on down to the tiny bundles for the very little hamlets. Each packet of parcels was bundled up and labelled, just as the postmaster wanted.

We agreed with the postal chief that our staff would be available to hand over the sorted mail within minutes of the strike ending and our warehouse would remain open night and day until clearance had taken place. He estimated that if the strike finished in the afternoon, all would be cleared by 3 am next day. Finally like all good and bad things, the strike came to an end. The postmaster was true to his word and the clearance took place rapidly. The incoming mail came flooding in with a huge accumulation of orders and cash; things began to look good, very good.

It was quite the opposite with our new associates who, it seemed, expected hour by hour statistics; emergencies are not handled that way. Apologies were offered when the money started to roll in and it was called a fantastic job. I had the feeling — *Too late the phalarope.* Relations never seemed the same again. But the press was much more understanding — *The Daily Express* banner headlines read:

'Housewives stay faithful to Mail Order . . .', followed by 'As the postal service returns to what it laughingly calls normal, the men who had more reason than most to shudder over the effects are beginning to learn to smile once more'.

Within our board room things were far from happy, the once jovial and encouraging atmosphere was gone. I sensed, as one does with experience, that there was an attempt to divide our happy camp; I felt we had a Trojan horse in the gathering. Someone else wanted the top place, that was very evident. I decided that there was no time like the present to deal with such matters.

At the next board meeting I raised the question of succession, just in case I became ill (shortly afterwards I was). I wanted to get this crystal clear, but met with no success. That eventually must have proved to be tragic to some, if not all of them.

We pressed on, despite feelings, for as the deputy managing director said to me, 'At least souls had been searched and some were found wanting.' In my opinion that meeting and all that followed was a disaster, and must have cost UDS dearly in the end. I think it is sufficient for me to recall that I had stated with some force that in the event of the chairman's and deputy chairman's departure, the loss to the business could be quite serious. The company might stand one going, few businesses could withstand both.

We published our annual accounts for the eighteen months ended 31st January, 1971, showing a more than useful profit. *The financial press* had got the position right.

> *THE TIMES*
> MYERS MAIL ORDER GAINS
> During the latest period Myers sales topped £27½m and pre tax profits were £1,030,000.
> The acquisition [Atlas etc] contributed losses in the early months of 1970 and profits at the end of the period. (Myers) share price has increased from 110p to 162p.
>
> *FINANCIAL TIMES*
> Turnover included 12 months of the acquired companies although they did not contribute to Profits until the end of the period. Although the profit increase is marked it would have been some £200,000 higher had not the Postal Strike affected January sales to a considerable degree.
>
> *DAILY MAIL*
> Mail Order Bounces Back . . .

And so it went on through to the Guardian, Scotsman, etc. I had my moments still, and happy they were!

The 1969 fall in profits was the only setback we had and we never made a loss.

* * *

Towards the middle of 1971 I had a most friendly telephone call from Bernard Lyons the chairman of UDS, who asked me to meet him at Ringway Airport for a private chat. Could Miss Adderley and the other directors be around say about an hour afterwards? We met at the Airport Hotel; he was very friendly, I was sure I knew what was coming, and I was right.

We talked about the crowded flights, our families and farms, eventually I said, 'So, what?' He commenced, 'We thought that it might be as well for all of us if we did things together, more together.' I seemed to remember thinking that's what the girl said to the soldier, and said, 'Shall I spell out what I think you mean. You mean an all-out takeover?' He said, 'Yes,' and coughed, 'You see you would still be chairman and of course we would like you to join our board, but *one of the vital points we would insist on would be retention of the present management.* If there was no continuity there would be no takeover.' Exactly the same creed expressed by Jack Sampson so many months earlier. In retrospect I wonder whether they regretted not sticking to this creed in the years that followed, or put another way round, how much worry and money it might have saved them had they done so. No! I have never understood why they moved from the original idea of the retention of all management.

My two colleagues arrived. My deputy was not sold on the idea at all. After the previous arguments early in the year, she firmly believed that they did not like women in business. (This was before the Sex Discrimination Laws.) Would I think it over? Yes, but I could not see what there was to think over without a price. It was agreed then that it would be mulled over until something tangible came forward. Again the management creed was propounded; that was very sound. In the meantime we did our sums, consulted Lazards, and then awaited developments.

* * *

I vividly recall the next move. My wife and I were at Wimbledon. Just before the players came on court for the first final, the loudspeakers boomed, 'Will Mr S G Cooke proceed to the telephones to take a very urgent call.' It was as I expected; could I attend a meeting with UDS, or our bankers, or both? I said no, I wanted time. I reflected that it was at Wimbledon I got news of our first dealings as a public company all those years ago.

I was told there was some concern in the City as Myers share price was rising rapidly. I remember saying, 'Well it certainly would not be our side that leaked, and there was little I could do about things in the absence of something concrete.' I was assured there was something concrete, so I concluded, 'I will see the match then I will come to the City.' Which I did.

I had heard that in early June there was buying in shares and loan stock at ever advancing prices; of course they were perfectly entitled to do so. Lazards as usual were kind and helpful, they had had a tentative offer but it was not to my liking. However, forgetting myself and my colleagues, I had a job to do for the shareholders.

I talked to Lazards and met them later that afternoon. They were aware of the suitor's ever increasing stake and agreed that very soon we would have to issue a statement; it had to be only simple but they advised that we ought to do so on the following Monday. I was asked to phone UDS with my reactions, and I did so saying

I did not like the way things were being done, neither did I like the price. I realised I was on slippery ground in view of their increased holding, therefore I would need time to think things over and arrive at a possible announcement.

I produced an announcement we could support. Bernard Lyons could not agree with me but he would consult his advisers further — ultimately we agreed.

The press got a release and they went to town. 'MYERS BID STIRS UP MAIL ORDER BOSSES — REDDISH JOBS ARE SAFE — UDS BACK TO MAIL ORDER IN A BIG WAY — A BALANCED CHOICE FOR MYERS SHAREHOLDERS — WHO LEAKED THE MYERS UDS MERGER TALKS?' This last one continued,

> And some angry ex-shareholders in John Myers & Co must be upset about the hole in the security at United Drapery Stores. Some 45 minutes after Stock Market dealing got under way yesterday morning, Mr Sampson and the Myers Chairman, Mr Stanley Cooke, issued a joint statement that in view of the recent rise in the price of the Ordinary Shares of Myers the two were talking about United taking over the 66 per cent of Myers which it did not already own. Just a week ago, the Myers shares were standing at 160p but they put weight on steadily through last week, and ahead of the announcement of the talks yesterday were up to $182\frac{1}{2}$p — what a leak! Those who sold Myers shares over the last week must be particularly upset that no one thought to tell them what all the interest was about. In fact United plans to make an offer worth 200p for each share in Myers half of it in Ordinary Shares of United.
>
> In spite of the hefty 34% holding United already has in Myers, Mr Sampson might find himself on the receiving end of a rebuff unless he does something about boosting the offer. Could it be that the bigger plans slipped out of Mr Sampson's pocket because his talks with Mr Cooke were proving tougher than expected? The bid was increased to 220p. Yet to judge by the Myers price it looked as if talks started some seven days ago at least, without a happy ending.

But I think the *Investors' Guardian* said it all succinctly

> The UDS bid for Mail Order Group John Myers unfolding this week is a classic case of allowing someone else to do the spadework and, providing you have the strength, claim all the advantages. It also says a lot for the benefit of scale.
>
> About fifteen months ago UDS ran a smallish Mail Order outfit and finding its size prohibited any real profits contribution, sold it off to Manchester based John Myers in return for about 30 per cent of the equity. Possibly John Myers realised it had taken a viper to its bosom but perhaps the advantage of rationalizing both businesses under one roof proved too tempting.
>
> Presumably UDS must have found the recovery of John Myers from a previous trough too tempting as well, hence the 200p.

Eventually the takeover was completed on the strict understanding that all the management would stay on. The original intention to ensure continuity was very sensible, but it was not carried through.

I have always felt sorry for those who are taken over — when a few men or women who have created a living thing only to see their fruits removed by money; in short the work of creation, is wiped out by the power of money. Money is not everything, it is certainly no food for the soul, but I suppose it is business.

My wife, son and close friends gave me strong advice that in the interest of my health I should not sign any long term contract. I decided to carry on for a while to protect the staff and secondly I was proud of what had been built and still wanted, even ached for, it to grow.

* * *

On joining the board of the new group I sketched out my views on the probable and possible development of retail trading, particularly those parts that affected mail order.

I surveyed the possible acquisition of one of the remaining independent mail order companies, which in that rapidly shrinking field would be difficult. By their very nature the individuals who controlled these remaining enterprises would fight hard for their autonomy, therefore even if a deal were possible the price would be extremely high. We had seen that happen before, so this was not on.

For quite some time before I met UDS I had contemplated the use of catalogue shops. To do this a lot of shops would be required. UDS had them! So now I turned to this idea. There was more than one approach to this scheme (these were the heady days of development), one idea was the creation of hyperstores with built-in catalogue offices, where both agents and customers would be catalogue browsers, and where their cash could be paid in, so very big savings would be effected in postal and transport charges and catalogue costs. Orders would be transmitted to the warehouse daily and goods would be delivered overnight by road trunker service to the shops, for collection by the customer; the economies can be imagined. There were many variations to the theme. Of course there would be difficulties but experiments could be made at a comparatively small cost, however this idea was not developed. I could understand the reasons and risks. As events proved I was not alone in thinking of the possibilities of one or other of the ideas. About that time Mr Tompkins of Green Shield stamps developed a slightly different operation with his Argos chain of catalogue shops. He scooped the pool, selling out in a comparatively short time and at a high price.

Maybe the system will be developed one day, but it needs two vital things—a great number of retail outlets and a sizable mail order rump—others may have failed in their effort—because of the missing rump.

In the autumn of 1971, my doctor warned me that I needed a serious operation. I tried desperately to settle a management plan which would enable me to retire. I offered to stay as a consultant, and I would be willing to reduce the time spent with the company gradually on the basis of a day less each year until I was sixty-five. I felt this would ensure protection for the company and its staff and a smooth transfer of authority. I thought it was ideal for all concerned but this idea was not accepted.

There is an old saying, 'You can't catch old birds with chaff'. While I was not old, I knew my way about and I was more than ever convinced that there was a move afoot to eliminate the two top directors; it may seem strange but it eventually happened that way.

I still hoped that perhaps better judgement would prevail. It was obvious that in the mail order field, the available top entrepreneural experience was very limited. Past excursions had proved there were so very few that knew the whole of any business. But mail order is a non-starter if the one or two at the top do not have the personal drive and full knowledge not only of the organisation, but the subtle approach to advertising and catalogue construction; they also need spirit, determination and dedication. So I guessed that while it would be possible for them to let one of the top two go, it could be dangerous to lose both.

I spoke to my colleagues in London and told them that in view of my impending operation it was important to get the command structure settled and that it seemed to me that my deputy with her wide knowledge and ability, was the obvious one to follow me.

Myers, like any other company, would need well defined and continuing leadership, or it would suffer badly. I went over the position once again, adding a warning that great damage would be done if that continuity was not assured by the appointment of my deputy to the chair. I spoke again on 2nd December; I got nowhere, then just a few days afterwards I had a letter explaining that due to both my ill-health and that of Freda Adderley they had appointed the third man as chairman and had head-hunted two other executives from a competitor.

I was surprised that they decided with one shot to let go their two top people who had made the business and had successfully brought it back to full profit after the disastrous post office strike. The action seemed unbelievable, unless of course they had been misguided or misled. Talking of the mail order business one competent city analyst afterwards said, 'They have no catalyst now.'

I had never been against a take-over company dealing as it likes with the company it has taken over; after all that is their prerogative—'Yer pays yer money and yer takes yer choice.' But it is not always wise.

With nearly eleven months of the financial period gone I left the company with a year that profitwise would be among the very best. I spent a little time in clearing up—and that was very sad. I went straight to the hospital. Next morning I was in the operating theatre and one's thoughts on the operating table set things in the right perspective. I made an excellent recovery.

CHAPTER SEVEN

Thereafter

My active business life ended prematurely; I couldn't grumble for, despite the great depression, it had from the beginning been exciting and exhilarating. I have my old headmaster to thank for that; he had the gift of inspiring the young with ideas that were not only material but also of the spirit.

Yet it was in those very conditions of a deep depression that human endeavour blossomed in brilliant fashion. Great industrialists emerged, probably not beloved by everybody, but they proved beyond doubt that it was spirit, ability and dynamic leadership that laid the foundation for work and wealth. There were the great motor car magnates like Sir Herbert Austin, who was as good with a draughtsman's pencil as with his baby car, the Austin Seven, selling at under £100. William Morris, starting in a bicycle shop, he eventually built the Morris Minor, the MG, and so many wonderful cars. There was Edmund Crane, who exported cycles to the world, became a multi-millionaire, and worked as hard as any of his minions. Sir Alfred Herbert, alas no more, of machine tools fame; in days gone by even the Japanese copied his machines, even to the name. There were many more men with vision and inventiveness, all responsible for the employment of so many thousands. All took risks, and few sought government aid.

I am not suggesting that entrepreneurs could do these great things alone, but as catalysts they were vital; if we could only use those gifts with the great modern inventions, robots, micro-chips, numbered tools, etc, and unify the whole with a dedicated work force, we might well make Britain great again. Above all we might remember that as the minutes tick away in disputes from whatever cause, the time wasted has gone for ever and we are all losers.

Earlier in this book I told of new approaches to production in the thirties with what we thought were great new machines. The mind boggles as to what could be achieved with the spirit of those days and tools of today.

As a boy I had seen the effects of the First World War, and the terrible times of 1919 onwards. I sometimes wonder if all the leaders of ASLEF were about then, for some of them seem fond of comparing the present year with 1919. True the country as a whole suffered in the twenties and the thirties, but we never seemed to lose our pride and spirit of fairness.

Young as I was then it would be untrue to say I was not depressed about the utter despair of the huge army of unemployed, but it would be equally true to say that the fear of being jobless never crossed my mind. I would have taken any job and I would have determined to do it better than it had ever been done before. That eminent American philosopher Emerson made a great impression on me, and I clearly remember the story of the mousetrap. *If a man write a better book, preach a better sermon or make a better mousetrap than his neighbour, tho' he build his house in the woods, the world will make a beaten path to his door.* If only now we could build better things than other countries, deliver them on time and at the right price, perhaps once more the world would make a beaten track to the British door!

I was also impressed by Emerson's words, *To believe your own thought, to believe that what is true for you in your private heart is true for all men—that is genius. (Essay on self reliance).*

I believe in those inspiring words; without that belief I do not see how a boy from a big family, denied the higher education which might have led along other paths, could have made progress in the appalling economic conditions of the times. Education leads me to a story* told by an eminent man at a Manchester dinner.

It concerned a down and out who was at the end of his tether and failed to get a job. He had made his way to the ship canal and was about to throw himself in to end it all. Along came a kindly chap and said 'What are you truing to do?' 'I ain't trying guvner, I'm a'going to do it and end it all,' he replied. 'Fred' said the kindly chap, 'It can't be all that bad, tell me about it.' Fred cooled down a little and explained his sorry story. No job, no hope! Just that morning he had lost his final hope; a job had been advertised by Manchester Corporation for an underground lavatory attendant in Albert Square. Fred had an interview, the questions and replies went well. 'An ex-serviceman with decorations? Good! Family man? Yes! Good! Clean and tidy? Good! Not afraid of long hours? No! Good! Don't mind work underground and some filth? No! Good record! Splendid!' said the interviewer, 'You've got the job,' and handed him the application form with a 'just sign your name there.' Fred stifled his sob, 'I can't sir,' he said, 'yer see I can't read nor write.' 'Then you can't have the job—out you go!' said the interviewer. So out Fred went. 'That's why I'm finishing it,' he concluded. 'Oh no, you're not,' said the kind friend, 'I'll tell you what to do, here's ten bob (50p), go outside to the fruit market and hire yourself a flat handcart, and with the rest of the money buy yourself as many apples as you can get, put them on your cart, stand on a corner and sell them off quickly, and take just a little profit, do that for a few days then with the profit you make you can get two or three different kinds of fruit and very soon you'll have a handcart full, and then you can take a bit of money out for yourself.' 'I don't know gaffer, but I'll try,' said Fred and went away. He did not see Fred again for many years, but one day walking across the open market at Stockport they met. Fred looked very prosperous, and our friend said, 'Well! Well! Fred, time's been very good to you.' 'Yes, guvner I followed your advice.' 'What's happening now Fred?' 'Well,' says Fred, 'I've got four stalls in market, four in Manchester and a few in Liverpool and a few here and there, and I've got half-a-dozen shops, a nice home and a car.' 'Good, so you're all set up,' said Fred's friend. 'Yes,' said Fred, 'You did me proud, I've med a lot of brass, that's me one worry, I've got it in boxes and bags underneath mattress, and bed.' 'I'll soon help you with that,' said his friend, 'Let's

*This story has been told in many forms—the message is always the same.

194

go home, collect your cash, and I'll take you around to my bank and that will be that.'

Home they went and loaded two cars with cash for the bank. The manager beamed, his eyes popping out as the cashiers counted so many thousands of pounds. When it was all finished the happy manager said 'Well, well! Mr Fred, you have done well, all this money and how successful too! I am delighted to open an account for you, here are your paying in books and cheque books.' He filled the forms in, passed them across to Fred and said, 'Just sign there Mr Fred, if you will, thanks!' But Fred stifled his reply, at last he said, 'I can't sign there, I can't read or write.' 'Good heavens! Good heavens!' gasped the manager, 'You've made all those many thousands of pounds and you can't even read or write?' Shaking his head in disbelief, he said, 'I wonder what you would have done if only you had been able to read and write?' Back came the answer like a shot from a gun—'I'll tell yer guvner, I'd 'a' been cleaning out lavatories underground in bloody Albert Square!' There is a moral in that story.

* * *

At Hercules no young man could have had a better chance than I had. It was there I really appreciated the meaning of honest endeavour, courage, determination and enthusiasm. Ted Crane gave me at the age of sixteen-and-a-half that dream chance to make a rapid climb up the ladder of success. I do not think I disappointed him. When I had outgrown a top job with Hercules it was with more than understanding that he realised and said it would be wrong to try and keep me, even with money.

I ventured north to Liverpool, and now I was married, two were taking risks. In those days the thoughts of a married woman going out to business was abhorrent to most men; it was a sign of a man's inability to provide and survive. I had the unfailing support of my wife Mabel, come hell and high water, and for her help, guidance and affection I am eternally grateful, for I must have been very trying at times.

I ventured north to Liverpool, where Littlewoods was already a company of considerable size, restlessly determined to diversify away from the Pools which could so easily be attacked by legislation. Senior executives were sought in large numbers; the 'starters' were always very much greater than the very few who came 'into the straight' and those arriving at the finishing post, were indeed very few.

So the struggle was intense, and although it was vital to have courage, determination and enthusiasm, they did not necessarily ensure survival. In common with many great national companies, there was much head hunting, and that is never easy to overcome, so political cells survived and flourished on the nerves of the new recruits. Many stories naturally were around which were never aimed at stabilizing the new man, or encouraging his affection for the company itself.

I just relate one well worn tale. All staff, executives as well, were remunerated on a weekly basis, and the then current tale suggested that the most popular and overcrowded place on a Friday afternoon between two and five pm was the men's lavatory block which was the only safe place from the foolscap envelope, the sign of the dreaded cards and the week's pay in lieu. It was best to keep out of the way until the afternoon of Monday, for then there would have to be another week's pay. There were those, of course, not so kindly disposed, who suggested that it also provided the cheapest way to hire and fire. I stuck my week out and said to the story tellers that it was only the people who did not believe in themselves who feared the system. I might add that that won me few friends among the politicians. My first few weeks in Liverpool tested my courage to the full, but then determination took over and I posed to myself the question, 'Why shouldn't I be the stayer?'

I reasoned that by the natural progression of things success must come to those with courage and enthusiasm rather than to the politicians. I admired John and Cecil Moores. It was John with whom I was in close contact in those early days; he certainly had tremendous courage, determination and enthusiasm.

True, times were dreadful, poverty appalling, and jobs almost non-existent. There was real suffering by any standard. On my first Littlewoods visit to Manchester I saw in Ardwick so many bare-bottomed kids running about in just a vest with no pants, shirt, or shoes, and with crusts of bread in their fists. But still men and women battled on to try and succeed; unemployment pay was meagre, and there was a means test to sort out the very needy. Compare those times with today (which many trade union leaders are fond of doing, some of them not even born in the thirties). The unemployed then had little to feed on, no generous handouts from social security, no television, and very few council houses. No sports and leisure centres, cheap holidays abroad, central heating, child allowances, or subsidised rents, and so on. But by and large people in general had one very great quality in abundance—the craving desire to work—while the more ambitious fought to get on.

It is both untrue and unfair to the many who have gone before, socialists, liberals or conservatives alike, to suggest that we are back to the thirties. If we were, there would be some pretty big dumps of unwanted tellies, motor cars, fridges, built-in wardrobes, double glazing, washing machines, dryers, electric kettles, the lot, all strewn across the land. It is both wrong and misleading to compare today with the 1930s. It may be politics but it is wrong, almost immoral to imbue the young with what at best are untruths and at worst downright lies. Perhaps part of our troubles start just there.

In Littlewoods, when the stress of war was over, the birth pangs of a rapidly growing business were felt, and it was then I had my real chance. It was a challenge, for I had the opportunity of studying in depth a big, fine and rapidly growing organization, admittedly some work was menial, and at times there were big disappointments. I am glad I accepted the challenge, and as the years went by life became very acceptable, while the organization made great strides and materially I benefited much and had many happy years. I never saw eye to eye with everything, but I learned to compromise in a hard school — that was essential — and after all that is business.

In the end I did have one of the two top appointments; naturally on leaving I felt the break, but I still look back with a great deal of affection on the Littlewoods days.

* * *

On leaving Littlewoods I accepted a new challenge, Myers. I again put a great deal at risk; many friends said it was foolhardy and certainly I laid my hard won security on the line. Once again my wife went along with things even though it must have been very hard for her. To change our way of life once in a lifetime must be hard, three times, with all the attendant risks, was almost too much to expect of her, but she rose nobly to it, as always.

I knew the strain would be severe both mentally and physically; perhaps I would have been just as well off in accepting one of the other offers made to me, but I still had courage, determination, enthusiasm and what was more important now, a very great deal of knowledge on the organization and *know how* of big business, in the creation of and the seizing of opportunities, both in manufacturing and in the latest and most rapidly developing retail sections, chain stores and mail order trading.

I had many friends in the city and elsewhere who put business opportunities my way, but I went for Myers, perhaps after all I wanted to prove the point that it could be done.

The rebuilding of Myers from a dying concern to a large and very successful public company in an amazingly short time was tough and exhausting, but it was exciting and thrilling.

Over and above all, Myers gave me the deep satisfaction of creating a business and seeing other people respond to teaching, of bringing employment to a district that was desperate, and in so many other ways encouraging enthusiasm with, I hope, happiness to others.

I would not forget my gratitude to all who helped in that big venture, some in big jobs, some in smaller, but all with spirit. So, *proving the point* was not the least of my rewards, but I now confess that retiring from the company was not very satisfying.

In the years that followed my retirement, I observed the elimination of policies on which Myers had been rebuilt. The dominant advertising seemed no more neither did the theme of the 1,000 page catalogue. The big competitions were no more, neither it seemed was the higher commission explored. I mention these merely for interest for of course the new powers were entitled to operate their own policy.

So it was no real surprise to read one August morning in 1980 just nine years after I retired:

JOHN MYERS
One of Britain's mail order firms collapsed last night.

197

The final annual loss, published for 1980/81 was £5.5 million. That must have been a horrible last year. It may seem strange but I felt sorry for UDS and for Bernard Lyons. It was and is a big business, and they were shrewd; while I did not always agree with their strategy and philosophy, I recognized their ability; perhaps something went wrong with the advice they got.

So in the end Sir Isaac got Myers, or rather the remnants of it. It was not *my* *Myers* though, and he got it much cheaper than when we met many years before; good luck to him. I have no doubt he will use that proud name to good effect, and I note with some interest the new approach of John Myers home shopping (shades of Orbit).

It is comforting to reflect that one of the most satisfying 'bouquets' we ever received was from our competitors was back in 1965, I quote:

The Statist

In the Trade it is John Myers which is admired more than any other company for sheer drive . . .

* * *

But it wasn't all work, even though I enjoyed success on so many occasions, as did my wife and son. I know they savoured the thrills, even though they had to keep cheerful during some of the disappointments, they were with me always and we got along very happily. Our son did very well at school, we enjoyed week-ends at Repton, speech days and all that went with them, eventually leading to lovely week-ends at Oxford.

In our time my wife and I have restored two old houses, a run-down Georgian farm that we built up into a lovely house, with one of the county's most beautiful gardens. In daffodil and tulip time we would have the most gorgeous settings with thousands of blooms, and were able to share this enjoyment with large crowds of people when the gardens were opened for the National Gardens Scheme.

We developed much of the land around, always we hope, with an eye to beauty. We took particular care with the heights that form the remains of two of the ancient quarries that provided the stone to build and restore so many of the very old churches in this part of Cheshire. The little handbook for our own church read:

> Alderley Church, now known as St Mary's but originally dedicated to St Lawrence. It was finally restored about 1330; the first Rector, Robert Byron died in 1328. This 14th century building today consists of the Nave with South Porch; and it is supposed that the stonework round the West Door is also of the same date, being moved to that position when the Tower was added early in the 16th century. The Chancel was restored in 1855. For all these constructions the material has been Alderley Stone, still supplied by the quarry on the hill.

Now the quarry works no more. In spring the old spoil heaps are covered with daffodils and narcissi, and the background of stately firs and beeches provide an abundance of colour in autumn.

One day I hope to write about restoring old houses, but I feel I must mention them now not so much from the wattle and daub point of view but from just the purely human angle, for it has been a deep and satisfying part of our lives.

Since we married we have lived in four houses. First we owned a plot of land, which in its way was very important to us; it was to have been the site for our first house, but, as the business challenge emerged, the building never happened, instead it became a temporary heartache, for it was in one of the most lovely spots in Warwickshire, and opposite the entrance to a lovely lane that really did bear the name of Lovelace Avenue.

Our first house was already built on land in the grounds of a mansion that once belonged to a friend of Horatio Bottomley. The house was none the worse for that. It was quite pretty, and we laid out a beautiful garden. It saw us meet with confidence the challenge of a very unsettled era, it knew some of our temporary disappointments and some of our early successes; above all, it was a happy house. We did all the usual entertaining, some might say showing off as young people do. The first Christmas though was a pretty tight financial affair for expenses on the company were very few, and we vowed then we would never owe anything or have a mortgage; we never did.

The time eventually came (probably too soon for Mabel), when I moved north for yet another challenge. We went to Upton in the Wirral, and an attractive house, but, I would say apart from the birth of our son, try as we might, it was a house rather than a home. The real reason I suppose was that we had the feeling that I might have made a mistake — many times I thought I had. An uneasy feeling rubs off, no matter how cheerful you both try to be; the house then seems to be just a staging post. Like the feeling I had in those few awful months at Brixton in my early days in the Littlewoods empire. The war came, the thoughts were right, it was a staging post, though not for the reasons we thought, and off we went to an outpost of the *empire* in Manchester.

We came to Alderley, and despite the war, the long hours, danger and shortages, the run down state of the farmhouse, and the difficulties of getting anything done, we knew for certain that we were coming home. The quivering trees, the scent of the good earth at night, even the frogs under the door — to say nothing of the driving snow, sometimes as much inside as outside, all were welcome. The farmhouse cradled in the countryside was always attractive; we saw the possibilities, and we were ever confident that one day we would buy it for a real home — we did.

Due to war time regulations, the licensing of building extensions and alterations was strict, it required almost a calamity to get permission. One wall of the farmhouse was badly weathered and very damp and there begins my story. I cannot recall how many times I painted that wall but they were very many. I would rise at four o'clock in the morning on the odd day off and toil till night time; we persisted but the wall stayed damp. Yet it was this damp wall that gave us our first break. One Sunday evening I went to the bathroom and, washing my hands, I felt a terrible tingling; I got little sympathy from Mabel or her mother. 'Must be rheumatism,' they said. Later Mabel's mother attempted to wash her hands, and she was flung across the bathroom; it was an electric shock. I phoned the electricity people and there was a stern reply, 'Touch nothing, don't even go outside near a wire fence. We will be there in next to no time.' True to their word, they arrived, and went through everything that was electrical—stove, radiogram, lighting system, immersion heater—with no luck. One chap said, 'Let's check the dining room, no electrical gadgets there—oh, but we'd better check the plug in that wall.' That was *the* damp wall.

He was right, the rising damp had penetrated and the socket was full of water, the lot apparently seemed at risk. The supply to this room was cut off—with a warning, 'Don't touch anything! You'll hear more tomorrow.' Next morning the chief engineer and later the surveyor arrived; and we were told, 'That wall's got to come down and smartly.' 'What about the licence?' I asked, 'There'll be no worry about that, best get an architect in and get cracking,' was the reply. We could barely conceal our excitement, while it was only a new wall, we could provide for doors and windows, which would be the starting point of the three major extensions we made. Electric shocks were soon forgotten.

We had bombs even in that remote part, which destroyed a farmhouse about three hundred yards away, killing both the mother and father of the family on a night we will not forget; my wife was up the stairs to fetch our baby and down again like an Olympic champion, even before the noise had died away.

For many years we never thought of leaving that home. Our son passed from a baby to manhood there, and I passed through two difficult periods, with few if any disasters, but some successes. Never once did we think of that farm other than as our home.

Even in this lovely house we now live in just across the fields from our original home my wife still sighs about the beautiful house across the way, *that lovely home*. I do not blame her. In fact I would quietly say if we could have bought the two fields between the two houses we would still be in the original; for the first real family home was that important. For nearly forty years we lived there, looking up to those lovely hills or down to the sweeping plain watching the twilight rise.

* * *

Finally we came across the fields to an adjoining farm we had bought years before, with its old house. Once the domain of the ancient family of Actons so it is believed, dating back to the time of Henry VIII, and its foundations to the fourteenth century. It was badly in need of major restoration, we completed this big job just over three years ago, after much luck and many thrills.

My wife discovered a Tudor fireplace which had remained virtually intact behind later additions in the form of various fireplaces from an old iron stove, to a white tiled modern fireplace with a surround of pseudo oak.

The discovery of that fireplace is a little story in itself; there were tell-tale marks of the changes that had taken place in fuel over the centuries. When all the spare bricks had been removed we could trace how the big fireplace, originally burning wood, had accommodated a very big fire. The black marks on the stone changed as the fires got smaller. Wood had become scarce, as a result of the continuous felling of the ancient oaks. Even now some of the great roots of those trees are still visible in our pastures. According to one record they were the boundary trees between the parishes of Nether Alderley and Over Alderley, dating back to the Conqueror's time. Later there was a change to coal which was available in Macclesfield, but that got dearer as the years went on and eventually the fire space contracted. It seemed to finish up merely as a hob hole for a kettle. The spare bricks had filled in the space.

When we arrived the windows were just plain glass, obviously Victorian and completely out of character. We and the architects pondered on what they originally looked like. What size were the frames, and what sort of glass? These questions may well have remained unanswered for centuries, however on stripping down yet more tiled fireplaces in the dining room, a wall at the back of the fire hole was exposed. My wife, ever watchful, noticed there was an opening in it lined with wattle and daub. She scrambled through and, searching around, found a screwed-up bundle of lead and glass. The lead was badly perished and only part of the glass remained; it was painstakingly flattened out, forming a whole window — that settled the problem of the windows. The very tiny leaded lights are seldom seen around here but now we knew the exact size of the panes and the experts very quickly identified the ancient glass. It was some of the earliest used in windows, and we were able to match it. The hole in the wall — well that was either a priest hole or an idiot's hole; our former rector adds for good measure, 'It doesn't matter much, there's so little to choose between the two!'

So the house is now back to much as it was so long ago (except for the addition of central heating, plumbing, etc!). The real joy in restoring was to see the old craftsmen, who were still about, joiners handling wood with loving care, masons chipping stone as if it were something very precious — I suppose it was really. The glaziers eyeing the little windowpanes almost in wonderment, above all the foreman, old Tommy, like a mother with her brood — this alone made the job worthwhile. I am sure that the old chimney, first repaired, it is said, ten years before the Armada sailed, nods its head in quiet approval. The gardens too, have been restored, all in keeping we hope.

* * *

No it certainly wasn't all work. Before Manchester lost (for a while) both its big theatres, the Opera House and the Palace, we spent so many pleasant and exciting evenings there, and during the war even the odd Saturday afternoon, for at the

Palace in the war days the great Irving Berlin, his orchestra and the American Army Singers played for charity.

Then there was the first performance of *Oklahoma* in England at the Opera House with the cheery Bill Johnson. He kept the audience entertained with much amusement while the costumes were being ironed; there had been a seamen's strike and the ship was late. The show went on till late too, but nobody minded that.

For more serious entertainment it was always the Opera House, with many great performances of ballet, opera and plays. It seemed to attract all the great artistes, Ninette de Valois, the red-haired Moira Shearer, magnificent Margot Fonteyn, John Gielgud, Richard Burton, Stewart Grainger, Dame Peggy Ashcroft, Owen Ayres, Edith Evans—all, or virtually all, the famous. In those days we even had coffee served by waitresses at our seats. It is a long time since we had great shows in Manchester, but we are promised them once more— now the new enlarged Palace has reopened and is capable of staging the greatest West End plays, grand opera, and ballet; we hope the old days will be revived.

If the crowds for some events were too great for normal theatres, then Belle Vue (that has gone now) was pressed into service, although I must agree that the competition between the lions in the zoo and the Hallé Orchestra and Choir with *The Messiah,* was a little disconcerting. Yet, when Gigli sang, that great voice stilled everything, including the lions outside. Finally when Markova danced the Dying Swan, all were reduced to bewildered silence.

The Free Trade Hall is part of Manchester's heritage, scene of great political land marks, and witness to so many great and inspiring speeches. Now the home of the Hallé, steeped in the traditions of its great conductors, Sir Charles Hallé, Sir John Barbirolli, Sir Adrian Boult, Sir Charles Groves and very many more. Great soloists have graced its platform: Kathleen Ferrier, Dame Isobel Baillie, Dame Janet Baker, Jacqueline Dupré, Menuhin, Ashkenazy, Clifford Curzon, to mention just a few. Its walls have echoed to the mighty works of Handel, Mozart, Beethoven, the haunting music of Elgar's first Symphony, and his soul-clutching *Dream of Gerontius* with its touching moments of soloists and choir. Two events at the Free Trade Hall stand out in my mind—the first the Hallé and its Choir with Nadia Boulanger conducting Fauré's *Requiem*; it was a wonderful performance with a great plus, the feeling of a continuity of Fauré through someone who had known him.

The second great event I recall concerned just a great singer and a pianist, and what a rapturous reception given to Paul Robeson. True, a number of his offerings had a pink or perhaps even a red touch, but the depth of sincere feeling he conveyed was soul searching, particularly the extract from Beethoven's Ninth. No, I shall not easily forget that evening.

* * *

Sport has always held attractions for us and in our early years it absorbed a lot of our spare time. Tennis or athletics in the summer, badminton in the winter. As business pressures got more intense we became mainly watchers, and where better for excitement and comfort than Wimbledon. Years ago it was not only the greatest tennis tournament in the world, it was not only a sporting event, it was an occasion. Lunch or tea or both served in the atmosphere of a garden, no regimented queues for coffee or tea in plastic mugs. Iced coffee was a drink to remember, and the strawberry teas, served on the well barbered lawns surrounded by glorious hydrangeas. That all seems to have passed into a super spectacle of performing professionals.

I reflect on some of the great players of the day. Lew Hoad with his tremendous service, Rod Laver who seemed to be unbeatable for most of the time, the evergreen Rosewall so beloved by the crowds, and the elegant Ashley Cooper. We also witnessed the first scintillating match and the emergence of perhaps one of the greatest but also one of the most contentious of players, Nastase — how soon they pass from the scene! They all played for peanuts compared with the golden grasps of today, and I cannot remember a player arguing with an umpire!

There were the women players, Maria Bueno, so very attractive; and Little Mo, in my opinion the greatest of all the American women players, we watched her emerge from a mere child to be a world beater, as brilliant as sunshine, yet as tough as old nails. There was that never to be forgotten match between Big Marge (Margaret Smith) of Australia and Billie Jean King of America, for my money the finest women's final yet.

Of course there was cricket at Old Trafford. I remember one great day when Don Bradman made his last appearance in Lancashire. He was quickly out for a tiny score. It made no difference to the feeling as the huge crowd rose to its feet crying 'the Don's gone', and the great batsman walked back to the pavilion amid tumultuous applause. As the newspapers confirmed, 'The Don has gone.'

The city of Manchester is only seventeen miles away from us. Football there meant Manchester United. My son and I went frequently and in the Matt Busby days it was great football with no beer cans, and we found the crowds nearly as interesting as the football — the critics with their trite remarks, particularly the bus conductresses in the ditch, providing running commentaries, on the player of the day. Albert Quixall came in for particular attention from the female of the species — he either got 'Good old Bert', for an excellent move, 'Come on Albert', if he missed a pass, or finally for what was reckoned a poor do, 'Thee get thee b____ cards, Quixall'. It was all good fun, and safe to take a child, with no fear of fights.

* * *

Over the years we have had so many exciting holidays in different parts of the world.

We felt that holidays should be not only a rest from the daily efforts but also a reservoir of memories for the days and years ahead; neither did we think the sole proof of a good holiday was a tanned torso or a freckled face. Ideally, holidays would be a mixture of things, suitable weather to enjoy glorious scenery, good food of the local variety as far as possible, and that depended where we were, but above all, for however short or long, an experience of foreign lands, particularly the great civilizations of the past.

That does not mean we ignored our own country, for on checking up, I find we have spent rather more holidays here in our country than we have abroad.

We spent our honeymoon in Bettws-y-Coed, Wales, which will always be a favourite. I remember the old *Royal Oak* there, and the story of its famous signboard painted in 1847 by David Cox, it became the centre of a legal affair, was it or was it not part of the freehold? Wales has so much to offer, verdant and rugged beauty, mountain ranges and deep valleys, lakes and castles. The great gardens at Bodnant are outstanding, and among so much beauty. Lovely Portmeirion, a creation of the late Clough Williams Ellis, reminiscent of Portofino in Italy, is sited on one of the most beautiful estuaries in the world. I like so much the fascinating play of the flitting sunbeams and the shifting shadows on the mountain sides reflecting, like us humans, so many moods. Of the brooding passes and the many waterfalls with their joyful *music,* I am so very fond of far-famed Aberglaslyn Falls on which so much of Kodak's production must have been used over the years. Yes, Wales is a microcosim of beauty.

Memories take me back to one of our earliest holidays in Northern Ireland, when the super train, the North Atlantic Express from Belfast to Larne was well-equipped in its blue livery. The glorious coastal scenery rich in history, was a joy to behold, with brooding Dunluce Castle; from a distance it reminded me of the advert for Knight's Castile Soap, or was it Gibbs Dentifrice?

Belfast, I remember, a stately and beautiful city, then untainted by the bombers, with elegant shops—not boarded up remains of the handiwork of the intolerants. I remember my wife was full of excitement to see that world renowned store Robinson Cleavers; at one time it seemed to be the standard bearer for the Linen of Ireland. The soothing touch of nature was provided by the truly beautiful glens of Antrim, then in almost undiluted peace. And the Giant's Causeway, a gigantic stone formation, described by many as the great monolithic organ pipes of nature. I remember too, the lovely shore at Ballintoy where a couple of university girls served tea for 1/- (5p) a time, with no cakes, but about a dozen different choices of bread—currant, potato, nut, you name it, they had it. Further away, there were the Mountains of Mourne and they really do come down to the sea.

I recall too the war-time journeys to and from Stranraer and Belfast, with the ferry loaded to the limit, threading its way through what seemed to me to be a forest of noisy ship yards—so many now silent.

Southern Ireland, to Dublin, a beautiful city, with its outstanding Georgian Square, its great cathedral, broad streets, the river and, for us, an easy but gracious life.

Then further south, and surely among the great gardens of these islands, if not beyond, the magnificent sub-tropical gardens at Garinish Island in Bantry Bay.

Onward along the coast road, with Hungry Hill on the right and its worked-out copper mines (the background to Daphne du Maurier's famous novel *Hungry Hill*), finally to the little harbour and the remains of the great derelict mansion of Dunboy, its eyeless windows brooding over a peaceful coutryside in the fading light.

The soul is almost stabbed with sorrow on what might have been; what I suppose could still be a happy place if all the people in general could learn to live together, according to the basic teachings of their creeds.

* * *

For short breaks London is a favourite, still the greatest capital in the world. I like to think of London on a spring Sunday morning, when the leafy squares put on their translucent show of pale green leaves, and above them the lovely houses raise their white façades. Whitehall stands stately with the sad window from which Charles I went to his execution.

The opening of Parliament, and many other royal and military splendours and ceremonials that we do so well, or the Mall and its distant views, the Palace and its milling crowds, awaiting a glimpse, if only a fleeting glimpse, of their Queen.

Further out, on a fine summer evening the *Son et Lumière* at Hampton Court is an experience, bringing back to life so many gay and tragic events in our history, from Henry VIII onward. The scented blossoms, drifting on the dying heat, with just a few hours crystallizing one of the most fascinating and exciting parts of the history of our land.

Royal Greenwich, dating from the 15th century, flanks the Thames with a dazzling array of glorious buildings, views that have inspired many painters, particularly Canaletto. The Queen's House, magnificently sited, contains many really great masterpieces. The Royal Naval College is an outstanding architectural triumph, with naval traditions harking back into history; everything is gracious, the gardens so neat, while the exhibitions at the National Maritime Museum are inspiring with the Nelson Rooms housing many of the great admiral's possessions, some of his silver, one of his uniforms and some of his battle equipment; while at the other end of the scale in the top-most room, when I went, was the Wrens' Exhibition, with that very touching notice 'The Missing', sent to the next of kin of a wren lost at sea, no grandeur here, but very much in the senior service tradition, it reads 'cessation of pay'.

There is the boys' delight, from toddlers to fathers, the *Cutty Sark* and *Gipsy Moth,* and for good measure, a little bit of old London in the shape of pubs and shops. There is the Thames Embankment, lined with magnificent buildings, and there is even a relic of early Egypt, Cleopatra's Needle.

Just to round off there are the great parks—Hyde Park (which must beat the Freedom Wall in China), with its Speakers' Corner, where some of the most violent, radical, stupid, funny and serious speakers have a go, only to be interrupted here and there with the odd heckle, groan or raspberry. That apart, Hyde Park is in the centre of a great capital, a slice of nature of which we can be proud with its beautiful trees swinging lazily in a summer breeze, well cut lawns, flowering bushes and beds of exotic flowers.

There are many churches with sustenance for the soul. St Paul's, the great masterpiece of Wren; some fashionable, like St Margaret's, Westminster; the mother church St Martin's in the Field; All Hallows (not big but full of history), where William Penn was baptized and where John Quincy Adams, the sixth United States president was married and Tubby Clayton's TocH Church, a very holy place to men of the first world war. There is the ancient and historic Temple Church serving the Inner and Middle Temples; that is a delightful place to walk around on a quiet Sunday morning, looking among the leafy trees almost prim and extraordinarily proper.

As for the theatres and concert halls, they are so numerous and so very varied, that I think they warrant a book all of their own — we have been to many. While awaiting a sleeper back north, it was at the Adelphi I saw Winston Churchill off duty in 1943 (I think) — he apparently loved the theatre as a diversion. The play was *Arsenic and Old Lace.* I was there when Winston arrived, my seat was in the next row behind him and very slightly to the right. The great man had to pass me, and I, like hundreds of others, cheered him, I also succeeded in patting him on the back.

One bitterly cold night I had some hours to wait for the Manchester sleeper from Euston. I nipped into the Westminster Theatre and saw a memorable war play, *The Moon is Down* by John Steinbeck, a most moving experience, about the Norwegian Army of Resistance. A point was reached in the play where a young man was being sent to his death at the instigation of the Nazis. From that still and hushed audience a piercing scream rang out, 'Don't let him! Don't let him!' It was both eerie and terribly moving, for it could have happened to us. Good 'theatre' too perhaps.

Another theatre that so many servicemen will not easily forget was the Windmill, with its wartime boast, *We never closed.* I must confess to seeing a show or two there while awaiting the over-night sleeper back home.

* * *

Away from London, there is Oxford, the historic centre of learning for many centuries, the second oldest in Europe, aptly put by Matthew Arnold, 'That sweet city of dreaming spires.' We have had many happy times there.

To anyone seeking a break from the world's cares, I suggest an early Sunday morning walk around Oxford, for then there is virtually no-one else about; when I look at my movies I find it hard to believe that this quiet and beautiful place is part of the same modern rush and bustle of the prosperous, modern, week-day city. My friends say I have a vested interest in Oxford, for our son went there. I remember our very first visit, when he was only a very little boy. Standing outside Magdalen Gate, he said, 'The Great Cardinal was here, I shall come one day,' and he did.

Another favourite is Cornwall, crammed full of history, yet above all abounding with great natural beauty, whether it be the waves pounding against the majestic headlands and cliffs, the worked-out tin mines, the moorlands, the lovely villages, or the beautiful isolated inlets, like so many nests holding a clutch of colourful little yachts.

Especially there is lovely Looe of pleasant memory. I took my wife there before we were married and naturally we had to row up the river, which has three main hazards, the arches of the bridge, other boats and many sandbanks, but all negotiable by good steering — if you know how! Sadly, I knew very little about rowing, but the kindly boatman gave us a good shove off; we narrowly missed several boats and headed straight for the main arch of the bridge to the accompaniment of the boatman's yell of 'Watch the bridge.' The afternoon ended none too quickly, for after pushing the boat off several sandbanks and nearly decapitating several fellow boating enthusiasts, we arrived back. Our dear old boatman was now wreathed in smiles, yelling, 'Well, Sir! If you don't mind me saying, yer came back better than yer went out.' Yes, we love Cornwall.

We have another favourite, the Cotswolds, those gentle rolling hills, with a whispering breeze that seems to say 'For ever England'. A countryside rich with villages, in glowing golden stone of unique beauty and bedecked with flowers. Hamlets ranging from the almost forgotten and isolated Stanton and Stanway to the American idolized Broadway, or to very ancient Chipping Campden — all full of history and beauty, as John Drinkwater wrote:

> 'Dark in the summer night my Cotswold hill,' and continued, 'I turn content that from my sires, I draw the blood of England's mid-most shires.'

Nearer to home lies the Peak District of Derbyshire and the upper reaches of Cheshire. After four years of sustained work during the war we had been told to have a break, if only for a few days in November 1943 and it was there we went.

We saved a little petrol from our meagre ration and offered it to a taxi driver who drove us to the little village of Alstonfield. He was a very careful driver, thank goodness, for to eke out his petrol he had to take many short cuts across roads which seemed more like cart-tracks, but being on high ground, they enabled him to coast down, spinning out his fuel.

We arrived in one piece at the farmhouse pub/hotel; fortunately for all concerned there had been two deaths in the farm family, a pig and a lamb, and the lush land had produced much vegetable. All transport locally was by foot and push cart. The surrounding hills were sublime and the quiet of the night, without bombers, was soothing. The weather was kind until the snow fell, enhancing the beauty, but restricting mobility

For us, with a young child, there was a desperate need for mobility, as great news was around in the pub that sweets (on coupons) and oranges (strictly one each) were available at the little store at Hope, a beautiful little village with an encouraging name. So for me it was to be over the hills now covered in deep snow.

I thought snow-covered hills would be no problem (particularly with the chance of an orange and a ration of sweets) but reality was different. I had fortunately taken the precaution to keep near an old stone wall, for as the snow got deeper and deeper, the going got heavier. At times up to my knees and very cold, I was almost devoid of breath. I hung over the wall gulping in as much air as I could, and gradually I made the top where the snow was much deeper but downhill it was easier now. At last, completely fagged out, I reached the village store and I got the oranges and ration of sweets. Then with little choice I decided to make a long detour back along the roads for the sake of safety.

* * *

Scotland for holidays was and still is high on our list. The wild beauty of the mountains and the lochs, the ravaged coast line of the north west, the lovely islands, the deep valleys, the heather covered moors and the great forests, soothe the soul and refresh the body.

Edinburgh is in my opinion one of the least spoiled of the world's great cities, with its Princes Street and the great castle rising from its very footpaths, and it is an experience, even for the most tired eyes, to see that great military tattoo performed on the castle ramparts in the fading light. Like Dublin it has its lovely Georgian buildings, both stately and well preserved. Loch Lomond is beautiful though being close to Glasgow it is sometimes dubbed as a tourist trap. I would not mind being trapped there for quite a long time.

The brooding passes, in sunshine, sunset or fleeting shadow, have always beckoned us. Glencoe always fascinated me, a scene of much bitterness for some, much beauty for others. Castles abound in this part of the world, including Balmoral, favoured by many monarchs. I picture once again too that lonely, and very moving battlefield at Culloden Moor — the separate lines of turf covering the remains of the various clans, all named except one, which bears the heading 'Of no known clan'. How reminiscent and yet different to the young who died on the Somme, 'Who know no known grave.'

On our first visit to the Kyle of Lochalsh we travelled there by rail from Inverness. It was a superb journey with views as good as the Italian Lake Maggiore. In those days the train pulled in almost alongside the ferry for the benefit of those going *Over the sea to Skye,* exciting in its loneliness and, viewed from Lochalsh, Skye is bewitching in the evening as the sun sets on the Cuillin Hills.

Back in England we explored East Anglia only recently. Many times I wonder why we left it so long? I suppose it is the cross country journey through a densely populated part of the Midlands, and it takes a long time to get there, but it is well worth it. There are the beautiful counties of Lincolnshire, Norfolk and Suffolk.

The city of Lincoln itself is delightful and full of history. Its magnificent cathedral, the third largest in England, is only outdone by York Minster and St Pauls. The majestic edifice rises above the city, yet its immediate surroundings are as silent as a country lane. The original cathedral was commissioned by William the Conqueror and was completed in 1092. Much of what we see today traces its glory back to Hugh of Avalon in 1192.

A musical weekend at the White Hart Hotel was food in good measure for both the spirit and body. But Lincolnshire is not only the city itself, for there is the beauty of its countryside alive with flowers particularly gay in springtime with fields of daffodils and tulips; with interesting towns and long forgotten hamlets set amid the smiling farmlands.

If I had to single out just one town or village in Eastern England, I would, without hesitation, go for Stamford, on the Great North Road. It is the town itself that impresses, the historic George Hotel, a meeting place of the Knights of St John of Jerusalem, the gracious churches, the quiet flowing river, and the Georgian squares. All the buildings constructed in that lovely restful stone make a very English scene, and just across the way is the great House of Burghley.

Norfolk, next door, has many old ports to roam around, particularly Kings Lynn, with its Scandinavian air. Norwich is full of history with its great cathedral, interesting and narrow streets, and not least its deep association with Nelson. The county has some wonderful bird sanctuaries and miles and miles of wild, lovely sands (a quiet wilderness), broken here and there with some lovely little harbours, still unspoilt.

Then there is Cambridgeshire, a lovely county with its great university city, the rival, yet the sister of Oxford. Like Oxford it is dominated by superb college buildings, and St John's and its backs in particular. Its old bookshops, churches, and the timeless river, contrive a haven for those who want to learn and those who are learned. Finally the splendour of that lovely King's College Chapel, claimed by many as the most glorious building in Britain, and by some as the finest perhaps the greatest achievement of Gothic architecture in the whole of Europe.

I would not forget a smaller place in Cambridgeshire of much trade and much beauty, that little riverside port of Wisbech, a flower port, a flower town, and an agricultural port, above all a place to see. Georgian squares not like those in Lincoln, Dublin or Edinburgh, they are of the country type. Quoting from the *Shell Guide to England*, 'The impression is of an Anglicized Delft with the terrace of mainly Georgian houses providing variety without sacrificing unity.' Having seen the beautiful town of Delft in Holland and Vermeer's great masterpiece *A View of Delft*, I have no complaints to make of that description.

I turn to Suffolk, the Constable country of delightful landscapes of bewitching light and shades. Constable was born in the village of East Bergholt, 'The church with the bells outside.' Eventually he was to become perhaps the greatest of all English landscape artists, and few little boys, girls, dads and mums would fail to recognise at least two of his works *The Haywain* and *Flatford Mill*. Flatford Mill in afternoon light and the great painting are uncannily alike! The light playing on

209

those quiet villages weaves the spell, and Kersey in autumn tints on an October morning with a bright blue sky is a feast. The great wool churches, as big as cathedrals and as lovely, are monuments to merchants of the past and lovely Long Melford must possess the biggest village green of them all.

I first saw Lavenham, a great favourite of mine, on a late autumn afternoon. It was a haven; it seemed a heaven. The medieval town is virtually complete; old hotels abound—my favourite is the Swan, half-timbered, secluded warm and welcoming. I recall a musical weekend there too that was so delightful and restful.

Yes, we have enjoyed so much of our islands. Oh! if only the years were longer.

* * *

The Lebanon and Syria we visited just once, for the unending war was about to start, resulting in the utter destruction of so much beauty and interest. There was just the first rumbling of catastrophe when we arrived in Beirut, for a newspaper editor had been assassinated. Now that wonderful St George's Hotel has gone for ever, the lovely waters of that superb bay go unlooked at, even the memorial to Rameses of Egypt on the Dog River, where he and all the conquerors that came after him stood and fought, is now devoid of star-gazers.

I remember so well the ancient towns of Tyre and Sidon beside the dark sea, the waves quietly breaking on the rocks and ruins. The Cedars of Lebanon in spring, huge trees of Biblical times standing among the ebbing snows, in stately, elderly grandeur, left lonely now, and the seed sellers bereft of customers; we have a pleasant reminder as the seeds they sold us did grow. Then Baalbek, the tremendous ruin, a dramatic site of seemingly endless columns, with the canopy of an eastern sky and the snow-capped mountains of the Lebanon as a backdrop. Or yet again, the remains of Krak, the most formidable castle in the world, with memories of the Knights of St John, a castle face that is eyeless now, but still nobly facing the sun-baked fields. It is easy to picture ancient Byblos the little port, once a great trading post of the Egyptians—said to be the birthplace of the alphabet, spelling, and the first books.

In Syria, Damascus is the queen of them all, the oldest continuously inhabited city in the world. We approached this lovely city in the early evening, the setting sun was colouring to pink, the snows on Mount Hermon, and on the narrow road winding its way in the fading light to the little spring which gives its water, as the Great Book says, to the oases around which Damascus was built.

There is much to feast on, the remains of the Great Souk, once the greatest market in the world; one might be forgiven for thinking it still is, for the noise of the shrieking traders offering their wide variety of merchandise, from beans to brass, silk to straw, carpets to chocolate, lambs to lilies, is truly a great cacophony of human vocalism. There is the Street called Straight, and the gate where St Paul was lowered in a basket, both dear to Christians. Nearby the great Mosque with its treasures, holy of holies to the Moslems, yet sheltering the tomb of St John the Baptist, making it just as holy to Christians. So, in unbroken sunshine, to the desert and the lonely village of Seidnaya and its historic convent where it is said miracles happened.

I remember one incident in Syria when we were walking outside the great French railway station in Damascus, Mabel is very fair, the Syrians are dark, and the locals stopped in their steps to eye us up and down, staring as if we were visitors from space; it felt as if the traffic had stopped while the inspection took place.

We travelled with some Americans in a small plane way over the desert to Palmyra, landing on the burning sands to be met by Ahmed the general factotum. We all asked for our private cars, as ordered. 'Yes,' he replied, 'It ees ready.' The *it* sounded ominous—it was, for Ahmed guided us graciously to his 'private transport', a converted lorry—all at the origional price of course. He knew, as did we, that the desert was not the ideal spot for an argument.

He had another little service to render, for he dispensed the *etiquettes,* which freely translated meant the wash basins and loos. He had a private service for *etiquettes* too when he could find a bedroom that was empty—that took him a little time, opening and closing doors. And the fee, 'Just an English pound, shall we say?'

I remember there was an American on that plane who was to survey a site for a new hotel. I asked Ahmed how he would get along. 'It ees no good—someone has let the farmer's goat loose. He will be away—the American will not see.' He didn't; I wondered!

Palmyra, still a ruin of mighty proportions and great colonnaded streets, once had a very beautiful queen Zenobia. It is said she was even more beautiful than Cleopatra. This impressed the Romans so much that they took her back a prisoner in golden chains. But when I reflect on Palmyra, my thoughts are not entirely on Zenobia, but on Ahmed, a lovable rascal.

* * *

So to the glory of Greece, with immortal Athens, parts of it now very modern, but still dominated by the Parthenon and its partners around the hill, guardians of great learning, deep philosophy and the like; buildings that have seen triumph and tragedy and now providing so much delight.

I remember a Good Friday in Athens with the solemn processions in the evening, the little girls and boys holding candles, providing virtually the only lights except for candles in the windows. The sacred music was moving, particularly Beethoven's *Eroica Funeral March,* while the floodlit Parthenon gleamed against a velvet blue sky.

As thoughts come flooding back on Greece it is difficult to make selections, but first I opt for Delphi recalling our first journey there so many years ago. I picture again looking across the Plain of Thebes, travelling towards Livadia and having lunch on the bank of the fabled stream, then on along the sacred way of the ancients, lovely and desolate then, and not a motor road in sight. Delphi nestles beautifully beneath the peaks, yes perhaps a dwelling of the Gods; as a sacred site it is reckoned second only to the Acropolis. The glorious treasury, so many ancient ruins, the historic theatre and the original stadium on the hill, still retaining its starting line intact, remind us that none of our pursuits are original.

We found Olympia so very beautiful; we were lucky for we first went in springtime when the beautiful blossoms were scattering their petals over the cheesecake masonry, watched by the mightly stone columns of the ancient temples; in Olympia it is rather like walking in a roofless cathedral, even voices are hushed, and if it is said that spirits of the ancient past abound, I would not argue.

I come now to Mycenae; and Argos seemed the most obvious place to stay, but the guide book didn't see it that way; it read:

> ARGOS — only if there is no accommodation in Nauplia would one spend the night in Argos.

On the first visit we stayed in Nauplia. On the second there was no room, so we spent the night in the little town of Argos. True, the hotel was not like the Amphitrion, but we were so well looked after, and showed so much kindness, that we were not disappointed and we were very close to many great sites.

Mycenae, I think, is the most gaunt and brooding, even dramatic of sites, yet exciting in its isolation and history. The Lion Gate dominates the entrance to the vast excavation carried out by Schliemann (1822-90), who revealed the great riches in gold of a very ancient race — this great but unusual archaeologist said he proved Homer was right! We were more than lucky for we had as our guide a very old man, by name Aristotles, who as a young boy worked with his father who dug with Schliemann. That dear old boy *made every stone live*.

Yet full of history as all the great sites and ruins are there is a memory that will never fade. It is a low grass mound, twenty or thirty feet high, lonely, in the middle of nowhere — the burial ground of the warriors of Marathon where the Athenians defeated the Persians in 490BC and stopped their advance into Europe and all that meant to the human race. The Marathon race (26 miles 385 yards) approximates to the distance run by Pheidippides from Marathon to Athens to announce the Greek victory.

* * *

> There is a land named Crete, fruitful and fair,
> Set like a jewel in a wine dark sea.
>
> (Homer's *Odyssey*)

It was on a return plane journey from Africa I had my first view of Crete. It was early morning and a fiery dawn was breaking the mist around the majestic mountains and reaching out here and there to tiny white villages and isolated farms. From the air it looked mysterious and exciting and it proved to be just that.

So we first visited Crete many years before bulk tourism arrived. Our plane, carrying Cretans with their Athenian purchases, including chickens, landed on the

212

sands of Heraklion (Candia). A blood-red sunset gave its light to the sea, surely Homer's 'wine dark sea'. It was a chilly night, the little cafés beckoning but the difficult Greek language does not make ordering easy.

It is an exciting island with Knossos the centre of its ancient civilization, famed for its treasury and throne room, the signs of the Double Axe, the legend of the Bull of Minos, and the remains of the first flush loo, and so very much more.

At one end of the island stands its capital, Chania (its old name Canea), with a lovely Venetian harbour dominated by the beautiful White Mountains. Even now I can feel the sticky Greek cakes as I picture that attractive scene from a very Cretan restaurant. At the other end (which tilted into the sea when Santorini was devastated so long ago) stands lovely Zakros — almost unvisited now. When we went there only very few names were in the visitors' book covering some half a century.

The island is renowned for its flowers, wild gladioli, chrysanthemums, cyclamen, iris, all growing in abundance. I recall the peasants gathering bitter herbs in Lent and their kindness, touching to a point with a gift of bread at Eastertime. The Cretans all seemed so British, indeed Crete's first travel agent continued for many years to send me Christmas greetings by Telex; we were among his very first clients.

* * *

Italy and Rome are almost indivisible, yet there are many other as historic or beautiful places in Italy that jerk the memories. Amalfi, an ancient centre of medical learning, approached by its stupendous coastal road, hugging the mountain-side, and on to Pompeii buried, as was Herculaneum, by an eruption of Vesuvius, with its relics of an early civilization unearthed many centuries later, showing a well organised, indeed, pleasure-loving people, with an early eye to town planning.

But after all it is to Rome that thoughts return. On a short visit to Italy I first saw the Eternal City; St Peter's was crowded to overflowing, and our guide told us we would be blessed by the Pope. 'How come? We are not Catholics.' 'Oh! But the Pope loves all people!' he answered.

In mid-afternoon we saw the Forum from the Capitoline Hill, the broken columns, the remains of the entrance, the great arch, and the Triumphal Way. It looked so small and majestic, and it left a feeling that the paper work of the Roman Empire must have been very small, so too must have been their civil service. I thought that if one of the greatest empires of all time could be run from such a small area, then the determined delegation of administration must have been of an extremely high order.

The Forum that night was bathed in moonlight. The lofty columns looked whiter, the tracery of the great arches more beckoning, even the broken stones and statues seemed to be saying in some mysterious way that 'we were and still are Rome.'

On a later visit we went to so many churches. One I remember very well. Outside it appeared quite a bit down-at-heel. I rudely said, 'Like a run-down jam factory'. Future visits proved I was more than a little wrong. It was at Eastertime again, and the interior of Santa Maria Maggiore, for sheer beauty, must rank among the

213

greatest of churches. Its towering altars, gleaming lapis lazuli, glorious gold and silver and above all perhaps its flowers, and those not only for beauty alone; for the scent oozing from the thousands of carnations perfumed the whole of that lovely building. By contrast there was the little church of Scala Santa, with, it is said, the steps up which Christ walked to be sentenced by Pilate, later taken there from Jerusalem — the self-same steps crowded now with pilgrims, moving to the little altar, with its picture ascribed to St Luke.

One Easter, I said to my family, 'Let's have one more look at the flood-lit buildings before leaving this thrilling city.' We went by cab to the Colosseum, but there was no flood-lighting, so back to the cabby, who through his very white teeth screamed, 'Eenside, Eenside.' So inside we went, for a wonderful experience. Mass was being celebrated; the priest was stationed at that dramatic position of the cross, marking the spot where the Christians were offered to do battle with the lions. Virtually the whole congregation consisted of boys and girls of all ages; the boys holding candles, the girls with lace coverings for their heads, a poignant and beautiful picture.

Florence too, a city of so much intrigue (the Medici would have called it business), but above all, it is the birth and workplace of many of the world's great masters in metal, painting or stone. It is one of the great treasure houses of the world, mothering so many masterpieces of the famous Michelangelo (especially his *David*), Raphael, Botticelli, Donatello, Cellini, and the famous doors of Ghiberti, the Duomo and Palazzo Vecchio, the Loggia of the Lancers, the ancient bridge with its shops intact, despite battles and floods. Then in the evening, from a distance, the beauty of the city itself, in the twilight.

Venice is so different, indeed unique. Built around the canals, every turn looks like a masterpiece; it holds so many creations of beauty to its bosom — not least that glorious view across the Lido captured in the great painting by Canaletto.

It was here we experienced a strike of the hotel staff at the lovely Royal Danielli. The early morning tea had not arrived, so we phoned 'management', only one word of English came across the line, 'Strike.' I had heard that word before somewhere in England. It certainly was an all out effort, with just the manager, chef and housekeeper on duty. They worked with a will, providing a breakfast of sorts, we were *invited* to make our own beds, and informed there would be no fresh linen. 'Please have lunch at the sister hotel across the Lido,' they advised. Somehow dinner was to be served; the three non-strikers must have worked very hard, for an excellent meal was ready in the roof top dining room. There were no waiters, but that made no difference, the visitors, Americans, Germans, French, British, all joined in, with one group serving soup, another the meat, and yet another the salads; I looked after the soup and cheeses with an American. I think we had something to do with the strike ending the very next day, for we discovered fairly early on, that our portions were far too generous and supplies were running out quickly. As for the city, I think Venice really deserves a chapter, if not a book, all to itself.

* * *

214

We visited the African continent many times. Starting in Ethiopia, we have twice been to this country shrouded in mystery, a land of very high mountains, deep gorges, arid deserts, much poverty, and great natural beauty.

Axum, its ancient capital, has its pre-Christian and unexplained obelisks towering seventy feet high; and the bath of the Queen of Sheba a muddy place, with cattle and peasants with their pathetic pots sharing the meagre supply of water. It is suggested that the Queen of Sheba was buried in Axum, certainly there are acres of stone slabs. I asked why they had not tried to find out; their answer was simple, 'She might not be there'. There was a lovely little guest house in Axum, sponsored by a princess of the royal family. It had been empty for some time and we were among the first visitors — probably the last too.

Lalibella was fascinating, with its many churches, carved from the living rock, and perfect in every detail, a place with more clergy than people. The children were in a terrible state with legs like sticks, faces covered with sores and masked with flies. It was hot, so very hot, and the local beer tasted like wine and was about as expensive.

Gondar, the medieval capital of Ethiopia, with its 17th century castles and buildings is so very well preserved. There is yet another side to this mysterious country, for near Gondar is the village of the Falashas, a black Jewish tribe whose origins have never been satisfactorily explained. Is there perhaps some truth in the love story of the Queen of Sheba and King Solomon? Indeed the main objects on sale to visitors were little crude clay models of Solomon in bed with Sheba!

The ancient walled city of Harrar had a mysterious feeling all of its own; the air was hot, the atmosphere seemed explosive, it was picturesque, but most likely unhealthy, its open markets not short on flies, and ablaze with a huge variety of food and merchandise, with cattle idling among the crowds and stalls. While there seemed to be many different races or groups, two religions were so easily identified, the Christians in their white robes contrasting so clearly with the saffron coloured garments of the Moslems. The shrieking market sellers were persistent in their enthusiasm with price reductions to tempt the hardened traveller as he walked away. I said to our guide it was an exciting place, he replied "Yes and dangerous in parts." I didn't doubt that.

Bahr Dar stands on Lake Tsna at the source of the Blue Nile, for the Little Abbai (river) is a sickly trickle flowing into the lake on one side and leaving it on the other as the Great Abbai, an ever swelling river eventually to crash over the Tississat Falls, where, as the Blue Nile, it begins its thousand mile journey to meet the White Nile at Khartoum. It has been truly said, 'On Ethiopia depends the life of Egypt,' for it is the Blue Nile that conveys the elements to fertilize the Nile Valley. It was at Bahr Dar that we met two boys, who, for a long time, sent me letters and cards, telling of their life and problems and asking for money for their school to buy books. We helped a little; I suppose that now they have been absorbed in the army, for the writing has stopped.

Lovely Eritrea forms part of Ethiopia, its Italian built road provides Ethiopia's only passage to the sea, a road weaving its way from a height of 7,000 ft with 800 bends in seventy miles to the Port of Massoua. The Italians did another brilliant job, for rich citrus and fruit farms abound; massive mountains and deep gorges frame a transport route that is vital to the life of Ethiopia, carrying petroleum, chemicals, raw materials and machinery to Asmara, where the spices, incense and all the other natural products begin the journey to Massoua and eventually all the corners of the earth. It was a dicey route to travel, with the army guarding all the important spots while the strict curfew at Asmara was rigidly enforced.

Addis Ababa was rapidly becoming an international city with skyscrapers, grocery supermarkets and Hilton-type hotels, but life for the native appeared to have altered little. When we first went there women seemed virtual beasts of burden, carrying eucalyptus leaves and branches down from the high mountains to the city. Certainly shopping in general has changed little, for the masses flocked in their thousands to the vast open market where there was a fantastic array of food and merchandise; the noise was terrific and the gaily clothed people provided a most colourful scene against the backdrop of mountains. But there is one view of Ethiopia that will stay with me for ever, for the Blue Nile Gorge breathes both history and the power of nature, it is staggering in its beauty, majestic in its loneliness and humble even in its solitary signpost declaring *The Road to Egypt*.

* * *

We travelled the great game parks in Kenya and Tanzania, and viewed lions, elephants, hippos, kudus, gazelles, wildebeeste, zebras, eagles, storks, hyenas and so much more. On one return journey from South Africa, I photographed the snows of Kilimanjaro from a plane so close as to be far from comfortable. I showed this film to some friends, they felt it frightening; certainly the tell-tale beads of my perspiration, mirrored from the window, appeared on the pictures.

The first park we visited in Kenya was Nairobi, it is unique, for it is only a few miles from the city centre. I called for a car, a taxi arrived, the driver was enthusiastic and said he would find *much game*. He certainly drove his taxi hard over the rough and bumpy grassland, braking here and there to a staggering halt, to listen and look. He scanned the skies with his big wide eyes in search of vultures, the tell-tale sign that a kill had taken place. He spotted them, and off the taxi shot, bumping more than ever, in time to find the lions gloating over their prey. Come to think of it chasing game in a taxi is unique, but not recommended.

Ngorongoro Crater was memorable, it has been variously described as a 'Wonder of the World', the remains of the 'Garden of Eden', or the 'Lost World'. Certainly it does seem another world, for winding down the steep gradients by jeep, wild animals of almost every description abound. I have vivid memories of huge hippos heaving their big pink snouts dripping wet, from the lake, to greet the morning. Lions, guinea fowl, duck, crested crane, the cruel looking water buffalo, hyenas, giraffe, yes as the guide says, 'name it it's there', as were the ever present monkeys galore. A favourite picture of mine is of flamingoes, so very pink, rising elegantly above the lake, the water falling from their bodies like pink jewels in the early light. I recall another lovely scene of a lioness guarding her young and another of a mother zebra feeding her foal way out in the grasslands.

Lake Manyara is a delightful park, famous for its animals and its birds. There are thousands of flamingoes, over three hundred species of duck, kingfishers, plovers, larks and most unusual blue starlings.

The lions of Manyara have a unique habit of sleeping in the acacia trees; we found this not only attractive but dangerous too, for as our jeep stopped a lion awakened and nearly landed on the bonnet — that was quite a shock. The park has another attraction too, with its luxurious hotel set on the edge of the Rift Wall; the view from the bedroom windows at daybreak across the vast shimmering landscape is breathtaking.

We approached Lake Nakuru down an escarpment; it appeared to be edged with pink rocks, like magic the rocks turned into flamingoes, the greatest concentration on earth, for some 2,000,000 of them inhabited the lake. They were everywhere and gliding among them like a fleet of dreadnoughts were the pelicans; storks abounded too, as did the sacred ibis. It was a great experience to sit for hours, wondering and watching this great beauty, the enormous variety of bird life and the marvellous colours that had been bestowed on them.

Close at hand was the Meningai Crater, which is supposed to be the greatest crater in the world, well over a million years old. The whole of this huge area of vision extends over one thousand two hundred square miles. The view is quite fantastic. The forests at the foot of the mountain are dark, dense and forbidding. Turn around and there are the vast farmlands; another turn, more brooding forests, fading into the vast farmlands stretching far into the distance to yet more brooding forests of eucalyptus.

Tree Tops is a different kind of park. Tea is served English style on the roof of the timber built hotel. At night after dinner silence is the order of the day for then the many wild animals come out of the forest to the water and the salt licks. Elephants to bathe, mongoose to swim, monkeys to chatter and rhinos to wallow in the water. It was at Tree Tops that we saw the Pennant Winged Night Jar — a rare bird at any time.

Another lovely park is Amboseli on the slopes of Kilimanjaro. Again great herds of elephants — herds that brought to mind the painting *The Elephants of Amboseli*, a lovely picture. The camp was tented, the dining room as well. It was delightful, with food and drink to match.

I remember that camp for sleeping reasons, for the beds we tired travellers fell on bore the tell-tale marks of deep dents in the mattresses where other travellers had slumped to sleep. I recall too, the semi combined loo and shower; you kept your hand firmly on the canvas to ensure a degree of privacy. The shower itself was a Heath Robinson affair; the water-filled canvas bag with cord was attached to the top of the pole, and at a tug of the cord the bag tipped, providing a very cool shower — elementary but refreshing!

217

As a schoolboy I often wondered if Dar-es-Salaam was as beautiful and exciting as geography books made it appear. I wondered if the silver sands were really so lovely, or if the palm trees really came down to the edge of that blue sea. Was there the heavy smell of spices and were the people really as black as the pictures? I was not disappointed, and as if to satisfy me fallen coconuts floated in with the tide.

Just north of Dar-es-Salaam there is the little coastal town of Bagamoya. It is a little port with two very different reputations. Years ago it was the end of the slave caravan route from the interior and the port of departure of so many thousands of slaves. The old stone and iron barred cages where slaves were kept awaiting shipment are still there for all to see, beside a beautiful beach edged by waving palm trees — horror side by side with beauty.

Its other reputation is quite different, for it was from Bagamoya that some of the great explorers, Livingstone, Stanley, Burton and Speke started their historic journeys to the interior of East and Central Africa.

We found it a most exciting little township which in the main seemed to be unspoiled. The little straw huts and marketplace, its very happy people and very naked children left little doubt that the tide of civilization had not quite overwhelmed them.

Our driver insisted we meet his father who he said was the local judge. We met him, a jovial figure, he was indeed 'the judge'.

Our first visit to the Rhodesias (now Zimbabwe and Zambia) was many years ago. Then the town of Livingstone was an elongated village with a famous signpost pointing the distance between the township and the great cities of the world. Nearby were the great Victoria Falls, breath-taking in their beauty, staggering in their force as the mighty waters of the Zambesi compress and fall over 350 feet to the continuing river below. A sight never to be forgotten as Livingstone, who discovered them, said:

> Scenes so lovely as must have been gazed on by the angels in their flight.

They are certainly dramatic; dancing rainbows are everywhere as the clouds of spray ascend to the blue skies. Before such a majestic and heavenly sight, yes, it was easy to understand Livingstone's words.

Rhodesia, as I saw it before the troubles, was a very beautiful country of smiling valleys, lovely cities, a vast river, well-ordered farmlands and plenty of land to roam around in. An article in the *Rhodesia Herald,* September 1968, recalled:

> There is no excuse for any tribal African to bemoan his lack of land in Rhodesia. Many of the Tribal Trust Lands near the line of rail and the European concentrations are crowded and their once fertile soil impoverished by bad farming. But in the Crokwe and Binga districts to the north, there is fertile, well wooded and sparsely populated tribal land, waiting for people with sufficient initiative to move.

* * *

In my letters to Mabel I have said much about South Africa. There is much to tell and for want of space much is left untold.

In South Africa, Johannesburg is a remarkable city with many skyscrapers, all developed in a short period of time, on a plateau some 7,000 ft high. This commercial hub of that vast Union is I feel, a brittle city like New York or Chicago, but apart from gold it has another great natural advantage, for it is very close to some of the most lovely country in the world. It is just a morning's run to the Kruger Park, the earliest of the giant game parks. Here we saw our first lion kill; even now I can see the pounding pride of lions chasing the hapless impala — with the lioness the first to strike.

Pretoria, South Africa's administrative capital, is revered by South Africans for its association with the Boers, and by nature lovers for its jacaranda trees with their glorious blossoms, spreading out their dying moments on the roadways. The old city houses, the striking Voortrekkers' Memorial, all enshrined as a part of its history, contrive a delightful city; and for all the Boers might have thought, quite a bit British.

Durban, a very bustling city and seaport, has changed much in the twenty-odd years I have been visiting Africa; not only has the city changed but the African also. I noted in my diary:

> Perhaps the most noticeable change of all was the number of well dressed Africans — Asians driving decent motor cars, fifteen years earlier they would have been scruffy and driving old Austin Sevens.

Gigantic waves beat on the Durban sands and the brave, and sometimes not too clever, fishermen go after the sharks and meet with trouble. Outside the city, the spectacular valley of a Thousand Hills is not ill-named — I did not count the hills, but there was pride in the deep-throated voices of old Zulus there. From my diary again:

> We drove back from the hinterland of the Thousand Hills into the setting sun. The dying rays, strayed on the hilltops and made a picture, unforgettable in its way, as those other great sights we had seen in East Africa.

On one occasion we boarded the *Windsor Castle* at Durban and sailed into the sunset for Port Elizabeth to start our crossing of Cape Province by car to Cape Town. It was a long journey through much beauty and history. We stopped for a night at Wilderness — lovely, lonely and wild — its shores at the mercy of the biggest breakers I have ever seen; and Mossel Bay claimed to be the first post office in the world, a piece of history in itself.

I quote again from one of my diaries:

> South Africa was and is changing all the time, Cape Town like all big cities changes too, when first I went there the road to Belleville, just about fourteen miles from the city, was a sprawling village approached through a straggling road amid great blue gum trees with magnificent mountains beyond. Now Belleville is just a suburb; thank goodness the beauty of the mountains remains. The most wonderful of gardens in Cape Town, bounded by the marks of the original settlers, is of course Kirstenbosch, probably the greatest garden in the world.

> There is the great coastal road, Chapman's Peak Drive. The old Governor's residence,
> steeped in history. Mighty Table Mountain, the huge rollers breaking on the beaches, and
> the timeless seas. This South Africa is a great and lovely country with its wide valleys, its
> magnificent mountains, the great vineyards, stately homes and shade trees, above all the
> air of eternal sunshine — no wonder it is called the Land of the Afternoon.

We looked out of our sitting room window, across the great bays watching the mists clear, the 'Table Cloth' of cloud slide from the top of the mountain, and gazing on the palm trees below we reflected on this great continent of Africa, stretching from Egypt in the north through the deserts and equatorial regions to this lovely haven in the south. This continent could be something great if only mankind would let it be.

* * *

It has been difficult to select the countries it has been our fortune to visit: India, Turkey, Spain, Corsica, Austria, France, Morocco, Kashmir, Nepal, Norway (so lovely), Uganda and recently the Canadian and American Rockies. In words I revisit just three more.

First, Austria and then most stately Vienna, with its great hotels, spectacular buildings and magnificent State Opera. A visit to the opera transports the lucky ones to a past era; the huge and lavish operatic productions, the stately parades, the grand stairways, the quiet dignity of it all is so impressive, while the spirits of the great composers seem to pervade the whole atmosphere — Mozart, Haydn, Schubert, Beethoven, Strauss, etc, all come crowding in.

On our first visit there we stayed at the Imperial Hotel and so did the Queen of Holland; the rooms were marvellous, the attention we had then seems almost forgotten now. The red carpet was still down when we arrived, it was an experience walking on it, and more was to follow. I had to pop down from our room to deal with tickets for the opera; coming back via the lift I pressed the wrong button and landed slap in the middle of the dignitaries and ambassadors and all those waiting to be received by the Queen. We were not to be received! I was soon off, never have I pressed the button of a lift so fast.

On our next visit we had the stately rooms of the dignitaries to ourselves, with all the antiques and masterpieces. I asked for the best suite and indeed I got it. It was unfortunate that on this visit the British were subjected to currency restrictions. I could have stayed in that lovely suite quite a few days longer; the great chandeliers and paintings and the thought that the famous and the infamous Khrushchev, Goering and the like had slept in those very rooms.

The restaurants and cafes, renowned for many generations, had a restful holiday-like atmosphere, for all business ceased at Saturday lunch time, so life there was not all business and shopping. The magnificent view of the mighty St Stephen's Cathedral dominates the fascinating roof-tops of the city and the historic churches, St Charles' with its huge cupola and double columns and the charming little St

Martin's, just two of the many; there is the Graben with its super shopping street and the plague memorial. The fountains, plenty of them, one in particular, the fountain of Raphael Donner, and the Spanish Riding School of great tradition. The Hofburg with its splendid and unique equestrian statues, linked it seemed with the stately buildings of the Ringstrasse was a most stately and imposing mark of a great city.

There is among so much, the fairy tale Palace of Schoenbrunn with its unique Gloriette, the final touch to a great vision.

Not so far away on the Danube there is the great Monastery of Melk where. Napoleon, it is said, paced around the Rose Garden before a great battle. For comparison the beautiful little medieval town of Durnstein lies sleeping alongside the Danube. The snow covered Alps, and scintillating lakes. The thrill of seeing before our very eyes crocus peeping through, as the snow recedes from the uplands in the benevolent sunshine and a still lingering view of beautiful Lake Carezza mirroring all those lovely things of nature.

Finally, there is Salzburg, the lovely city on the River Salzach. It is claimed to be the most perfect example of Baroque architecture, embracing the enchanting cathedral, its ancient university, the street of the metal signs and attractive fountains, a city cradled in the beauty of majestic mountains. Above all it is the birthplace of Mozart, his little violin can still be seen, indeed you can sample your ice-cream where Mozart partook of his. Somehow the feeling, even the presence of the great composer, is in the air. Particularly at festival times, the city reveals the universal link that Austria has with all nations — the language of music. For me and mine, it was a satisfying and uplifting experience, a bridge between the exciting past and the dignified present.

It is also worthwhile remembering that Austria gave to the modern world at least two great inventions. One of the most original of all typewriters was made there by a Tyrolese carpenter Peter Mitterhoffer, in 1866, and it had all the main features of the typewriters built in America shortly afterwards.

Secondly, and probably more important to both industry and the welfare of the masses, the sewing machine, built by Madersperger, in 1815, and known as the 'Iron Hand', it was a discovery of great importance for the whole world and one of the most outstanding technical achievements of Austria. For the first time the eye was transferred to the point of a needle, a device that made it possible to sew by machine.

Alas Madersperger died in the poor-house.

(Both the above are quoted in part or whole from *Wien* by L C Freidlander, published by Verlag fur Jugend und Volk, Wien, 1961.)

* * *

India, as many have written, is a great continent full of contradictions; great wealth, appalling poverty, glorious buildings, awful shacks, amazing beauty and abject squalor — all creating (so it is said) a feeling that is India.

In Delhi, the smell of spices, kerosene and petrol, mingled together as we stood outside the airport restaurant awaiting the plane to Kashmir. The taps in the airport washroom ran to only a sickly trickle, the attendant waited with both hands outstretched, one for the money and one with the towel, a ten inch square of cloth still damp from previous users; the ladies fared even worse, no water and no towel. The children were begging everywhere, and outside the airport, swapped around a legless child, which I suppose was an excellent begging ploy but an impelling wrench at the heart.

The tired ceiling fans failed to keep pace with the heat, and with the flies. Eventually the plane left—it had seen better days and nights. True I had a seat belt, but unfortunately the connection to the strong point was broken. We landed first of all at Islamabad, but we did not see the city for guards with rifles were at all plane exits. They had their guns at the ready; we did not mind as it was hot and we were tired and hungry. The plane took off again, the lower hills gave way to loftier heights, and eventually to mountains, with much higher peaks in the distance. At last the plane throttled back and glided to the tiny airport of Srinagar, where a van was waiting for our luggage, and little cars conveyed us to the shikaras (little boats) to take us to our houseboats on Lake Däl. We were in Kashmir.

Emerging from the airport I was not at all excited, I quote from my notes:

> No promise of the beauty of Kashmir—in fact it all looks barren. I turned to my wife and quietly said, 'Hardly guide book stuff.' We passed the squat little cubes that went for houses, plastered with birth control (and how they need it) graffiti, sketches of mum and dad with two kids—and the message, 'You have two—two will do.' The scruffy little apple trees seemed poor compared with the promises of Kashmir, the Orchard of India. Suddenly we turned a corner near a bazaar and there was Lake Däl shimmering in the sunlight, great mountains rearing from its banks, rich in colour and beautiful beyond belief, across the water were the houseboats. One was 'our residence', and it was marvellous with the restful silence of the night and the attentive service of the boys; as good as any first class hotel. The boys (servants) repeatedly asked, 'When will the British come back?' 'Why did the British leave us?' We tried to explain—they would have none of it. 'You will come back!'

The following morning we were to see the city of Srinagar, so in the shikara promptly at 8.15 am, we set off for the River Jhelum. We passed a whole collection of wooden boats lined up by the dozen; they provided houses for the many, and stuck in the middle of them all was a temple. After a short while we arrived at the lock gates, operated by a venerable but very shrunken gatekeeper, the boats passed through swinging slightly to the right; then a sight to behold, the complete medieval city of Srinagar. Many storeyed half-timbered buildings and temples flanked the river, grass was growing on the roofs of some, and it was apparently useful in their bitter winters. This was not, of course, the city that Alexander saw when he fought the first battle of India on the banks of the Jhelum River at Srinagar, yet it is still told with pride that in those far off days he knew the danger of snow from the high mountains, for he forbade his trumpeters to sound, or his troops to sing for fear of avalanches.

Kashmir is the land of kingfishers, of lovely lakes, majestic mountains with views so beautiful no artist can paint; looking again at a picture taken by my wife of Lake Däl in the early morning I think that most people would settle for the title 'The Jewel of Asia'. There is another and darker side with distrust of one for the other and poverty so grievous it seems almost immoral to feast on the beauty. Seldom have I seen such poverty in the midst of so much beauty.

Men seemed to take it as their due, that idleness is for them, and work for the women. Certainly it was the women with babies who collected the vegetables that grew on the floating islands of the lake and carried them in their boats to the lakeside markets. Not that all markets were lakeside — some mini-mini-markets on boats ply around the lake offering everything from razor blades to radios, flowers to toothpaste and if they have not got what you want they know somebody who has.

Stretching out from the lake are fingers of water, the crowded navigation roads, the trees alive with glittering kingfishers, and the water bordered with rich vegetation. The river banks, like the city, are clustered here and there with many half-timbered houses, a general shop, a tailor here, a baker there, vegetable shop or furniture maker, and ever present are the floating gardens.

Near Srinagar there are more beautiful gardens, those of Shalimar made so well known by Amy Woodford Finden, the composer with her *Pale Hands I Loved*; she apparently never saw Shalimar, she just felt the mood. Shalimar was originally built by the Mogul Emperor Shah Jehangir in 1619 for his queen. Designed originally as water gardens, but now the water is missing like so many parts of India. The petals once dropped as a pastime in the twinkling waterways by the ladies of the house no longer pass that way. Alongside the pavilions of love one pool is still left, beautifully reflecting lovely blossoms and the dramatic scene of the mountains beyond.

The Persian emperors must have had a passion for gardens for Nashit and Chesma Shabi are beautiful, not as big as Shalimar, but each offering a superb haven for the wonderfully sited red chinar trees brought from Persia, complemented with enormous beds of beautiful English flowers.

In Kashmir there is Pahalgam, the Valley of the Shepherds, where we saw the descendants of an ancient tribe bringing their cattle down from the high hills to the lower slopes for the winter. Legend has it that Jesus walked through the meadows — the very name Kashmir means 'Like the Syrians'. The rushing streams, the flower carpeted valleys, the snow-capped mountain peaks, some of them very high indeed, might well impress any god, Christian or Hindu.

I do not forget lovely Gulmarg, about 8,000ft high, set amid so many more high peaks and flower strewn meadows, the resort of the British when we were administering India; alas, St Mary's Church is now boarded up. Then as if to make peace, a truly wonderful vision of the Valley of Kashmir, stretching far out into the distance like some magic carpet, with a magnificent view of Nanga Parbat rising from the plains, the mountain that has been so cruel to climbers.

Delhi has some very great buildings, not least the Qutb Minar in the centre of the 12th and 13th century area, the great victory towers of the Persian world, while across the way the stupendous Tomb of Humayun, his library, the Pearl Mosque, the Mosque of Sher Sha, and the magnificent fort, a great edifice, a living memorial to the changing powers of so many pasts.

In the very first city of Delhi the past always seems present as streams of transport go by — the not so modern, bundles, even bundles of straw, carried on human heads, pack animals so heavily loaded and staggering as if about to crack, handcarts, loaded to breaking point. Then the really well off with their bullock carts, poor bullocks, they had to pull great loads and great quantities of families, the odd motor cycle and not so new car; the crumbling ruins of this old city of the East has much to tell.

The British can be rightly proud of the New Delhi they built, the Viceroy's Palace, the President's dwelling and vast administrative buildings, all in red sandstone, stand majestically beyond the impressive Houses of Parliament, exquisitely set amid lawns on the hill, the well kept roads drift down to India Gate, their Menin Gate, a memorial to the dead of the first World War. It is a magnificent group, a great achievement of the British architects, Baker and Lutyens.

In the other Delhi, the Jami Masjid — the Friday Mosque, is a magnificent edifice, it seemed to be crowded at all hours of the day, perhaps it was for free; but it was not for us. There is, too, the very remarkable observatory built in the early 18th century by Maharajah Jai Singh. The exhibits are extraordinary, all that time ago they must have seemed the frontier of the space age. Above all there is, alas, the impression that never leaves your mind, the teeming crowds of the eternally poor.

The emaciated faces are sad; spitting, which seems to be aimed at no one in particular, but spreads everywhere, together with so much disease, is appalling. John Keay, in his book *Into India*, sums up the feeling that I and many others had, 'The fantastic problem, untouchability, has been abolished for twenty-five years. Instead of fifty million Untouchables there are now seventy-five million ex-Untouchables of whom nine-tenths are no better off than before.'

That is the problem of India, words come by the thousand and children by the million, and agriculture, the means to keep them, despite all good speeches, fails to keep up.

While this feeling is ever present in Delhi, it is really nothing compared with Calcutta; it is no good pretending, for here the human race drinks the dregs. The poverty in that very damp and overheated atmosphere is awful, families are huddled near the gutters of the 'go downs' under a tattered piece of plastic or cotton material with dad, his frail body exhausted, sleeping away, with his head almost in the gutter.

There are kids prising open rotting water melons, to extract the pips for food, and begging. Oh, the begging! — and even more regretfully, some of it is quite professional. I will never forget a scene near the bridge over the Hooghly River on a very damp evening, many families were bedding down for the night on the rain-sodden earth, and lighting fires which produced the most appalling fumes, while the children, without a stitch on, played about like little skeletons.

Yes, Calcutta has some very beautiful buildings and some very fine streets but they do not assuage the feeling of the utter degradation of the human body and soul. Again I quote from John Keay — I could do no better.

> Inured as one becomes to poverty and squalor, I was still stunned by the chaos and
> desperation. The plight of the poor is often dignified, almost beautiful, but in Calcutta it
> is neither. Always it is tragic but the loss of dignity, the debasement of the human spirit,
> was somehow new and infinitely more terrifying.

I agree, it is the spirit, or lack of it, which is stupifying. I have travelled much abroad, but somehow it plumbed the depths of sorrow and suffering. Yet, for a complete view of life, I would not have missed the experience.

A doctor friend said, 'It is impossible, the population is growing so quickly, the means to feed them so slowly, and the means of contraception, for one reason or another, are ignored.'

Calcutta lists a curious tourist attraction in the great cemetery of lofty memorials holding down the dead; I was assured these were more for security than for memory. Maybe it is a point but surely part must be in memory of so many young mothers and their many children who died from cholera and other terrible diseases in the early days of the occupation. Some of them never even made Calcutta alive.

India has tremendous problems, yet even greater opportunities, for there are a great number of influential, clever and wealthy people around, but against the black canvas of poverty so little seems to have been done, and we the British were, after all, told to go, and that evacuation at the time was hailed as a victory for the Indian race! Yet there still seems to be both great hopes and fears.

India has, in the Taj Mahal, one of the most beautiful buildings in the world. The Taj is just a day's outing from Delhi on the super train — air conditioned, I think — I do not know, because even though we were booked, it did not run. We went by air conditioned coach to Agra, this would have been all right, except the air conditioning did not work! The journey was very hot and tiring but did not dim for one moment the glory of the Taj.

The monument is fashioned from gleaming white marble, built in the 17th century by the Mogul Emperor Shah Jehan as a tomb for his beloved wife, Mumtaz Mahal. It is a monument to a queen whose king never recovered from her death. That in itself, is curious, for he had the reputation of being a very cruel man.

The Taj, like other memorials to those who have died, be it the Cenotaph, the Menin Gate or the village cross, is sad, but there is a difference, the Taj was a memory to love, the others alas to sacrifice.

The approach to this glorious edifice through a seedy part of Agra is anything but encouraging; there is little to see from the first stone gateway, but nearing the second portal, a blinding light seems to fill the opening, revealing the first view of this great spectacle. One step further, and the experience is breathtaking, the whole of this lovely building seems to be floating between a blue heaven and a green and verdant earth. A marvellous piece of architecture has fashioned calm reflective water to form an open nave, then in some mysterious way the vision is mirrored and transfixed to the ethereal monument, towering it seems to the sky. There is a feeling of the eternal, the nearness of heaven to earth, and a bewildering paradox of how so much cruelty begat so much love.

Nepal is so different and a never to be forgotten experience. As a boy, the name of Katmandu sent my mind reeling with imagination—for real it does just that. Standing at the valley entrance to Katmandu is Swayambhunath with one of the oldest Buddhist Stupas or Temples, a huge tomb-like edifice erected to the Great Lord Buddha—He of the all seeing eyes—for eyes were indeed painted on all four sides. Prayer wheels abound, you spin them around to offer your prayers. Prayer flags fly in the breeze with yet other thoughts to their God.

So under this guardian at the end of the lush valley stands Katmandu, whose name is derived from Katmandap, a pagoda structure near the Durbar Square which is believed to have been built from the wood of one single tree; it must have been some tree.

The first view of Durbar Square is sensational—the schoolboy imaginations of Katmandu materialise. It is very full of temples, many large, some small, most of them gilded, one has a golden ladder to heaven, another, the Cobra Temple, has a golden snake rising above. The Monkey Temple is fascinating, much frequented by men for there is quite a bit of erotica around; many of the temples are not short on that. One of my friends described it as the most detailed exhibition of sexual acrobatics that he had ever seen.

I remember a little Indian boy, who did a spot of voluntary guiding at one temple, assuring me that his father said there was nothing wrong in these rude carvings. He explained that in the winter months the Valley of Katmandu is covered in deep clouds of mist. The men, so his father said, then went into the temples and thought those bad things and this prevented them doing the bad things for real—well that is one explanation—one would hardly get away with it here.

Close at hand is the Temple of the Living Goddess, a virgin child isolated during her reign from all but the inmates of the temple. Her palace is a heavily carved structure with many windows; at certain times of the day the courtyard is opened, the isolated child framed behind on glass, is on view, but no photographs please! The ancient ceremonial carts are still around, fascinating markets abound, rich in produce for people poor in money. Above all there is an air of mystery, the teacher or priest lectures his squatting students amid all the noise arising from an Eastern market; they seem to get by.

At nearby Bhadgaon there are yet more temples, the palace of fifty-five windows, a golden gate and the five storey Nyatapola showpiece, and so much more medieval art to attract even the most tired tourist. The feast of temples and gilded decorations might in itself cause mental indigestion were it not leavened by the glorious mountain scenery of the foothills of Everest. One afternoon we drove through the high hills to Kirkani to gaze across the fabulous range of mountains guarding Everest; the light began to fade, the setting sun's rays split the clouds with gold, revealing the snow-capped peaks in the distance— a mighty, sensational, yet unearthly scene—what food for the soul. The magic of that scene was perhaps confirmation of the spirit's supreme triumph over all things material.

* * *

Our Indian trip ended at Darjeeling high up in the mountains, claimed in the time of the British to be the Queen of the Hill Stations, in short the holiday place for the tea planters, government officials and others. The town still bears much of the British influence, although there are a lot of Tibetans there now; here we met Tensing, a jolly unassuming little man, despite the sad and unfair graffiti chalked on the walls about him.

The exciting journey from Bagdogra to Darjeeling, with just seventy miles of roads of so many bends, twists and turns. The little railway (then out of action) is quite miniature but has carried so many thousands up that tortuous trail — some of the ascents are so severe that the train winds around the mountain to gain only a few feet at each turn. The monsoons had destroyed much of the road and many of the bridges. Whole families maintained their allocated part of the highway, toddlers, mum, dad, grandpa and grandma, all making their contribution. On the lower slopes of the mountain were some of the great tea gardens, the pickers were returning to their stations on the flatlands in long trails, each picker with his or her leaf collection of the day. Today there are no British tea planters left.

Our jeep struggled up the mountain, through rain, mist and water, magnificent mountain views one moment, thick menacing clouds and fog the next, the little waterfalls gulped their surplus supplies on the cracked mountain roads — fostering an abundance of wild flowers, particularly the moon flowers *Datura suaveolens,* a shrub carrying very large white trumpet flowers that are very poisonous. After some hours we reached the first stop, the railway sheds, the little pre-war engines were all neatly stored, their beautiful headlights carefully cleaned and blinking in the fading light. Here and there along the mountain roads the little lonely shrines to their gods were afforded a posy of flowers; perhaps their gods sometimes smiled on them in thanks.

Darkness fell; as we reached Darjeeling the mist was clearing, the air felt clean, and we were surprised to find a warm fire in each of our rooms, but we had no change of clothes as our suitcases were in a couple of jeeps, apparently miles away, and hours behind us. The luggage jeeps had toppled over in a river, cases and all. When they did arrive at 2.00 am the luggage was saturated and our clothes were hardly dry; the thoughtful fire was more than useful.

Darjeeling is a little faded, but still has great charm, with hallmarks of the past. A lovely hotel, an abundance of high schools for girls and boys. As one native pointed out the obvious, leetle black children were there but no leetle white chidren anymore.

The 'pan' sellers were much in evidence whether the leaf be filled with sweet meat, real meat, candy, the ever popular betel, or whatever, the resulting red spit on the pavement seemed just the same.

Some of the shop signs bore witness to the past, all the old English adverts — Pears soap with 'Bubbles', Wills Gold Flake, Fry's Cocoa, Ovaltine and others; a number of picture postcards on sale were of a similar vintage.

Photography must have known some boom years in Darjeeling (and why not with its scenery), for the photography shop was the biggest store, its offerings displaying much of the past. As we moved through the little square, we were conscious of a change, was it the people? It was, the sloping hillside of the town was populated by Tibetans, and was gay with colours, particularly during the day when everything seemed to be put out to catch the air, bedclothes, curtains, and pants; the Tibetans are a very clean and soulful race.

At Town End we visited a world authority on rhododendrons and azaleas. Dr Goshe was at home in his little house among all his diplomas, cups and medals from the world over. No, he could not do business that day it was Ghandi Day, but he could take the money and would send the seeds to his nephew who was the receptionist at our hotel. He invited us to coffee, which his servant produced, with much bowing. The doctor was a charming and interesting old boy. The seeds did arrive on time, and back here in England some of them grew.

The tea gardens were set on the misty slopes with innumerable little pathways between the bushes, trodden so often and for so long by the comings and goings to the station. Over all this was the brooding mist, broken here and there by a splash of red, a robe caught by the wind, providing a picture no artist could really paint. Nearby the great Monastery of Ghoom houses great quantities of ancient writings all carefully wrapped up, and guarded, as it were, by the carvings of fearsome creatures, and monks heralding the dawn with bursts from extra long trumpets.

Physically and literally above all were the mountains. At dawn we turned out to see the miracle of day-break on the great Himalayan Range, including Everest and Kanchenjunga, all waiting to be kissed by the sun's first rays. One memory of mountains will stay with us for ever; on our second morning in Darjeeling, the room was full of blinding light, I said to Mabel, 'We're late for breakfast, it must be past nine o'clock.' Actually, it was quite early. I swished back the curtains and there it stood, the great mass of Kanchenjunga rising from the valley floor and dominating the whole sky, a vision so white, so vast, so unearthly, it was hard to imagine the great mountain was fifty miles away across the valley. Majestic Kanchenjunga, the world's third highest mountain (28,168 ft) seemed even mightier than Everest.

* * *

Of all the holidays we have spent abroad it was ancient Egypt that impressed so deeply. It is very true there are trials and tribulations to cope with on the trip. Accommodation reserved months before may not be available, or air tickets paid for had no seats to match; but as the mind becomes dominated by the wonders of that ancient race, the petty things are taken as acceptable and part of the price paid for a great experience — so wonderful that no words of mine can convey.

It has been known for a very long time that the existence of Egypt depends on the flow of the Blue Nile out of Ethiopia. Both countries knew that if Ethiopia denied the water, Egypt as a nation would die, conversely Egypt and her allies with their superior armies could invade, and Ethiopia would die. *Neither did either* so they both exist today. From so long ago is there a lesson for us all in this Nuclear Age that with both countries having an ultimate deterrent they both still live on? So *The*

Nile flows through Egypt for some six hundred miles and nowhere is it ever much more than a mile wide; yet, it forms the umbilical cord of the greatest and most continuing civilization the world has ever known. At the great bends of the river ruins of this tremendous past are strung out like pearls against the blue of the eastern sky.

From Aswan to Cairo history unfolds *before your very eyes*. First Edfu with its Horus Temple, built by the father of Cleopatra, the last of the pharoahs: it is still almost complete with the Sacred Birds guarding the portals. When we were there it was lonely, and the excavation of a Roman town was still in progress to yield yet more treasures.

The vast Temple of Luxor with its towering Pylons and columns and still filled with its statues, hugs the river bank; here not only the great buildings impress, for this ancient city stands witness to the belief in Almighty God; for at Luxor God the Creator has been worshipped without a break for more than three and a half thousand years. The name of the faith has changed over the centuries but the basic belief has scarcely altered.

Luxor and Karnak form a mighty temple complex which seems to be dominated by a huge statue of Rameses II—his Queen remembered by a little carving on his leg.

But another Queen is much in evidence at Karnak, for the great Hatshepsut had two enormous obelisks erected there (they still stand today)—her words ring out down the centuries.

> I was sitting in the palace and thinking of my Creator, when my heart urged me to make for him in the Hall of Columns two obelisks whose points should reach the sky. . . . Verily, these two great obelisks that my Majesty has wrought with electrum, they are of a single stone of hard granite without any joint or division.

The last sentence is interesting, for in the great quarry at Aswan there is a third column with *a fault*—therefore imperfect; it was never lifted. We were fortunate to have as our guide in Luxor and Karnak, Peter, who as a boy had dug with Howard Carter at Tutankhamun's tomb. It was evening when we made our final visit to Karnak—the fading golden light was reflected in the Sacred Lake, reminding us of the death rituals of the ancient pharoahs whose bodies were rowed around the sacred water nine times, before their last journey across the river to Thebes.

Their great tombs are carved out of the living rock in the now desolate Valley of the Kings that was once *alive with dead Pharoahs* for virtually every tomb was robbed in antiquity and at least one of them bears the tourist graffiti in Greek of so many centuries ago. The magnet is of course the tomb of Tutankhamun; yet as magnificent as the paintings, coffins and death masks are, it was a much more human thing that made the impact on me for I do not forget the faded remains of a goodbye bunch of flowers (now in the museum of Cairo) left at his feet by his Queen.

Down river again Abydos is the most revered place in Egypt. Its primary association was with *death,* which to the pharoahs was very important. Here are the remains of the Natron Baths required in mummifying, so essential to the funeral rites; fascinating, but awesome of course. The first Temple to Osiris the God of Death and Resurrection was built there over 4,000 years ago. So into the sunshine and on to the delightful Fayum Oasis, with its pigeon houses, farms, ancient water wheels that still work, providing part of the irrigation to the fruitful oasis. All this was made possible by Amonemhat III who engineered a great dam 20 miles long to hold the flood water for the dry season — or as Herodotus recorded:

> The water in the Great Lake at Fayum does not spring from the soil . . . but it is conveyed through a channel from the Nile and for 6 months of the year it flows into the reservoirs and for 6 months it flows out again.

This, one of the greatest engineering feats in history happened 2000 years before Christ. The vision, the effort and construction — so breathtaking.

Just along the Nile sleeps Maydum with its unique pyramid, the link between the step Pyramid of Zoser and the true Pyramid of Cheops; it is so huge and so different that some think that the Pyramids at Gizeh only rate second class, I don't know about that; but I do know it is set in the middle of a very big stretch of desert in its lonely glory, and wasn't visited very often then. We came to it on a very hot day, the soldiers on guard seemed (at least later) so pleased to see us that they might have thrown their hats over a rainbow had there been one about. Certainly our last view of Maydum was of the chaps — who at first had drawn guns on us — dragging at *our* cigarettes and waving a cheery goodbye.

I remember us coming at last to the Great Pyramid and Sphinx complex at Gizeh, the mightiest site of the ancient world and claimed by Cheops to be built *to last for ever* — certainly of all the Seven Wonders of the World it is the one that can still be seen today.

No one is quite certain as yet when it all began, perhaps 12,000 to 15,000 years ago; what is known for certain is that in those early civilizations were the beginnings of the sciences, physics, astronomy, engineering, religion, laws and government, for Egypt is credited with the first political act in history — the uniting of Upper and Lower Egypt.

Yet it is in *our very own knowledge* of the achievements of the ancient Egyptian race that the wonderment lies, for they left us indelible proof of so much written on papyrus or carved on stone. Margaret Murray in *The Splendour that was Egypt* a most wonderful book, puts it succinctly — I quote

> The splendour of Egypt was not a mere mushroom growth lasting but a few hundred years. Where Greece and Rome count their supremacy by the century, Egypt counts hers by the millennium and the remains of that splendour can even now eclipse the remains of any other country in the world.

So it wasn't all work, and while I subscribe to Winston Churchill's view that life is whole and good, it must be accepted together, the journey has been enjoyable and well worth making once. I would just add, for me at least, just once more please!